ARCTIC ICONS

*How the Town of Churchill
Learned to Love its Polar Bears*

EDWARD STRUZIK

Fitzhenry & Whiteside

Published in Canada by Fitzhenry & Whiteside, 195 Allstate Parkway, Markham, ON L3R 4T8
Published in the United States by Fitzhenry & Whiteside, 311 Washington Street, Brighton, Massachusetts 02135

10 9 8 7 6 5 4 3 2 1

Fitzhenry & Whiteside acknowledges with thanks the Canada Council for the Arts, and the Ontario Arts Council for their support of our publishing program. We acknowledge the financial support of the Government of Canada through the Canada Book Fund (CBF) for our publishing activities.

Library and Archives Canada Cataloguing in Publication
Struzik, Edward, 1954-, author
Arctic icons : how the town of Churchill learned to love
polar bears / Edward Struzik.
Includes bibliographical references and index.
ISBN 978-1-55455-322-8 (pbk.)
1. Polar bear--Manitoba--Churchill. 2. Human-bear
encounters--Manitoba--Churchill. I. Title.
QL85.S77 2014   304.2'7   C2014-902106-2
Publisher Cataloging-in-Publication Data (U.S.)
Struzik, Edward.
Arctic icons : how the town of Churchill learned to love its polar bears / Edward Struzik.
[320] pages : col. photos. ; cm.
Includes bibliographical references and index.
Summary: For nearly a quarter century, the polar bears of Churchill were routinely run down and shot by the military, by residents and by conservation officers who were brought in during the late 1960s to protect the people. In the '70s, the residents of Churchill decided that it was time to find a more peaceful way of living with polar bears. This book describes how the 1,000 mostly aboriginal people living on the west coast of Hudson Bay found a way to co-exist with the polar bears, and how these bears became the most studied group of large predators in the world.
ISBN-13: 978-1-55455-322-8 (pbk.)
1. Polar bear – Manitoba – Churchill. 2. Human-animal relationships – Manitoba – Churchill. I. Title.
304.27 dc23   QL737.C27.S878 2014

Text and cover design by Kerry Designs
Printed and bound in Canada by Friesens

CONTENTS

Biologist Peter Clarkson peers down at a bear that had been waiting for someone to take a walk on the tundra.

ACKNOWLEDGEMENTS

The idea for this book came from Mike Spence, entrepreneur, longtime mayor of Churchill and descendent of a remarkable group of aboriginal men and women who grew up on the west coast of Hudson Bay.

I was tempted, but inclined to turn down the offer to write it when the idea was presented to me by Lorraine Brandson, the long time curator of the Eskimo Museum of Churchill, who was a member of the committee that was established to get the book published. I was busy enough with other books, magazine articles and university research projects. The prospect of squeezing in another tome into what was already a crowded field of books on polar bears did not particularly appeal to me. Lorraine, however, persisted in convincing me that this book could be different. Many books had been written on Churchill's polar bears, she noted, but none focused on the unique relationship between the bears, the town's residents, and efforts by scientists and Manitoba Conservation personnel to find a way for the two to co-exist.

After giving the matter some thought, I accepted and put pen to the subject.

I'm glad I did. Thanks to Pierce Roberts, the director for the Northeast Region of Manitoba Conservation, I was given access to more than forty-five years of records that described, in remarkable detail, how many polar bears had been shot, deterred, interned and sent off to zoos, and what was done to prevent the deaths of animals, injuries to people, and destruction of property. The data was raw and unfiltered. I got to read everything.

Pierce seemed to be as excited about this project as I was. Nothing I asked of him was refused. I was allowed to spend considerable time with conservation officers on the job in Churchill, with biologist Vicki Trim, helicopter pilot Justin Seniuk, and the incomparable Daryll Hedman in the field. Once again, there were no strings attached. I was given the freedom to write all that I saw and heard, which was a great deal, as readers will see.

Many people read and commented on the manuscript. Pierce Roberts and Lorraine Brandson spent an inordinate amount of time doing so, as did Steve Kearney, the former director of the region. Not one of them insisted on changing anything other than that which was not factual. Thankfully, most of my mistakes were minor in nature, and every one of their suggestions was spot on.

Scientist Ian Stirling also read and commented on the manuscript. For that, I am extremely grateful. I had accompanied Ian in the field for the first time in 1989 when he and Ph.D. student Becky Sjare (now a Fisheries and Oceans scientist) were drilling holes in the sea ice, listening to the spooky, descending trills of bearded seals and the bell-knock codas of a male walrus searching in vain for a mate that never

came. It wasn't the first time that Stirling had given me the opportunity to join him the field, and it wouldn't be the last; a survey of polar bears in the Beaufort Sea in 2006 was one of the most recent highlights. It was, however, typical of the way Ian went about dealing with journalists who showed more than a passing interest in the research that he has been doing for the past four decades.

Many others graciously read parts of the book for accuracy; among them were Doug Webber, former mayor of Churchill and owner of Webber's Lodges. Fred Bruemmer, the great photographer and the first professional to photograph

Bear peers into a cage in which the author has taken refuge.

polar bears in Churchill, offered advice before he passed away in the fall of 2013. Fred was a great artist and he will be missed.

University of Alberta polar bear scientist Andrew Derocher, wildlife specialist Roy Bukowsky, former conservation officer Wayde Roberts (now a regional director), and Mike Spence, the long time mayor of Churchill were also extremely helpful. Roy, as well, provided me with records and magazine articles that proved to be invaluable.

Along with Doug Webber, a number of current and former residents of Churchill also shared their recollections. The list is a long one, but those who stand out include: Carol Rogers, Maureen Osland, Al Chartier, Bonnie Chartier, Bob deMeulles, Eileen Jacobs, and Tim Hawkins. Tim recalled being mauled by a polar bear nearly a half century earlier like it was yesterday.

I would also like to thank Canadian Wildlife Service scientists Nick Lunn and Paul Latour, as well as biologists Brian Knudsen and Ricki Hurst for their insights and recollections. They were all involved in polar bear research in Churchill at one time or another (Nick is still doing research). Special thanks go to biologists Gordon Stenhouse and Peter Clarkson who allowed me to spend several weeks with them in the Polar Bear Tower at Cape Churchill over a three-year period in the 1980s. I still have wonderful dreams and the occasional nightmare about the time I spent there among so many hungry bears.

I'd also like to thank past and current conservation officers, wildlife technicians, biologists and helicopter pilots stationed in Churchill at one time. I got to meet and talk to most of them. Two, however—Dale Cross and Ian Thorleifson—stand out for really digging deep in helping me.

Not everything has gone smoothly with the polar bear management plan over the past forty-five years, but I give credit to the Government of Manitoba for acting swiftly when things went awry, as they sometimes did, and for daring to experiment with bold ideas that had the potential to backfire. Their management of polar bears, in conjunction with scientists and the residents of Churchill, is truly one of the great conservation success stories of our time.

ARCTIC ICONS

INTRODUCTION

Ed Struzik

In 1949, a "top secret" plan was hatched to detonate twelve Hiroshima-sized atomic bombs along the west coast of Hudson Bay during the autumn months, when the winds could be expected to keep the fallout from migrating south to more populated centres. Had the plan been approved, the bombs would have laid waste to a huge stretch of tundra in northern Canada. The blasts, and the fallout, would have also killed most of the 1,000 polar bears that are forced to spend the summer and fall there, waiting for cold weather to bring the ice back to Hudson Bay.

"The Technical Feasibility of Establishing an Atomic-Weapons Proving Ground in the Churchill Area"[1] was not the brainchild of terrorists or madmen, but the work of C. P. McNamara of Canada's Defense Research Board and William George (later Lord) Penney, the scientist who had participated in the Manhattan Project before moving on to direct Great Britain's Atomic Weapons Establishment. They decided on Churchill over several other similarly remote places in Canada because they considered it a "waste land suitable only for hunting and trapping." Only the "occasional hunter or trapper," would be affected, they reasoned in a proposal that would have had the highest level of attention in the two governments.

The Churchill plan, of course, was never approved; the winning bid went to Australia[2] because the British felt that northern Canada would be too cold and uncomfortable for their scientists. But the idea did reflect just how out of sight, out of mind, and thoroughly unimportant the polar bears of western Hudson Bay were back then, and in the decades that followed.

Personnel at Fort Churchill, the enormous Canadian–American military base that was established eight kilometres east of Churchill in the 1940s, often viewed the region's polar bears not as great hunters of seals as the Inuit did, but as vermin. In an effort to keep them off the base, soldiers dug long trenches on the tundra and filled them up with garbage. Occasionally, men would be sent out to chase the garbage-eating bears with helicopters, trucks and all-terrain vehicles. No one could say with certainty, but both residents and conservation officers working there in the 1960s and 1970s suspected that dozens of furry white souvenirs were taken home.

By the time the military began pulling out in the 1960s, there were so few bears left in the region that it was rare for someone in Churchill to see one. The disregard for the welfare of bears, however, continued into the 1960s and 1970s when the polar bear population began to bounce back. On any given Sunday, families could be seen at the town dump, tossing refuse out and pushing their kids in front of the garbage-eating polar bears so they could take pictures. On more than one occasion, men got liquored up and chased the animals around in their trucks and snowmobiles. Not everyone in Churchill approved. Carol Mackenzie, a longtime resident, wrote a letter to the local newspaper calling for all this to stop. "Despite my conservative outlook, I feel very strongly that a more liberal attitude could be adopted towards Churchill's Polar Bears," she wrote.[3]

Police mostly ignored this kind of behaviour, however. Government authorities were indifferent to, and misunderstood, the plight of the polar bear. One man in Churchill even got a grant to set up a chicken farm in the middle of the polar bear's migration route. Another raised pigs and shot a couple of bears that tried to get a free dinner.

When American biologist Chuck Jonkel was hired by the Canadian Wildlife Service to study the polar bears in Churchill in 1966, he was appalled by what he saw. "Polar bears are apparently not looked upon by these people as the 'Great White Bear of the North,' but rather as creatures akin to rats," he wrote in the scientific journal, *Biological Conservation*.[4]

In spite of Jonkel's pleading, nothing was done to stop any of this until the bears started turning on people. When one young man was killed, and several others injured, by polar bears between 1966 and 1968, wildlife officers were sent to Churchill to patrol the streets during the fall months. They were there, however, not so much to deter bears from coming into town, but to shoot them if they did. As many as twenty-nine polar bears were being destroyed each year.

By the early 1970s, it was apparent to all that, if nothing was done to address the problem, this situation was going to become a lot worse before it got any better. Remarkably, science, sanity, public opinion, and the involvement of the International Fund for Animal Welfare, a fledgling international animal welfare organization at the time, turned things around. When every adult in Churchill was asked in 1976 what could be done to solve the polar bear problem, there were those who predictably suggested that all the animals should be killed. To the surprise of Roy Bukowsky, the wildlife specialist who put a copy of the survey in every mailbox, a significant number of people desperately wanted to find a way to live with the animals.

Sign at a Kaskattama goose-hunting lodge near the Ontario–Manitoba border.

Many of the letters weren't simple responses from ordinary people who, for the most part, led unextraordinary lives, as Bukowsky had expected, but long thoughtful reflections on what had happened in the past and what needed to be done in the future. One elderly lady who had experienced more than her share of troubles with polar bears sent in a hand-written note that was four pages long. She apologized for being so verbose. Bukowsky was so impressed with the quality of her insights that he asked her to be a member of the committee set up to devise a plan to solve the polar bear problem.

The plan that Bukowksy and the Churchill Polar Bear Committee penned in 1977 resulted in what amounted to a polar bear jail for so-called "problem bears" that would otherwise be shot. A more humane protocol for deterring bears was also recommended, and opportunities for wildlife viewing were envisioned. The committee insisted that scientific research and public education needed to guide future management decisions. In short, they wanted people to regard the polar bear not as a great white rat that ate garbage, but as a majestic animal that deserved respect.

The plan was not perfect by any means, and unofficially, it has been a work in progress ever since. There has, however, never been anything quite like it. By 1984, the polar bears of Churchill were such a hot tourist attraction and a cash cow for the town's businessmen, that *National Geographic, Audubon, Smithsonian* and *The New York Times, TIME Magazine*, London's *Daily Mirror*, and *Le Figaro* had all already devoted considerable space to the subject in magazines and documentaries. In 1984, the editors of *Life Magazine* sandwiched a 5,000-word article about Churchill's polar bears in between one on the Shroud of Turin and another on the 20th anniversary of the Beatles coming to America.

In the years that followed, Churchill became the centre of some of the most advanced, and sometimes controversial, research on polar bears, thanks in part to the creation of the Churchill Northern Studies Centre, which housed and fed scores of scientists when they came into town. They conducted studies on the polar bear's social behaviour, their responses to sound and pain, and the impact that three to fourth months of fasting has on their health. Bears were studied at the dump, in their dens, on the sea ice, and in an

After some time in Churchill's "polar bear jail," problem bears are airlifted far from town in the hopes that they won't return.

© Edward Struzik

experimental chamber set up in an old laundry room at one of the abandoned military buildings. Polar bears were put on giant treadmills (which they apparently loved) and hooked up to respiratory machines to measure the amount of energy they burned off. Some were soaked in oil to see how they would respond to a spill. With the help of the Born Free Foundation and advice from the San Diego Zoo, experiments were done to provide orphaned cubs with surrogate mothers. In relatively short order, the bears of Churchill became the most studied group of large predators in the world.

The world's infatuation with the polar bears of Churchill hasn't waned since then. Each year some 10,000 well-heeled tourists—most of them from the United States and Europe—make the trip to town of 1,000 or so (mostly aboriginal people) to see some of the 1,000 or so bears that inhabit the region. There would probably be more tourists if the town could accommodate them.

Churchill's polar bears have long been a favourite for television wildlife shows such as Mutual of Omaha's *Wildlife Kingdom,* and the Canadian Broadcasting Corporation's *The Nature of Things.* Television crews from Japan, France, Germany, and other countries routinely visited the town. But the celebrity "hot" factor has ramped up in recent years with stars such as Martha Stewart, Ewan McGregor, Ryan Seacrest, Dan Aykroyd,

and Rob Reiner coming to town. Diplomats and high level bureaucrats such as David Wilkinson, the U.S. ambassador to Canada, and Janet Napolitano, the Governor of Arizona and future Secretary of the Department of Homeland Security, have also made the pilgrimage. Nine times out of ten, Manitoba government leaders choose Churchill when they are looking for a way to entertain visiting dignitaries.

Recognizing the marketing value of polar bears, Nicola Kettlitz, the president of Coca-Cola Canada, visited Churchill in the fall of 2011 to give the World Wildlife Fund $2 million over the next 5 years for a joint polar bear conservation campaign called Arctic Home.[5] This campaign seeks to raise awareness and fund the protection of the polar bear and its habitat.

Kettlitz was living up to a commitment that the global CEO of Coca-Cola had made two years earlier when he came to Churchill promising to support any measure that might save the animal from the effects of global warming.

The World Wildlife Fund's latest effort to save polar bears is nothing new. Polar Bears International has been doing this kind of thing since its inception in the 1990s. Since then, the non-profit organization has worked with corporate sponsors, scientists, and Manitoba Conservation to do anything and pretty much everything that can be done to help polar bears.

The International Polar Bear Conservation Centre at the Assiniboine Zoo in Winnipeg represents one of the biggest and most ambitious projects focusing on Manitoba's bears. The centre, which opened in 2012, serves as an international hub for education and zoo-based research as well as a quarantine, holding, and transition centre for orphaned polar bear cubs, injured sub-adults, or bears affected by oil spills and other catastrophic events. It's part of a $200-million redevelopment, and includes a "Journey to Churchill" polar bear exhibit that will eventually be home to six polar bears.

Money and scientific advice, however, may not be enough to save the polar bears in this part of the world. If an expert panel appointed by the U.S. Geological Survey is correct, there will not be enough ice left in western Hudson Bay by mid-century to sustain this population.[6]

Difficult as it is to believe, Ian Stirling, the polar bear scientist who has been conducting and facilitating research on polar bears in Churchill for the past 40 years, believes that it could happen sooner than that. Not only are the bears here getting skinnier and producing fewer cubs, some are resorting to cannibalism, maybe because they are now spending an additional three weeks or longer fasting on land.

Up until a few years ago, many of the town's residents had doubts that a population of 1,000 or so animals could disappear so quickly. But

The Inuit represented a small but significant part of Churchill's population until the 1970s, when the Canadian government transferred services for Inuit to Frobisher Bay (Iqaluit).

A family of bears feeds on a seal killed in the shallow waters of western Hudson Bay.

© Edward Struzik

now that the bears are spending a lot more time fasting on land in the ice-free months, they are causing more trouble. The number of calls to the Polar Bear Alert line has nearly doubled in the past decade. Conservation officers have been able to minimize the number of bears they need to handle or euthanize, but that is proving to be a challenge. An increasing number of residents in Churchill are beginning to acknowledge that they may live to see the day when the last polar bear of western Hudson Bay goes back on the ice and does not come back.

Helicopter pilot Justin Seniuk examines the carcass of a dirty polar bear, killed by another bear in the region.

CHAPTER ONE

POLAR BEAR SLAUGHTER

On September 7, 1619, two small Danish ships—the *Unicorn* and the *Lamprey*—entered the Churchill River on the west coast of Hudson Bay with 64 men on board. Theirs was as sad and miserable a story as has ever been recorded in the five hundred year search for the Northwest Passage—the fabled shortcut to the Orient. Only three men made it back home the next year. The rest succumbed to disease and starvation. They were buried or left to rot in a small cove southeast of the present day Churchill town-site.

Their fate had been set that first week of September when Jens Munk, the Danish leader of the expedition, realized that they would have to overwinter. Some of the men were already showing signs of scurvy, and the snow, the unrelenting wind, and the bitterly cold weather that usually comes six weeks later in the 21st century only made their miserable state worse. Recognizing the need for fresh food to augment their dwindling supplies, Munk ordered his men to gather berries and harvest what they could catch or shoot.

Shortly before settling in for the winter, a polar bear came in to feed on a beluga whale that Munk himself had killed the day before. Munk would then do what most Europeans who followed him did when they encountered such a large and imposing creature.

"I shot the bear and gave the meat to the crew with orders that it was to be slightly boiled, then kept in vinegar overnight," Munk wrote in his journal. *"I even had two or three pieces of the flesh roasted for the cabin. It was of good taste and quite agreeable."*[1]

The European traders, the American whalers, and the thousands of military personnel that followed, however, were rarely looking for food or trying to protect themselves, as Munk and his men had done back then when polar bears came into view.

More often than not, polar bears in the western Hudson Bay area of Churchill and York Factory were souvenirs and hides, or simply targets to shoot at, to take home to England or the United States.

Missionary John West was one of the first to describe the mentality that prevailed for nearly two centuries. Sailing from England to York

Factory in 1820, he describes how the chief mate alerted the captain to a polar bear and two cubs swimming towards them:

"He immediately ordered the jolly-boat to be lowered, and asked me to accompany him in the attempt to kill her," West wrote with uncharacteristic cheeriness in a journal that is very Protestant in its piety. *"Some axes were put into the boat, in case the ferocious animal should approach us in the attack; and the sailors pulled away in the direction she was swimming. At the first shot, when within about one hundred yards, she growled tremendously, and immediately made*

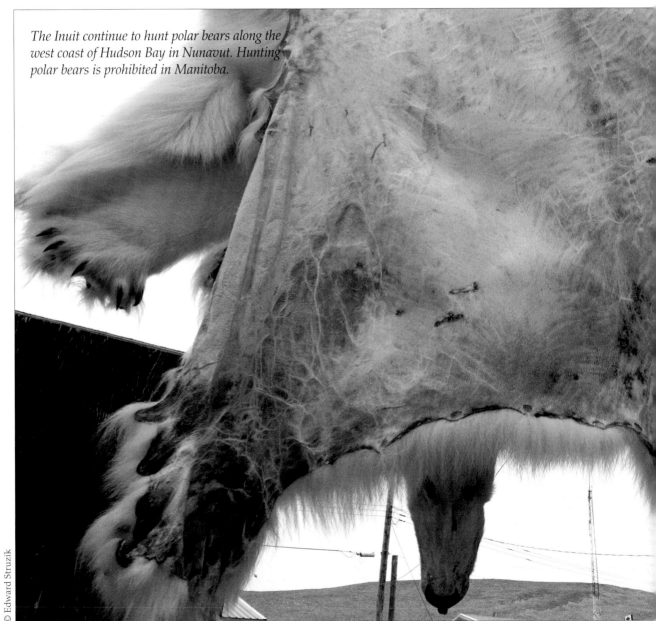

The Inuit continue to hunt polar bears along the west coast of Hudson Bay in Nunavut. Hunting polar bears is prohibited in Manitoba.

© Edward Struzik

for the boat; but having the advantage in rowing faster than she could swim, our guns were reloaded till she was killed, and one of the cubs also accidentally, from swimming close to the mother. The other got upon the floating carcase (sic), and was towed to the side of the ship, when a noose was put around its neck, and it was hauled on board for *the captain to take with him alive, on his return to England."*[2]

Heartless as West was in the telling of this tale, he proved to have been a keen and prescient observer of the natural history of the polar bear in this part of the world. Travelling 200 kilometres by horse and by foot from York Factory to the Prince of Wales fort, the Hudson Bay post along the Churchill River, he and his guides came upon the fresh tracks of a polar bear on July 12th.

"The bears are now coming off the ice in the Bay, on which they have been for several months past, to live upon seals, which they catch as they lie sleeping by the sides of the holes in the drift ice, when it dissolves or is driven far from shore," he wrote. *"They seek their food among the sea-weed and every trash that is washed up along the coast, or go upon the rocks, or to the woods, for berries, during the summer months."*[3]

West's observations were correct. Ice, or the lack of it, is the reason why there were, and continue to be so many polar bears congregating along the coast of western Hudson Bay near Churchill. Polar bears use sea ice as a platform to hunt seals, which comprise more than 95 percent of their diet. Due to the Bay's counter-clockwise current, the last of the winter ice melts near the Manitoba–Ontario border. As a consequence, hundreds of polar bears have no choice but to fast and hunker down there along the sandy, boulder-strewn beaches until the saltwater freezes, as it begins to do at Cape Churchill where a spit of land juts out into the tidal flats of Hudson Bay. The fasting season was three and a half months in West's day. Today, it's more than four, sometimes five months.

Polar bears are the largest non-aquatic carnivores in the world. While females normally weigh between 150 to 250 kilograms, males can weigh 350 to 650 kilograms or even more. Polar bears, especially the big males, preserve their energy throughout the hot summer months by resting and occasionally socializing with other bears, particularly on the capes and offshore islands where it tends to be cooler. Sometime in late July or early August, pregnant females will travel up to eighty kilometres inland to den sites that stretch 50 kilometres south of Churchill to the Ontario border. The tracks that West saw that day were probably those of a female on her way to give birth to one, or as many as three cubs.

West also accurately noted that *"savage as this animal is, it is not so much dreaded by the Indians as the grizzly bear, which is more ferocious and forward in his attack."* West would have been correct had he included the Inuit in that assessment.[4]

To the Inuit living along the coast of western Hudson Bay and elsewhere, the polar bear was more than just a source of food and material for clothing. For many of them, *nanuq*, as the animal is called by the Inuit of Canada, was nomadic, resourceful and such a good hunter of seals that it became a powerful symbol of who they were as a people, both in life and in death. The Inuit weren't so much afraid of the polar bear as they were in awe at how much it was like them—great hunters of seals.

Imagine, if you will, the Thule, ancestors of the Inuit who lived in Hudson Bay, seeing a bear up on its hind legs walking like a human. Or consider what they thought on those rare occasions when they were able to kill and skin an animal with only a snow knife and spear. In this state of undress, the similarity of the skinned torso of a bear to the appearance of the musculature of a human is superficial but spooky. In a skeletal state, a polar bear cub can look positively human.[5]

According to Inuit legend, the polar bear has the ability to transform itself into a human when it enters an igloo, reverting back to the animal form again when it goes outside. In the many stories that have been told and passed on, some bears could fly, disappear into thin air, or listen into conversations taking place far away. That's why Inuit children in some western Hudson Bay communities are told not to mention the name of *nanuq* when they come along on a hunt. If the bear hears them, their elders would warn, it will come and steal them away in the night.[6] Even today, many Inuit hunters firmly believe that a

Inuit hunter searching for polar bears, seals and walrus off the west coast of Hudson Bay near Rankin Inlet.

ARCTIC ICONS

17

© Lynn Holden

polar bear will not give itself up in a hunt unless it knows that it will be treated with respect after it is killed.[7]

Not surprisingly, the polar bear was often the spiritual guardian, or *tornaq*, of the shamans who were mediators between humans and spiritual beings. On his remarkable journey from Greenland to Alaska in 1923–24, ethnologist Knud Rasmussen described one encounter with an Inuit shaman, named Igjugarjuk, who countenanced the souls of a small group of people living inland in the region that straddles what is now the Manitoba–Nunavut Territory border. In one of many stories that Rasmussen tells, Igjugarjuk sees his sister-in-law, Kinalik, as a candidate for shamanism after she reports dreaming that a member of her tribe will become seriously ill. Recognizing this talent for prophecy, Igjugarjuk tests her spiritual powers by having her spend five days outside in the cold, tied to tent poles so that she would be noticed by *Sila*, a powerful spiritual force that controls wind, weather and all life on Earth and in the heavens. When the five days are up, Igjugarjuk throws a stone, striking her in the heart and causing her to collapse into a state of unconsciousness. The following day, Igjugarjuk attempts to revive Kinalik. She wakes up from her brief visit with death and explains that the polar bear, one of the guiding spirits that she has embraced in the form of an amulet that she wears, had protected her through the ordeal.[8]

Up until the time that Rasmussen arrived on the scene, there was no evidence to suggest that the Inuit were overharvesting these animals. Even with the establishment of a trading post at York Factory in 1684, and another at Churchill in 1717, very few polar bear hides came in from the north during the early years. *"In the course of many years residence at Churchill River, I scarcely ever saw a winter skin brought in from the Northward by the sloop,"* wrote explorer Samuel Hearne, who was for a time, governor of Prince of Wales Fort at Churchill. *"Probably, the Eskimaux, if they kill any, may reserve the skins for their own use, for at that season their hair is very long, with a thick bed of wool at the bottom and they are remarkably clean and white."*[9]

The Dene (Sayisi Dene) and the Maskekowininiwak (Swampy Cree), who also live along the coast of western Hudson Bay, were more interested in hunting caribou and moose than they were in *Sas Delgegiq* or *wâpask*, their names for polar bear. They valued the animal not so much for spiritual or cultural reasons as for the meat, fat, fur, and decorative items it provided them.[10] According to Andrew Graham, a fur trader who worked at Churchill, York Factory and Severn House, *"the Indians likewise eat the flesh of all* [polar bears] *they kill and mix the fat with cranberries, pounded venison* [ruhiggan] *etc., which constitute one of their great dainties."*[11]

By many accounts, there were a lot of polar bears back then. According to James Isham, who was based in Churchill in 1744, there were *"more polar bears about this fort this fall than ever was knowne* [sic]."[12] In 1783, William Falconer, the master of Severn House, claimed that there were so many bears around that he had difficulty getting the Swampy Cree to return to York Factory. All they wanted to do, he reported, was to hunt and eat the fat and meat of these animals.[13] Two years later, David Thompson marvelled at seeing twelve to fifteen polar bears daily when he walked from Fort Churchill to York Factory in the company of two Cree guides.[14]

While the Cree may not have held the polar bear in as high esteem as the Inuit did, the animal did have their respect. Thompson recalled an incident in which the two Cree guides killed a polar bear that had been cooling itself in the tidewater. When, with great effort, they dragged the animal ashore as the tide rolled in, they pointed its nose towards the open sea and prayed to the Bear Manitou.[15] According to Thompson, they interpreted the sinking of the skin as a signal that the Manitou did not want them to go back to Churchill and sell it for three pints of Brandy.[16] Thompson was relieved.

During the first few days of that long walk to York Factory, Thompson was clearly puzzled by the lethargic nature of most of the bears. One or two, he noted, would raise their head, but none rose up to *"molest"* them.[17] The strategy, his Cree guides advised, was to walk briskly past them and pay no notice.

On the sixth day of that long walk, however, Thompson learned pretty quickly that not all bears are as passive as those he had observed previously. The big bear they encountered that day was in the middle of a stream, feasting on a beluga that it had either killed or scavenged. When Thompson and his companions attempted to cross some fifty feet away, the bear growled like a *"Mastiff Dog…showed to us such a sett* [sic] *of teeth as made us turn upstream."*[18]

Thompson saw a lot of strange things during his stay at Prince of Wales Fort. The men who were employed at the trading post turned one cub that had been captured into a pet. The relationship did not last long, however.

"At first he had to be carefully protected from the dogs, but soon increased in size and strength to be a full match for them, and the blows of his forefeet kept them at a distance," he wrote. *"This Bruin continued to grow, and his many tricks made him a favourite, especially with the sailors, who often wrestled with him, and his growing strength gave them a Cornish hug… On Saturday, the sailors had an allowance of rum, and frequently bought some for the week, and on that night, Bruin was sure to find his way into the guardroom. One night, having tasted some grog, he came to a sailor with whom he had been accustomed to wrestle, and who was*

drinking too freely, and was so treated by him so liberally that he got drunk, knocked the sailor down and took possession of his bed. At fist-cuffs, he knew the bear would beat him and being determined to have his bed, he shot the bear. This is the fate of almost every Bear that is tamed when grown to their strength."[19]

The killing of polar bears intensified dramatically when American whalers began sailing into Hudson Bay in the 1860s. At one point, there were as many as sixteen ships in the region in a single season.[20] Initially, the whalers were interested more in sport and collecting souvenirs than in procuring hides. But as the bowhead whale numbers began thinning out, the whalers increasingly relied on these bears to augment their income. Polar bear hides fetched a good price from the Hudson's Bay Company in those days. Between the late 1880s and 1935, an estimated 15,500 hides were traded at posts across the Arctic.[21]

Up until 1935, there were no laws protecting polar bears in North America, or any other place in the world for that matter. Manitoba's decision to limit the hunt from May through October that year was one of the first attempts at conservation, but one that was not enforced in any meaningful way.

In 1938, the All-Russia Environmental Protection Society persuaded the Northern Sea

Wildlife Specialist Roy Bukowsky removes a leg snare from a tranquilized bear. The snare line was built to prevent bears from reaching town.

© Roy Bukowsky

Route Authority, Glavsevmorput, to prohibit the hunting of polar bears from ships and at polar hydrometeorological stations. A year later, the government of Norway followed suit with the establishment of the Kong Karls Land Polar Bear Reserve in Svalbard. Canada made its mark in 1949 when it restricted the hunting of polar bears to the holders of a General Hunting Licence. Then in 1956, the Russian Soviet Federated Socialist Republic Council of Ministers decreed, *"no polar bears could be hunted in Arctic waters and on islands and shorelands bordering the Arctic Ocean."*

In spite of these regulations, and other similar measures taken by the United States in the ensuing years, the numbers of polar bears continued to dwindle dramatically. By the 1960s, hunters in Alaska were killing so many bears that as many as 30 bush planes were lining up on the ice in Kotzebue waiting to take trophy hunters out onto the sea ice. In 1965, sports hunters accounted for more than half of the 386 bears killed that year,[22] leaving the writer of a *New York Times Magazine* article to ask: "Are the Days of the Arctic's King running out?"[23]

The decline of polar bears in the twentieth century was linked, in large part, to technology. The automatic high-powered rifle, and then the commercialization of the snowmobile in the 1960s fundamentally changed humankind's relationship with the polar bear, reducing the classic confrontation between man and beast to an arcade shooting game. In 1948, only an estimated 148 polar bears were killed in Canada. By 1960, that number rose to 509. In 1967, when the snowmobile overtook the dogsled as the primary means of Arctic transportation, 726 bears were reported killed. The trend, which was worldwide, was exacerbated when sports hunters and trappers joined the harvest using aircraft and preset guns to help them take their prey.

By the middle of the 1960s, scientists such as Dick Harington, who was assigned the task of studying polar bears for the Canadian Wildlife Service in 1961, estimated there might be only ten thousand bears left in the world—less than half of what there is today.[24] The Russians suggested that the numbers could be even smaller. The alarms led to the first circumpolar meeting on polar bears in Fairbanks, Alaska, in 1965.

Fortunately for the scientists attending, there was, by this time, genuine political interest in the plight of the species. *"If, as some people fear, the polar bear is in danger of becoming extinct, the world will be less for the loss,"* Alaska Senator E. L. Bartlett told the delegates on behalf of the President of the United States. *"If man can still take the time to see and understand the dignity and magnificence and uniqueness of polar bears, there is a good chance that man will meet and pass the necessary moral test."*[25]

It was a remarkable meeting, considering the Cold War mentality that prevailed at the time. At its conclusion, a resolution was passed calling for the protection of denning females and their cubs. In addition, the United States, Canada, Denmark, Norway, and the Soviet Union—together under the auspices of the International Union for the Conservation of Nature—agreed to pool their resources and research efforts to ensure a future for the species.

The Government of Manitoba did not stand by idly during these years. Recognizing the vulnerability of fur-bearing animals such as denning female polar bears, trappers were encouraged in 1949 to limit the number of polar bears they harvested. Then in 1954, regulations were brought in to ensure that non-natives did not trade in polar bear parts. In 1963, the hunting of a polar bear was limited to native people who rarely exercised that right.

In spite of these regulations, it was clear that polar bears in the Churchill region did not fare well in the 1960s, as they had in the decades before and after. Amy Lundie, an elder who lived on both sides of the Churchill River, says she rarely saw a polar bear in those days. Neither did Bob deMeulles, who was a young boy when his father got a job at the Port of Churchill in the

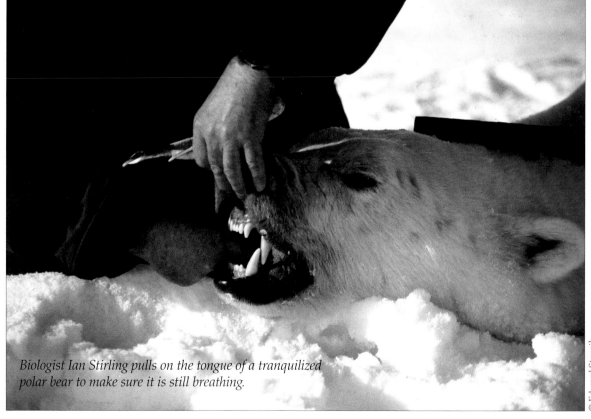

Biologist Ian Stirling pulls on the tongue of a tranquilized polar bear to make sure it is still breathing.

© Edward Struzik

Polar bears testing the thickness of the sea ice near Cape Churchill

1940s. The bears that residents saw back then, he recalls, were few and far between and usually just dots out on the ice. "Nobody seemed to be too worried about bears in those early days," he told me when I met with him during the height of the polar bear season one fall. "The big thing back then was caribou, which often stopped trains dead in their tracks or migrated by the thousands right through town."

The chance of being confronted by a bear was so slim that deMeulles remembers being completely caught off guard one day in the early 1960s when he was walking home from the Igloo Theatre and spotted a bear in the middle of town. "I first saw it out of the corner of my eye," he said. "I just froze in my tracks, I was so scared. I had never seen one so close. Fortunately, the bear just kept walking past the train station."[26]

No one knows exactly why there were so few bears back then; the whaling was long over by this point and the depleted bear population should have recovered from those slaughters.

The Inuit hunt for bears farther up the coast likely accounted, in part, for the small numbers. Once Hudson Bay freezes over, many of Churchill's bears travel as far north as Arviat, Rankin Inlet, and Chesterfield Inlet. Up until 1968, when harvest quotas were first issued for each of those Inuit communities, hunters could shoot as many bears as they wanted.

The hunting of females in dens could have also been a factor. In the five years preceding the closure of York Factory in 1957, an average of seventeen polar bear hides were brought in by native trappers each year.[27] While that may not sound like a lot of animals, it takes very few adult females to be removed on a continuing basis to have a significant dampening effect on a polar bear population.[28]

The build-up of thousands of men, machines, buildings, artillery, rocket ranges and the requisite garbage dumps at Churchill was likely the main reason for the paucity of bears.

The military build-up in the region began in 1942 when United States Air Force came up with a plan to ferry planes and material from southern California to Europe along a series of landing strips that extended from The Pas to Churchill, and from Churchill to Coral Harbour, Fort Chimo (Kuujjuaq), Frobisher Bay (Iqaluit), Greenland, Iceland and eventually to the United Kingdom.

Although the railway was shipping grain to the port by this time, there were no more than a few hundred people living in, or near, Churchill.

In relatively short order, however, some 83 officers and 2,152 enlisted men from Louisiana set up a tent camp in the middle of town. By the end of 1942, two runways, a hospital, three mess halls, and a receiver station had been built at a site about five kilometres away. The so-called Crimson Route never proved to be of much use, however. After just two years, the U.S. turned the site back to the Canadian military, which used it in cooperation with the Americans for the next quarter century. For a time, it was the largest jointly managed military installation in the world.[29]

The military never did launch any atomic bombs in the Churchill area as was once envisioned, but personnel did test 280-millimetre cannons and 106-millimetre recoilless rifles to see how they would fire in extremely cold conditions.

Experiments were done on insect control, cold weather clothing and on Inuit who were apparently worthy of study because of their ability "to take off and replace nuts and bolts at extreme temperatures far faster than white men in similar conditions."[30]

The northern lights were of particular interest to the military because of their apparent ability to block out radar and radio signals. U.S. defence research scientists went to bizarre lengths to figure this out. In 1950, a consignment of seventy Army Signal Corps carrier pigeons was sent to Fort Churchill to see how the birds would react to the magnetic pull of the northern lights.[31]

Recently vacated polar bear maternity den.

© Edward Struzik

While the military did its best not to disrupt local routines, it was virtually impossible to keep everyone out of harm's way, given the vastness of the landscape. Forty-nine-year-old Henry Johnson, a father of seven children, found this out the hard way when he got caught in machine gun crossfire while out collecting traps. So, apparently, did Simeon Spence, a trapper with six children.[32] There were so many close calls that the military ended up compensating a number of trappers in exchange for them giving up their trap lines in the region.

The welfare of polar bears, however, was a different matter. They never figured into the plans of the military. Against the advice of Canadian Wildlife Service scientists, a major manoeuvre on the west coast of Hudson Bay was staged during the fall months one year when the polar bear migration was at its peak. Shortly after the troops arrived, a blizzard blew in, preventing them from going out onto the land. With little to do, the soldiers chased the bears around on their snow machines. The bears, however, got their revenge. In the middle of the night, a number of them came into the base and tore apart three snowmobiles. One officer was apparently so upset he vowed to use the War Measures Act to go out and kill them.[33]

In an effort to keep polar bears off the base, soldiers dug long trenches on the tundra and filled them up with garbage.[34] There were numerous reports of planes leaving with polar bear hides along with trophy heads on board. Anecdotal reports suggest a number of bears were dispatched to protect people or to keep them away from the dumps.

Rev. Jock Davidson was the military chaplain in 1958 when Fort Churchill faced what he called a "polar bear invasion." According to his account, there were, at any given time, as many as twenty bears hanging around that November. Military personnel tried to drive them away with lights and thunder flashes, but the bears kept coming back. No one got hurt, but one young seaman on duty in the wireless station was left bug-eyed when the enormous paw of a polar bear came smashing through a window by his desk. When the animal's head followed, the seaman managed to fend off the bear by shooting the contents of a fire extinguisher into its face.[35]

Officers in charge of the base apparently took this all in stride until one of them nearly lost his life while walking through camp with his head down in a snowstorm. When the officer looked up momentarily to get his bearings, he spotted the figure of a polar bear standing up glowering at him and another officer who was walking behind. It was decided then that the military had to be more diligent in its use of helicopters to keep the bears away from the base.

Polar bear on the west coast of Hudson Bay near Churchill.

© Edward Struzik

Most times it worked, but in one case, the pilot was surprised to find a "great big daddy of a bear" turn on him and the machine, "wildly shadow-boxing for a time."[36]

The relationship between soldier and bear wasn't always a hostile one. Like the voyageurs who were stationed at Fort Churchill with David Thompson in 1785, some soldiers managed to turn a polar bear into a pet by regularly feeding it. The relationship got to be so cozy that the bear was invited to join the enlisted men for meals in the mess hall on a regular basis.

The beginning of the end of the strange relationship between the military and the polar bear began in 1964 when it became clear that conventional defence strategies for the Canadian north were no longer what they were when the base was set up. So when austerity

Occasionally, polar bears will try and break down doors in Churchill, as one did in the fall of 2011.

© Edward Struzik

measures led to major defence cuts that year, Fort Churchill was among the first to be put on the chopping block.[37]

With the closing of York Factory and the decline of the military presence in Churchill, the bear population began to rebound. In relatively short order, the animals quickly became a nuisance as well as a danger. Bears were breaking into houses, killing dogs, and terrorizing people on the streets. Residents responded by shooting the bears, or running them off with trucks and snowmobiles.

Inevitably, some of the more aggressive bears did what polar bears do in the wild. In some cases, such as the occasion when trapper Angus MacIver crawled under the lumber building to deal with a particularly troublesome polar bear, it ended with only a few stitches. The day, however, was soon coming when a confrontation like this one would end more tragically.

Before the town of Churchill closed its dump, many polar bears would wander in, attracted to the smell of garbage.

Polar bear cooling off on an iceberg.

CHAPTER TWO

GREAT WHITE RATS

In 1966, Churchill was a backwater port town that had been in steady decline since the military began pulling out of the area two years earlier. The prospects for the future did not look good. One could walk from one end of the town to the other in ten or fifteen minutes. Along the way there was the Eskimo Museum, the Churchill Hotel, the Hudson Hotel, Chez Gizelle, Bay Motors Garage, the Masonic Hall, the Hudson Bay store, the RCMP office, and Sigurdson and Martin's Supermarket, whose owners kindly carried customer debts until they had the money to pay. That was about it for commercial enterprises. The Igloo Theatre had closed its doors for the last time that summer, as did the Steak House, the town's only restaurant.

The housing situation was even worse. Many of the homes were tar paper, bare-framed shacks with additions that had been slapped on without any observance to municipal codes. Water was trucked in and stored in fuel drums. Heat came from oil, coal or woodstoves, many of which would never have met current safety standards. Voluntary firefighters were busier than they would have been in any other rural community.[1]

Port and government workers, Pan Am airline employees, local entrepreneurs and a handful of military families that had no other choice but to live in Churchill were better off, but not by much. Eileen Jacobs recalls having to share a tiny tar paper shack in town with another couple because her husband, a navy man, hadn't been in the service long enough to qualify for married residence. Their half of the

house was once a coal bin. No matter how much she cleaned, she says, she could never remove all traces of the coal dust.[2]

There were no sewers in those days. Honey buckets, chemical toilets, and outhouses served as toilet facilities. It was not uncommon for raw sewage to be floating down the street during the spring thaw. According to consultant Murray V. Jones, who was sent up to Churchill by the Government of Manitoba, the town council, and the Canada Mortgage Housing Corporation to evaluate the living conditions in the late 1960s, health hazards had been underscored many times before he arrived on the scene. He blamed the federal government for not preventing the "unparalleled squalor" that he saw in the community. Living conditions in Churchill, he reported, were "among the most wretched in Canada."[3]

Residents, which included a long list of colourful characters both from the region and from far-flung places, apparently agreed. In telegrams inviting the leaders of the three major federal parties to come to Churchill, they noted that "The Jones Commission agreed with the townsfolk that Churchill is forsaken by God and government…and that while there is no control over God, there may be hope the government would offer aid."[4]

It didn't do any good. Instead of offering aid, the Canadian government was preparing to announce that 250 people who were employed at the Rocket Range were going to lose their jobs and that the federal services being offered out of Churchill were going to be moved to Frobisher Bay in the Northwest Territories. Gordon Beard, the Independent MLA for the riding, was so distraught when he heard the rumours that he suggested that the government should "lock the whole show up and leave Churchill to the polar bears."[5]

Polar bears, however, represented another serious problem. Since the military began pulling out in 1964, more and more of the animals began venturing into town looking for food in one of the community's dumps. "Employees hauling the garbage were increasingly reluctant to deposit it into the pits," one government employee noted at the time, not because of the danger it posed to them, but because "it created a hardship for the human scavengers."[6]

When Canadian Wildlife Service scientist Chuck Jonkel first showed up in Churchill in the fall of 1966, some twenty bears had wandered into town at one point, including one young female who had made a nuisance of herself hanging around the Rocket Range looking for the handouts routinely offered to her by staff members who didn't know any better.

It was not uncommon for him and others to see cars and trucks lined up at the dump in semi-circles with the headlights trained on the animals. On one notable occasion, a group of 80 people formed a human ring around the bears.[7] Observing this dangerous practice, and the reckless and sometimes abusive manner in which some other people were interacting with polar bears, Jonkel felt that it was just a matter of time before something terrible would happen.[8]

He didn't have to wait long to be proven right. On the morning of October 1, 1966, four teenage boys set off from Churchill with plans to bag a few ptarmigan along a trail where the forest meets the open tundra near the Royal Observatory. Tim Hawkins, Roy Oliver, Ron Lockyear and Barry Pidskalny had been doing this pretty much every Saturday that fall without incident.

Five kilometres out of town, however, they ran into a polar bear that was apparently in no mood to give them a wide berth.

"We were walking along single file, when all of the sudden the other guys started yelling and screaming and then running off in all directions," Hawkins recalled 47 years later, as if it were yesterday. "I was last in line, so when they cleared off, I was left standing there alone, and there was this big bear coming towards me. I turned the other way and ran as hard as I could until I couldn't hear it chasing after me anymore. When I stopped and looked around, there was nothing there. I thought I had given it the slip."

Trying to figure out the whereabouts of his companions, Hawkins continued along the trail until he got to a small crater, which he figured had been created by mortar shelling during

A group of adult male polar bears congregates in Kaskatamagan Wildlife Management Area.

The Polar Bear Alert team skids a large tranquilized male across the ice to where they can load it in the truck.

© Brian Barton

previous military exercises. At the end of his run down to the bottom of the crater, Hawkins froze when he saw the bear coming down towards him from the other direction.

"I had no chance," he said. "He gave me a good swat and literally took the top of my head off. The next thing I knew, I was on the ground half-conscious with blood pouring out everywhere. The bear then came over to me and started chewing on my foot. I curled my toes back in my boot so that it couldn't bite me. I don't remember much about what happened next because I kept coming in and out of consciousness. Each time I opened my eyes, though, I could see the bear lying down in the corner of the crater looking at me. It was strange, like a bad dream that wouldn't go away. There must have been something wrong with it. Otherwise it would have eaten me, I figure."[9]

Hawkins' pals eventually caught up with him after backtracking and calling out his name. Seeing the predicament he was in, one of them—he can't remember which one—fired a few bullets from a .22 rifle into the rump of the animal. It was the only gun they had. All that did was make the animal more ornery than it already was.

Hawkins would have almost certainly died had there not been anyone at the Observatory to come to his rescue and rush him to the hospital.

He can still remember the look on the face of his mother, a nurse, who happened to be on duty in Emergency that day.

Hawkins lived to tell the tale. The bear, however, ended up dead after an RCMP constable arrived on the scene and tracked the animal down.[10]

Tragic as this incident was, Jonkel had a theory as to why this bear acted so strangely. While conducting a necropsy on the animal in the days that followed, he discovered old scars, along with the fresh wounds that the boys had inflicted that day. The scars suggested the bear had been shot a number of times before.[11]

It was not a pretty sight. One of the earlier shots had driven a canine tooth into the nasal passage, leaving the bear blind in one eye. In Jonkel's view, the attack on the boys was not unprovoked, as the RCMP had concluded. The bear, he felt, had been tormented or used for target practice.[12] This was an animal that saw humans as a threat. So when Hawkins and the other boys came around that day, it instinctively attacked to defend itself from further pain. Being a newcomer, however, Jonkel bit his tongue, at least until he could get a better handle on what was going on.

Jonkel had earned his stripes in the scientific world with a groundbreaking study of black bears in northwestern Montana, which tested the theory that extrinsic factors such as climate and the availability of food were responsible for fluctuations in populations. The three-year field study led to a fundamental rethinking of the management of black bears, which at the time consisted largely of ranchers, miners and lumberjacks shooting them whenever they came near livestock or humans.

When John Tener, the head of the Canadian Wildlife Service was looking for someone to replace Dick Harington after Harington decided to become a paleontologist and moved to the Canadian Museum of Nature in 1965, Jonkel came highly recommended. In addition to the legendary Ian McTaggart-Cowan acting as his thesis supervisor at the University of British Columbia, Jonkel had the great Aldo Leopold as an external advisor, and Canadian geneticist David Suzuki as a teacher. All three encouraged the application of scientific methods to wildlife management.

The west coast of Hudson Bay near Churchill was not Jonkel's first choice to begin his polar bear studies. Instead, he headed up to Southampton and Coats islands at the north end of Hudson Bay, hoping to continue the work that Harington had started in the region. With him was his assistant Ken Coldwell, University of Manitoba student Brian Knudsen, and Fred Bruemmer, a Latvian-born, Canadian photographer who was

well on his way to becoming one of the country's finest photographers.

There was really no protocol or strategy for handling polar bears at that time. Harington had tried using a "Cap-Chur" compressed air gun that was supposed to drive a drug dart into an animal. But the first time he tried putting one into a denning female, the dart made a slight "pop" and fell to the ground near the tip of the air rifle. The gun, it seemed, was not designed to operate in the extreme cold. When Harington tried strapping a drug dart onto a seal lance and jabbing the mother with that primitive tool, she let out a growl and chomped on the lance, leaving it bent at a right angle.[13]

Biologists working on polar bears in Alaska hadn't fared much better when they embarked on the first survey of the state's beleaguered population in 1965. To his dismay, Vagn Flyger, a University of Maryland scientist who had successfully used syringe guns to immobilize deer in Maryland in the 1950s, found that he had to get within 13 metres of a polar bear in order to effectively fire a syringe into the animal. "This is a little too close for comfort," he told *The New York Times*.[14]

Darting bears in this way was so harrowing that Flyger confessed that he had asked himself on more than one occasion, "What am I doing out here?" He did, however, manage to shoot seven bears in this manner the first time up, but four of the bears died, and two ran away without any noticeable effect. Only one bear was captured, marked and released.

With a new generation of drugs and projectile syringes at his disposal, Jonkel was a little better equipped to take on the challenge when he took over from Harington in 1966. Things, however, did not go his way when he headed north to the Arctic. In the ten weeks that he and his colleagues were camped on Coats and Southampton islands, they managed to catch just one bear.

With time running out before winter set in, Jonkel and his team headed south to Churchill, hoping for better luck. It was a good decision. In six weeks, they caught 20 bears with baited traps that had been set out on the tundra.

Given the fierce reputation that polar bears had at the time, Jonkel and his colleagues were a little surprised to see how most of the polar bears were resigned to their plight once they were trapped.

The first animals they caught, for example, were a female and a two-year-old cub. Except for a low growl the mother made when they approached to put a syringe into her, neither one seemed to be the least bit aggressive.[15]

Jonkel and his colleagues were so smitten by the gentle nature of another female that was captured that first week, they called her "Sweety." The bear they got attached to the most, however, was "Linda," the animal that had made such a nuisance of herself begging for food at the Rocket Range. She was accidentally snared a second time that fall while Jonkel was on his way to Ottawa to pick up some radio collars. When informed by phone of what had happened, Jonkel told Bruemmer and Fred Anderka, the Canadian Wildlife Service radio technician, to keep an eye on her until he got back.

Having travelled 1,800 kilometres by dog sled for two months photographing Inuit from Grise Fjord hunting polar bears in the High Arctic, Bruemmer knew a little more than most about the nature of polar bears. The gentle character of this animal, however, so caught him off guard that he was left enchanted. Linda became so accustomed to his twice-daily visits that she readily ate meat from his hand and allowed him to pet her.[16]

In addition to being fitted with ear tags and lip tattoos, polar bears like Linda were equipped with radio transmitters that would allow Jonkel to follow their movements. The strategy proved to be useful a lot more quickly than he had imagined.

As it turned out, one of the polar bears they caught and tagged was shot and wounded a short time after mauling two Chipewyan residents at the Dene Village outside of Churchill.

The plight of the Chipewyan, or the *Sayisi Dene* as they call themselves, had been a sorry one up until this point. Churchill was intended to be a new home for about 200 of them after they had been forcibly relocated from Duck Lake in 1956 so that the government of Canada could better provide social services to them. Government bureaucrats, however, never properly planned for their welfare. For the first ten years, home for

most of them was a tar paper shack overlooking a graveyard on the rocky, windswept shores of Hudson Bay.

When a senior bureaucrat saw how wretched their living conditions were in 1966, he had them

moved to a new site in the muskeg, five kilometres southeast of town. Life in Dene Village, as it was called, was no better for a variety of reasons. Unable to hunt for food because government officials feared that they would kill too many moose and caribou, many of the Dene were forced to go to one of the dumps in the area to find their supper. "You got along with polar bears so long as you didn't dig in the same pile or fight over the same piece of meat," Dene chief Ila Bussidor recalled many years later.[17]

Traditionally, people living in Dene Village came out at night to socialize, even in fall and winter when it was cold and dark. On some nights they would walk to "Camp"—the name they gave to Fort Churchill—to see what they could scrounge up.

On one of those dark nights in November, twenty-eight year old Adolphe Thorassie was confronted by a polar bear at around 9 p.m. The animal ripped out a piece of his scalp before Thorassie took refuge in a nearby house. Adel Nalge wasn't so lucky. Alerted to the screaming, she ran outside only to find the bear turning on her. The bear dragged her by the head for several metres before two neighbours arrived and shot the animal.[18]

Having tracked and occasionally observed this bear for two months, Jonkel knew a little about its history. During that time, he saw that

One orphaned cub became so accustomed to Norwegian biologist Nils Øritsland that it followed him everywhere on an island in Spitsbergen.

the bear had been photographed, stoned, fed, and chased by trucks, dogs, and snowmobiles at various times while feeding at the dump.[19]

Once again though, Jonkel decided to bite his tongue rather than speak his mind. When four bears were found dead at the dump in what some interpreted as an act of revenge, however, he could no longer remain silent.

"Polar bears are apparently not looked upon by these people as the 'Great White Bear of the North,' but rather as creatures akin to rats," he wrote at the time. "Should the present trend continue, this view of polar bears will prevail as it has in regard to the Black and Grizzly Bear in some southern regions."[20]

It was one thing back then for a scientist like Jonkel to vent his frustrations in private and on the pages of a scientific journal, but when a polar bear killed a 19-year-old boy in the fall of 1968, members of the Chamber of Commerce in Churchill suggested that something needed to be done to avoid a "wholesale slaughter."[21]

Paulosie Meeko was a vocational student from Great Whale River in northern Quebec. His fate was sealed on the afternoon of November 17th when he and two friends came across a polar bear that had been sleeping in the sun behind the recreation centre. The bear had apparently become habituated to the town-site because hospital workers were in the habit of feeding it scraps. Seeing the bear lying there quietly, Meeko and his friends played a game of "Chicken," trying to see who could get closest to the animal. Meeko won the contest when he got near enough to kick the sleeping bear in the butt, but lost when the bear got up and ran him down.[22]

Tim Hawkins remembers it well because he was in the gymnasium playing basketball at the time. "Like everyone else, I headed out to the scene to see what had happened when I heard the screaming," he recalls. "I didn't think about what had happened to me two years earlier until the RCMP officer who eventually showed up told me that I, of all people, should have known better than to be out there with a polar bear on the loose. I didn't care though. Like everyone else, I wanted to see what was happening."[23]

As it turned out, there was too big a crowd for Constable Jim Madrigga to get a clear shot. So he fired into the air, hoping to scare the animal off. The bear took flight as he had hoped, but unfortunately, it dragged the boy with him. By the time the bear was put down, the boy had lost too much blood to be saved. He died two hours later, after being taken to hospital with a badly slashed throat.[24,25]

Churchill's problems with bears didn't end then, however. Ten days later, local government administrator Doug Ritchie and his wife found themselves trapped in their cabin, 15 kilometres away, by a polar bear that had broken in.[26] Their ordeal only ended when Ritchie picked up a broom and whacked the bear over the head a few times.

The growing tension between polar bears and people in Churchill reached a breaking point the following spring when local Cree trapper John Spence lost his arm to a bear that had pounced on him in the bush.

The winter of 1968–69 had been a hard one for locals like Spence who still relied on hunting and trapping. To help make ends meet in a year in which the caribou did not come around, he, his father Alec, his uncle Jimmy Spence, and his cousin Frank went out trapping beaver along the Rupert Creek in what is now Wapusk National Park. After the tent was set up, John went out on his own, looking for beaver houses when he stumbled on a bear and her two cubs. Out there alone, there was nothing he could do when the bear rose up on her hind legs and swatted Spence across the head, knocking him to the ground and taking several bites out of him. Fortunately for Spence, the bear backed off when he screamed and fought back.[27]

He was left bleeding badly though, and barely made it back to camp. "Oh boy, talk about a mess," Spence's uncle recalled a few years later. "He was all covered with blood on one side. No mitts, no cap. His arm, from the shoulder down to the elbow, was bare to the bone. The flesh was hanging down. Everything was frozen."

Realizing that his son needed help badly, Alec Spence set off at 5 a.m. the next morning and ran his dog team for 18 hours straight before getting to the railroad siding at M'Clintock, 50 kilometres away. There, he asked a section foreman to send a telegram to Churchill for help. There was, however, no aircraft available in Churchill to conduct a rescue and it would be a day before a pilot could fly in. Knowing that the pilot would need directions, Spence hopped into a boxcar and rode the rails in the bitter cold that night.[28]

When Spence's story, and his eventual rescue, made front-page news in Winnipeg, Manitoba government officials were already well-aware that they had a problem on the west coast of Hudson Bay. A few months earlier, conservation officers Mike Kotyk and Cecil Smith had flown up to investigate, and what they saw, even before Paulosie Meeko was killed, was disturbing. Not only were bears injuring or threatening people, they were killing dogs and destroying property. In their opinion, however, people were a bigger problem than the bears were. Warning signs, public notices, and radio and television announcements advising people to stay away from bears went unheeded. "If anything, it has encouraged people to visit

Polar bears play-fighting. Battles such as this rarely end in serious injury, unlike during mating season.

© Edward Struzik

the dump where they photograph, feed, stone, shoot, and even try to pet the bears," they wrote in their report. "Anyone can drive out to the pit and do so in much the same manner we go to the corner drive-in theatre... There even appears to be a resentment toward those carrying out scaring and live-trapping operations to protect the public. The live trap had to be locked to prevent it from being pushed over the dump edge. Tires had been punctured and trapped bears released."[29]

In many ways, Gordon Emberley was the right man to deal with this increasingly volatile situation. As a bush pilot and animal control officer working for the Manitoba government, he knew the lay of the land and a little about the people who lived in Churchill. He had also participated in wildlife surveys in the region with game warden Joe Robertson.

Over a period of two days, Emberley sat down with Jonkel, RCMP officer Jim Madrigga, officials from Indian Affairs, Public Works, and Doug Ritchie, who was the local government administrator.

"There was no doubt in my mind that we had a very serious situation on our hands," Emberley recalled when I tracked him down 43 years later. "People in Churchill were getting fed up with the situation, even before the death of that Eskimo schoolboy (Meeko), and they wanted something done. I was there to see what the possibilities were."[30]

No shortage of solutions was offered in those two days of meetings. The most extreme—killing all the bears—was rejected without serious debate. Many of the participants supported the idea of building an incinerator, or relocating the dump at Fort Churchill five to ten miles down the coast to keep bears and people a safe distance apart. One person suggested that a ton of whale meat be dropped off annually along the coast at La Perouse Bay to keep the bears away.

There was talk of sending problem bears to zoos and introducing legislation that would make it illegal to feed the animals. Emberley himself favoured the idea of guided big game hunts that would dispatch problem bears and bring in revenue.

Emberley was disappointed when the government failed to act on most of his recommendations. He believed it was because he was not a biologist. He may have been right. But the situation was not that simple. Relocating the dump so far out of town would have been extremely expensive for a small town like Churchill, and it already had more than its share of infrastructure problems. Snow, which comes often to the region, would have had to be cleared regularly for garbage trucks, and studies would have had to be done to make sure that the new site would not contaminate groundwater. Pan American World Airways officials, who managed the Churchill Rocket Range, also objected, because the location of such a dump might attract bears that were a lot more dangerous than Linda or Sweety.

Bleak and hopeless as Churchill's future looked to be at the time, not all was lost. In the end, the Department of Public Works agreed to at least bury garbage in Churchill with sand and to look into the possibility of building an incinerator. Manitoba government officials also committed to the idea of sending wildlife officers to Churchill during the fall months to scare off and live-trap problem bears, as well as to help educate the public.

Dick Robertson the regional wildlife biologist and Paul Rod the senior conservation officer responsible for the region, were sent in during the summer of 1969 to get a feel for the situation. Conservation officer Dale Cross followed shortly after. Once there, it was obvious to them that Jonkel was right. Polar bears were

Young polar bears like this one are the animals that are most likely to cause trouble in Churchill.

© Edward Struzik

too often viewed as great white rats—as some people at the time called them—rather than the great carnivores that they are.

Just 23 years old at the time, Cross took over for David Buck in 1969 after Buck was transferred out as conservation officer for the Gillam–Ilford district. Green behind the ears as he may have been at the time, Cross was skilled in the outdoors, as most young men from Flin Flon were. He recalls having no fear when he hopped on a train for Churchill that fall, even though he had never seen a polar bear before.

It wasn't easy getting the polar bear control program up and running. Manitoba Conservation had no physical presence in the community. There were no government trucks, no offices to work out of, nor any lodgings for Cross and his colleagues to live in. With no other choice, for the first couple of years, they worked out of a two-room patrol building downtown, renting what they dubbed "Rent-a-Wrecks"—two-wheeled machines with bald tires—from a local establishment, before they started shipping up four-wheel driver vehicles on the train.

At the peak of that first season, there were as many as four officers working 12-hour shifts and sharing in the duties of manning the radio, setting up traps, working with the media, educating the public and patrolling the streets.

For Cross, Paul Rod, Bruce Molberg, Roy Reinke, and university student Bill Harper, it was mostly a matter of learning on the job that first year, just as it was for Dick Robertson who spent 23 days at Churchill that fall. No one else in the world had attempted anything similar in the past, so there was no model for them to follow.

The protocol that emerged that first season, however, was relatively straightforward. Working with the RCMP, a radio communication system was eventually set up to direct reports of polar bear sightings to the patrol house. Residents were asked to keep their garbage indoors, putting it out only on collection day. A chain-link fence was erected along the school grounds to prevent bears from coming in out of the forest. Many of the high-risk areas were posted with "Out of Bounds" signs.

When a bear was observed anywhere near a residential area, Cross and his colleagues would use giant firecracker-like devices such as cracker shells, bird bombs, and bear bangers to scare it away. In the event the bear returned, a live trap was set up. If the bear couldn't be trapped, it was shot and sent to Jimmy Spence who lived on the outskirts of town. After skinning the animal, Spence would then feed the meat to his many dogs.

Trapped bears were transported and released at Bird Cove, 20 kilometres away, and almost as far east of Churchill as the officers could drive before

running out of road. If that bear returned, every effort was made to transport the animal to a zoo, so long as zoo officials were willing to pay for the cost.

There wasn't much in the way of polar bear sightings in September, and not much more in October. Only one bear had to be destroyed: it was dispatched by the RCMP at Fort Churchill in September. That gave Cross and his colleagues some time to get the safety message out to residents and to school children.

One of the things that surprised Cross was how most of the school kids he talked to knew as little about polar bears as kids from towns like Flin Flon or Winnipeg. They all wanted to know how fast a polar could run, how large its teeth were, how big they grew and whether it was true that polar bears could only turn in one direction. Many of the children assumed that if attacked from one direction, they would be safe if they zig-zagged the opposite way.

Not everyone paid attention to the advice Cross offered in classrooms, on the local radio, and on sign posts. One day, Cross found a group of unsupervised kids skating on the outskirts of town in an area where there were fresh polar bear tracks. He sent the kids back home. Later that same day, an employee at the Fort Churchill weather office was seen checking instruments outside the building he was working in, with bears all around him. People were still going out to the dump on Sunday to get pictures of their kids standing in front of a bear eating garbage. And a few people were still taking pot shots at bears. One of the animals Cross handled that year suffered from a bad limp. When Cross darted the bear and checked its condition, he found the animal's paw had been shot full with pellets.

Quiet as it was in the first several weeks, the situation changed dramatically after a four-day blizzard blew in. The number of problem bears jumped from just 22 in September and October, to 92 by November 16th. In almost all of these cases, officers simply chased the animal out of town. One young animal, however, could not be deterred from returning to the residential area to which it seemed to be habituated. When it was caught in a culvert trap the fourth time, it was considered "delinquent" and shipped off to the Assiniboine Zoo which, to the surprise of many, was one of the few zoos in the world interested in receiving a live animal.

The big scare, however, came on Sunday, November 16th when Cross and his colleagues were just finishing up their lunch after unsuccessfully tracking down a bear that had killed the local doctor's dog that morning.

Greta Cook was one of the town's school teachers. She was driving home that day when

Signs are placed all around Churchill to remind people of the possibility of a polar bear in the area.

ARCTIC ICONS

53

she spotted a boy cornered by a bear on the steps of the Catholic Church. It was bitterly cold and 50-kilometre per hour winds were whipping up clouds of snow on the streets. With one eye on the road, and another on the bear, Cook made a quick U-turn. The next thing she saw was the boy lying on the ground. He looked like he was dead.

Seven-year-old Bradley Whyte, however, was just playing possum. The bear had swatted him on the back and knocked him down. Bradley lay motionless until the bear walked away. Cook picked the boy up and took him home to his father who then called the RCMP. By the time the RCMP and wildlife officers arrived, there was nothing left to do but to track down the animal and kill it.

Two days later, Cross and Robertson flew east along the coast of Hudson Bay to survey

Polar bears routinely wander in and out of the treeline near Churchill.

© Edward Struzik

the situation. It was surreal, Cross recalls. Along the way they counted 70 polar bears.[31] Most of them were concentrated around Cape Churchill where the ice was beginning to form much more quickly than it was along the town site. It was apparent to him and Robertson that these polar bears must have sensed that this location was the best place to be in order to get back onto the ice and hunt seals.

It was difficult to evaluate how well that first season went, given the fact that nothing like their project had ever been attempted before. At least some people in Churchill were beginning to embrace the idea of reporting a bear, and,

more often than not, wildlife officers were successful in driving the animal away with cracker shells and bangers. Still, a total of ten animals, including two that attacked biologist Dick Russell while he was working in the field, had to be put down. Protecting people, it seemed, meant that a lot of bears would have to die in the future, unless some other methods of management were found. Although they had no way of knowing it, Dale Cross and his colleagues would face an uphill battle in the years ahead. It wasn't going to be easy convincing people that polar bears were not the great white rats that some considered them to be.

CHAPTER THREE

OPERATION BEARLIFT

In the fall of 1971, Jack Howard, the chief of wildlife operations for the Manitoba government, hopped on a single-engine bush plane in York Factory to take a trip along the west coast of Hudson Bay to Churchill. With a journalist on board, he wanted to assess the polar bear situation firsthand, now that the polar bear control program was making headlines on radio, television and in newspapers down south. No one had ever seen anything like it. Three weeks earlier, Canada's *Globe and Mail*, London's *Daily Mirror*, the Canadian Broadcasting Corporation, and a CBS television crew from Chicago were in Churchill with several other reporters sending out stories that were being published all across the western world. Even *The New York Times* called in at one point to assess the situation.[1] An estimated 300 million people had tuned in to learn about a controversial program to airlift two-dozen problem bears out of the community.[2]

This wasn't the first time that polar bears along the west coast of Hudson Bay had made international news. The unease that reflected the relationship between bears and people in the region first caught the attention of the foreign media in 1915 when a group of engineers was setting up a wireless station on the coast. In an effort to get back to their camp ahead of a looming storm, the men got lost in a blizzard before finding themselves stranded on a massive ice floe that happened to be inhabited by two-dozen hungry bears. With only one gun between them, the men spent the night huddled on top of a huge chunk of ice. By the time the sun rose the next day, one bear was dead and several others were injured. *The New York Times* reported that the

frightened and hypothermic men were eventually rescued.[3]

Churchill's bears had also made world headlines in July 1970, when the Queen of England came to town. Buckingham Palace had been warned about mosquitoes.[4] But no one in the Manitoba or the Canadian governments, it seemed, contemplated the possibility that the Queen and her entourage might run into a polar bear, even though the animals traditionally start coming off the ice around the time of her scheduled arrival. As a result, it was left to the RCMP to haze the two bears that wandered within a half mile of the ceremonies. Neither of the animals was killed, but a nine-year-old local girl presented the Queen with a polar bear rug. The gift was made courtesy of the Girl Guides and Boy Scout associations of Churchill.[5]

What happened in the fall of 1971, however, was even more extraordinary. Media coverage of the plan to airlift twenty-four polar bears out of Churchill bordered on the hysterical. Reports about the relocations were either full of praise or full of rage about the amount of time, money and effort being spent on those bears causing trouble in town. In Churchill, journalists from Canada and from other parts of the world jockeyed for opportunities to see the bears up close. Many of them pleaded with conservation officers and local residents to share their wildest tales. "There are only 12,000 polar bears left on earth," a headline in London's *Daily Mirror*

screamed. "This story might save some of those sentenced to death."[6]

The idea of using a DC-3 to relocate 24 polar bears 200 kilometres away from Churchill was the brainchild of Brian Davies, the founder of the International Fund for Animal Welfare (IFAW), which was also behind those images of baby white seal pups being clubbed to death off the coast of Newfoundland and Labrador, and in the Gulf of St. Lawrence. Davies was a British college dropout who had come to Canada from Wales in 1955, before joining the Canadian military for a short spell. He was volunteering for the local Society for the Prevention of Cruelty to Animals in Fredericton, New Brunswick, when he and several directors of the SPCA founded IFAW in 1969.

Brian Davies, founder of the International Fund for Animal Welfare (IFAW) suggested using a DC-3 to airlift 24 polar bears 300 kilometres away from Churchill.

© Dale Cross

The ensuing campaign to save the baby seals from being clubbed to death had not made Davies many friends in Canada during those early years. Canadian Embassy officials at one point had to be dispatched to the four corners of the world to control the damage his anti-sealing campaign was doing to Canada's reputation abroad. Newspaper editorialists and politicians loathed him. At one point in the debate, Newfoundland Premier Joey Smallwood called him a "bigoted, biased, and badly informed fool."[7]

Notorious as he was, Davies wasn't quite the lightning rod he would come to be several years later when he brought French actress Brigitte Bardot and other celebrities out onto the sea ice to stare down the sealers and accuse them of being "assassins" and "murderers."

Manitoba was in the midst of a dramatic political transition when Davies arrived on the scene. For the first time, a social democrat—Ed Schreyer—was premier and his government was busy implementing a socialist agenda that included public automobile insurance, a more affordable medicare system and the creation of the Department of Northern Affairs, which aimed to help impoverished frontier communities such as Churchill.

Still, the fact that his government even considered allowing Davies to airlift polar bears out of Churchill is remarkable, given Davies' hardcore, unconventional stand on animal rights. Politically progressive as Manitobans may have been back then, many of them were avid hunters and fishers.

Unlikely partners as Davies and Manitoba Conservation seemed to be, there were reasons for the alliance.

The Manitoba government had spent a lot of money—$40,000 the year before—airlifting problem bears forty kilometres out to the coast by helicopter. Not only was this extremely expensive, it proved to be futile. Most of the bears found their way back to town within a few days.

The government also had a potential public relations nightmare on its hands. Jack Howard himself had publicly predicted that if a solution to the problem bears was not found, as many as thirty animals would die that year. "Every year we have this problem of keeping bears and people apart," he told the *Winnipeg Free Press*. "And with live trapping, it was getting to be a pretty expensive business."[8]

Davies' offer to spend about $20,000 to fly problem bears out of town was one that could not be refused. Even if the relocations didn't work this time around, Howard figured, it would be better if the money was wasted by Davies than by the government.

Andrew Szklaruk and Mike Sitko load a tranquilized bear into the back of a truck.

To his credit, Davies didn't disguise what it was that he was trying to do when some skeptical members of the media initially questioned his motives for trying to save polar bears and seals instead of other threatened animals that perhaps deserved as much, or more, attention.

"One of the great weaknesses of animal welfare is that people try to do too much, and as a result, nothing ever gets done," he said when he announced the launching of "Operation Bearlift," the name he personally gave to his polar bear relocation plan that October. "We believe in seizing an issue. This [polar bear] situation developed this way. It has to be something that appeals to the media. Besides," he pointed out matter-of-factly, he liked seals and polar bears and this campaign appealed to him.[9]

For conservation officers Dale Cross, Brian Wotton, Paul Rod, and nine other colleagues who were being rotated in and out of town in

1971 to work on the Polar Bear Control Program, Operation Bearlift was a bit of gong show. They had been busy enough dealing with an increasing number of bears that were breaking into houses, killing dogs, and terrorizing people in residential areas. Since the start of the Control Program in 1968, the number of problem bears showing up in Churchill had risen from 20 to 57. Sightings of polar bears had increased from 92 to 184. "We didn't need the media parachuting in at any given time asking us silly questions and trying to get us to do stupid things such as dressing up in white coats so that we would look more photogenic," Cross recalls.[10]

It was obvious to Cross, and to pretty much everyone else by this time, that the garbage dumps of Churchill were the main attraction for polar bears. There were several dumps scattered about. As many as forty bears could be seen feeding on the waste, at any given time. Beautiful as a polar bear can be hunting seals on the floe edge in spring, they are often not a pretty sight in the snowy, muddy days of autumn in Churchill. It was not unusual back then to see bears with tin cans stuck to their tongues or chewing on car batteries. Many of the animals were blackened by soot from fires that had been started in an effort to burn the waste. Sadly, the

Baited culvert traps such as this are still used around Churchill's perimeter. Manitoba Wildlife Technician Dale Cross pictured.

© Dale Cross

great white bear sometimes did, in a perverse way, resemble a great white rat.

Garbage wasn't the only issue; there were other attractants as well. One Rocket Range employee, for example, came up with the idea of raising pigs along the coast near the Boy Scout Camp, using restaurant and butcher waste to feed them. In relatively short order, some fifteen bears had been drawn to the site. They were breaking into buildings, terrorizing people and, of course, eating pigs. The pig farmer was incensed when he was given a stern warning about killing the pig-eating bears.

There was also the issue of dogs, which are, like pigs, a tasty treat for a seal-eating polar bear that hasn't consumed much more than seaweed, berries, and maybe a few goose eggs for three or four months. Like most northern communities in the 1970s, dogs could be found everywhere in and around Churchill. People used them for hunting and trapping, and for recreational purposes in winter. In summer, they were tied up on the coast, or on the outskirts of town, often with 45-gallon drums filled with rancid whale and seal meat to feed them. Left to fend for themselves, the dogs were easy pickings for an animal that has the ability to lift a 700 pound (318 kg) bearded seal out of the water.

While no one in Churchill had been killed since Paulosie Meeko was mauled to death in 1968, most everyone thought it was only going to be a matter of time before something as tragic as that would happen again. A few weeks before Howard arrived on the scene, conservation officers were so busy dealing with problem bears that it was left to the RCMP to kill an animal that had smashed its head through a window while a family was eating at the dinner table.

None of this was conducive to employee morale. There was, as Howard noted in a letter to his boss, a "sour note" and "a general feeling of frustration," among conservation officers who were being rotated in and out of Churchill during the fall months to deal with the bear problem. With eight animals dead in 1969, ten in 1970, and already seven by the time Howard arrived, some officers felt it would be more effective, and just as humane, to allow big game hunters to harvest the bears instead of just killing the more troublesome animals.[11]

The idea of thinning out the population was nothing new. Doug Beiers, editor of the local weekly newspaper, suggested to *The New York Times* that he and most residents in Churchill believed a cull of fifty to one hundred bears was necessary.[12]

Beiers and others like him were in good company, however. Now five years on the scene, Chuck Jonkel had already convinced Canada's newly established polar bear technical committee to recommend a harvest of fifty bears in the Churchill region. He predicted that conservation officers would eventually have to kill that many if a hunt were not allowed.

No one in the government, however, was interested in dealing with the public backlash that would inevitably follow, should a big game hunt be sanctioned. Howard said as much in October when he told a *Globe and Mail* reporter that even though he personally believed a "stringently controlled hunting season would effectively thin out the bear population," he also believed that the fallout from the public would be "damning."[13]

There were, however, other issues at play which may, or may not, have affected the decision to forego a cull of the population. Manitoba's jurisdiction ended at the low tide mark back then, just as it does now. Therefore, any hunt in the province would have to take place when the animals were on land—hardly a challenge given how lethargic the bears are at that time. It would be like shooting fish in a barrel.

Hides would also be of low value because the bears are generally thin in late fall and their fur is often ratty and yellowish. And since it wouldn't be a meat hunt per se, sportsmen would want to shoot the largest animals—the big males that tended to congregate at places like Cape Churchill. No one other than Dale Cross and the

'There will be a further delay on flight . . .'

Making the fur fly

Globe and Mail editorial cartoon October 12, 1971.
conservation officers fully appreciated it at the time, but it was the young animals that were causing the majority of the trouble.

There were also political issues to consider. In the long lead-up to the International Agreement on the Conservation of Polar Bears that was still being negotiated in 1971, representatives from the Soviet Union had repeatedly made proposals to stop the worldwide harvest of polar bears completely. The Soviets were supposed to be the bad guys, as Premier Alexei Kosygin found out in October of that year, when he was manhandled by protesters during his visit to Parliament Hill. Where polar bears were concerned, however, the Soviets had taken the high road. They had become so frustrated by the slow pace of conservation negotiations with Canada, Norway, Denmark, and especially the United States, that Savva Uspensky, a biologist and a member of the Rare Species Commission for the International Union of the Conservation of Nature, declared that "only the Soviet Union has come out in defence of the polar bear."[14]

The Soviets, however, were not the only force that had to be reckoned with. Groups such as IFAW were already up in arms about the Canadian government's decision in 1970 to allow an Inuit-guided sports hunt in the Northwest Territories. Both they and the Soviet Union would have gone ballistic had local residents been given the same opportunity in Churchill.

Brian Davies may have been a lot of things to different people, but the one thing no one could dispute was his ability to raise money and generate publicity. "Buy a Share in a Bear," was the slogan he cleverly used to get people to donate to the cause.[15] "Thirty-five of some of the most magnificent wild creatures in the world are going to be shot here in Churchill if we don't meet this challenge and fly them out," he declared.[16]

While some people scoffed at what he had to say, a significant number were genuinely sympathetic. On a twelve-day visit to London, The Hague, Paris, and St. Louis that fall, Davies raised $7,000 for Operation Bearlift. Two schools in St. Louis and one American school in The Hague each paid for the cost of one flight. Three conservation organizations in Switzerland offered to pay for several more.[17]

After some negotiating and planning between Davies and Howard, Kaskattama was chosen as the relocation site, mainly because it was the only place far enough along the coast with a decent dirt airstrip. Located at Cape Tatnum, near the mouth of the Kaskattama River in northern Manitoba, it was a little over an hour flying time from Churchill, depending on which way the wind was blowing.

Along with Dick Robertson and Brian Wotton, Dale Cross participated in these relocations. By this time, Cross had transferred over to the Wildlife Branch and was, in concert with the control program, involved in the capture–tagging program. Experience had made Cross comfortable working with bears, if comfortable is the right word. Still, he, Wotton, Bruce Molberg, and Paul Rod, who also participated in the capture and relocations that year, admit that it was a bit of an adrenaline rush—jab-poling a snared bear with a tranquilizer syringe, loading it onto a DC-3, and sitting there for an hour or more in the dark confines of a cargo hold with one, and sometimes two, live bears in cages fashioned from galvanized steel culverts, four feet in diameter and eight feet long. In the beginning, none of the men were convinced the cages would hold if a bear pounded hard on them.

The pilot, co-pilot, and cargo handler were so concerned about the possibility of bears escaping from their cages, they insisted on the animals being tranquilized during the flight. This proved to be problematic because a "top up" was often necessary once the animals arrived at the site. Drugging bears even once was risky business. Some polar bears didn't respond well to these injections. One bear even stopped breathing on the flight, after being drugged. Conservation officers spent three hours on the ground resuscitating it before it finally recovered and walked away.[18]

Complicating matters more was the absence of a forklift at Kaskattama. Cross and Wotton, therefore, had to manhandle the drugged bears in order to get them safely onto the ground. Fortunately, the pilots and employees of the airline

Two males bears wrestling along the coast of Hudson Bay.

© Edward Struzik

eventually realized that non-tranquilized bears would not escape and eat the pilot en route, so the animals could then be induced to walk down a ramp onto the tundra upon arriving in Kaskattama.

Both Cross and Wotton had had their share of dealing with big black bears in the boreal forest of Manitoba, but none of those experiences could compare to those they had with polar bears. Resigned to their fate, as polar bears sometimes are, when snared or trapped, the power of some was often humbling. One big male that Cross had leg-snared and tagged in 1971 weighed an estimated 1,400 pounds (more than three times the weight of the average black bear in northern Manitoba), and was far too big an animal to be a candidate for relocation. In this case, the snare that caught the bear had been anchored to a 45-gallon fuel drum filled with rocks. The animal dragged the drum for three quarters of a kilometre before the snare got wrapped around a spruce tree. "Otherwise," said Cross, recalling the experience many years later, "who knows how far it would have dragged it?"

Resuscitating polar bears was one thing, but the experience that really had Cross shaking his head was the relocation flight in which reporter Alan Gordon and photographer Kent Gavin of the *Daily Mirror*, were allowed to come along. *Globe and Mail* reporter Martin O'Malley, who was in Churchill at the time, suggested that they were chosen over other reporters like him because they were "intimate" with Davies and sympathetic to what he was trying to do.

Gavin does not dispute this. Davies, he recalls, courted them because of the terrific publicity they had generated for him during his anti-sealing campaigns.[19] Be that as it may have been, the flight to Kaskattama was, by all accounts, quite the show with a "mean and ornery" polar bear on board. Dale Cross called the 350-pound (159 kg) male Oscar. He had snared the animal with beef that had been marinated in rancid whale fat. Shortly after the bear was tranquilized, it was tagged and sprayed with a green paint so that it could be identified, if the occasion arose, in the future.

Not all went according to plan, however. Shortly after taking off, the journalists started throwing up violently because of the turbulence. Making matters worse was the absence of air-sickness bags.

Once the plane landed, the seats were removed so that the cage could be dragged to the cargo door. As anticipated, Oscar was more than happy to get free of his confine.[20] But once he got to the cargo door, he simply stood there staring quizzically at the photographers below before retreating to the cage. It was a good hour before Cross and Robertson were able to coax him down the ramp to freedom.

Davies, however, was not amused when Oscar began bee-lining it northwest along the coast of Hudson Bay. "Jesus Christ, he's headed back to Churchill," he said at the time. Standing by with a grin on his face, Robertson predicted that it would take a week for the bear to get to Churchill.

Robertson wasn't about to make any apologies if that turned out to be the bear's destination. "These bears are increasing by 100 or so every year and some of them are becoming a real problem," he told the reporters when he got back to town. "So far only an Eskimo boy has been killed, but wait till a white kid gets it and then the people will just want to go out and start killing them."

"We've tried everything," he added. "We're spending $40,000 a year right now protecting the people from the bears and the bears from the people. We caught problem bears and put them in trucks and driven them miles away by helicopter, but some of them almost beat the helicopter back to town. They can run at thirty miles an hour and we just haven't the money to airlift them far enough out."

Coming as this did from a government biologist, Davies couldn't have written a better script.

In 1971, IFAW paid to have problems bears airlifted out of Churchill. Shortly after being released, the first bear headed straight back.

Conservation officer Andrew Szklaruk removes the dart from a tranquilized sub-adult.

ARCTIC ICONS

Nor could he have anticipated the friendly reception he received from the locals when he got back to Churchill. Instead of threatening to run him out of town, as might have been expected, the community hosted a reception for him and the journalists that night.

Not everyone who attended agreed with what Davies was doing. "We are very angry about this threat to the bears," local Margaret Evans told the *Daily Mirror*. "The general local opinion is that people don't mind them. I'd like to know who started all of this fuss."

"We know the rules and I don't let my kids out after supper," added Nancy Zolen, a 26-year-old mother of two children. "I'm all for the bears … they were here before people. They are beautiful animals and I respect them."[21]

But there was at least some goodwill. John Kristiansen, Port Authority chairman, quipped that Operation Bearlift had succeeded in doing at least one thing: "creating instant experts."

"Polar bears have been around here for 300 years that we know of," he told a reporter that night. "If we leave them alone, we will get along all right. I've lived here for 15 years and only seen bears twice."

Dick Robertson and Jack Howard had genuinely hoped that Operation Bearlift would work.

Some of the relocated animals, however, had different ideas, as Howard and Roberston discovered a week later on a flight along the coast. Four of the bears that had been flown out to Kaskattama were already on their way back to town. Remarkably, Oscar covered the distance in just 20 days. He and other polar bears, it seemed, instinctively knew where the first ice would return and where the garbage was.

Not surprisingly, Howard was a little red-faced when the media asked what he thought of Operation Bearlift since some of the relocated animals had come back.

"We knew it was possible that they might return this way," he said, making the best of it. "But we never thought that they would make it from so far away. It may be only 150 miles by air, but it's more than 300 miles by the way the bears travel. It just goes to show that some of those things [polar bears] have real stamina."[22]

Controversial as the relocations were at the time, Howard privately concluded that supporting Operation Bearlift had been worthwhile in spite of the setbacks. "Only two bears had been killed to date by our staff," he wrote in a memo to A. O. Jardine, his boss. "This is partly at least the result of Operation Bearlift, which removed all the bears that our men had to capture, so that the problem of 'repeat,' trouble-making bears did not exist this year."[23]

Davies, for one, took this, and the media coverage he got from the *Daily Mirror* at least— Canada's *Globe and Mail* was clearly not on his side—as a sign of success. Back home in New Brunswick a few weeks later, he was already talking up plans to do the same thing the following year. Even if the government built an incinerator, as promised, to keep the bears away from garbage in the future, he said to Howard by way of a telephone call, it would take time for the animals to outgrow the habit of coming into town to find a meal.[24] The Manitoba government, Davies strongly suggested, would need him and his money for years to come.

There were those in Manitoba Conservation who admired Davies and what he was trying to do, while others thought he was the greatest con artist who had ever lived. Howard himself realized that continuing on with the program could end up being a waste of money. But, after some thought, he once again concluded that the government was still better off wasting IFAW's money than wasting taxpayers' dollars.

Howard also realized that the story had become too big to kill with the pen of someone like him. Remarkably, some 300 million people had tuned into what was going on in Churchill in the fall of 1971. Thrilled, Kristiansen and other councilors passed a motion at a regional development board meeting calling on the Manitoba Government to create a polar bear sanctuary in Churchill that would serve as a tourist attraction.[25] Operation Bearlift, Kristiansen noted, had produced the kind of publicity for Churchill that no amount of money could buy.

The *Winnipeg Free Press* seemed to think so as well. In picking the best "Good News Stories of 1971," editors chose "Operation Bearlift" as one of their personal favourites.[26]

In the end, Howard persuaded A. O. Jardine, to invite Davies back the following year. Even if it didn't work, he reasoned, Operation Bearlift could ultimately resolve the waste disposal problem that was at the root of the polar bear issue.

"I believe he [Davies] would prefer to use his power of persuasion to encourage the government agencies involved to either move the garbage disposal area farther from Churchill or to build an adequate garbage incinerator. This should cut down on the attractiveness of the immediate Churchill area to wandering bears. If some action is not taken on this project by next year," he warned, "he [Davies] will in all likelihood be criticizing us and other government departments for not moving on the proposal."

Davies wasted no time when Howard gave him the go-ahead to come back in 1972. That January, Davies took out advertisements in the *Winnipeg Free Press*, *Montreal Gazette* and other newspapers across Canada, soliciting donations from the public, claiming that fifty bears faced a "firing squad" in Churchill if people didn't help raise the funds that were needed to relocate the animals.

It is difficult to say just how effective Operation Bearlift was in 1972. A total of thirteen bears were killed or found dead that year, just three more than the year before. Conservation officers had dispatched ten of them. Locals had shot two of them at the dump. The number of problem bears, on the other hand, was down by about fifty percent, possibly because of Operation Bearlift, or because freeze-up came early.

There was also some reason to believe that a few of these deaths were unnecessary, delivered as they were by a small number of conservation officers who may have been a little trigger-happy. "Bear chasers" is what Cross called them—young guys who hadn't quite bought into the idea that they were there to protect the community, not to harass the animals at every opportunity. A few couldn't wait to get off the train so they could shoot a bear, he said. The bigger the bear, the better.

If there was unambiguous good news, it was in the data that was beginning to trickle out

Female bears and their cubs tend to avoid being anywhere near male bears.

© Edward Struzik

of the tagging program. Those data were giving Chuck Jonkel and the conservation officers a profile of those bears that were prone to causing trouble. Previously, residents, biologists, as well as conservation officers, were under the impression that most of the troublemaking bears were outcasts—male bears that had developed bad habits and preferred to live on garbage rather than seals. The tagging data told another story: most of the tagged animals were between two and three years old. Many of those that were captured—eleven out of twenty-nine—were

repeat offenders that had been caught in previous years. Only one of the thirteen animals that had been destroyed was an adult.

As promising as this was proving to be for future management decisions, both Chuck Jonkel and Dick Robertson had come to the conclusion in early 1973 that a solution to the polar bear problem in Churchill was still a long way off. Bears could not be deterred easily, they realized. And relocating them was not going to be economical or practical in the long run. What was more, the attitude of the pig farmer and other local residents suggested that a significant number of Churchill residents weren't going to change their ways or their attitudes towards bears.

The thing that really troubled them was the federal government's decision in 1972 to lay off 200 federal employees working at the Rocket Range. That meant that the incinerator, promised a year earlier, was deemed to be expendable. There would, it turned out, be garbage galore for the polar bears of Churchill for some time to come.

Furious, the two men expressed their frustration in a report they both penned in early February of 1973.

"The balance between polar bears and people at Churchill has survived partially on good luck these years," they wrote. "But this is hardly a policy we should continue to follow."

A polar bear tries to find a way into a cage that has been partially buried in the permafrost off Hudson Bay's west coast.

© Edward Struzik

CHAPTER FOUR

POLAR BEAR JAIL

In the summer of 1975, the government of Manitoba decided that it was time to put some people permanently on the ground in Churchill to deal with the polar bear problem and to work with the Sayisi Dene who had been relocated yet again—this time by their own choice—to the wintering grounds of the Qamanirjuaq caribou herd at Tadoule Lake.

Roy Bukowsky and Steve Kearney were the two wildlife specialists who were hired to work with conservation officer Brian Wotton, and wildlife technician Neil Hickes.

Bukowsky was just twenty-seven years old. Like Kearney, he was moulded by a much different world than the one that Wotton and Dale Cross had grown up in. His hair was long and his mustache was Frank Zappa-like without the soul patch.

Like Kearney though, he had won the job contest in the most traditional of ways. Bukowsky had worked in the Yukon for a year and a half before completing a two-year Natural Resource Management program in Saskatchewan. He never dreamed that he would someday be working on polar bear management on Hudson Bay's west coast. The only polar bear he had seen up until this time was in a zoo. He was so hyped when he got word that one of the two wildlife specialists jobs was his, he couldn't sleep for weeks.

The dream, however, turned into a bit of a nightmare almost from the get-go. Finding a place to live proved to be problematic. Thanks in part to the publicity that Murray Jones had generated when he reported on the squalid living conditions in town a few years earlier, Churchill was in the final stages of a complete reconstruction. Housing in the townsite was not readily available. The Canadian Government had promised to supply accommodations and furnishings, but as days turned into weeks, and details about where Bukowsky and his colleagues might be living were not forthcoming, he called the Ottawa-based federal bureaucrat who made the promise to see whether any progress was being made. The Public Works official assured him that four houses were in order and that both electricity and running water were available.

In Churchill for a meeting the following February, Bukowsky decided to have a look for himself. As it turned out, the house he was assigned was located in the tiny outpost village of Akudlik, which was conveniently located 3.5 kilometres southeast, between Dene Village and Churchill.

Akudlik had originally been built in 1954 to house forty-two Inuit from northern Quebec who had been relocated after a famine left many of them destitute and starving. By 1976, the town had been transformed into a housing complex for Inuit from the Northwest Territories who were being ferried in and out to learn various trades.

It was snowing hard the day Bukowsky made the drive in a beat-up, half-ton truck to see which of the fifty pan abode-style houses would belong to him. The building at the address he was given, however, didn't quite turn out to be what he had expected. The front picture window was broken, and the place was partially filled with snow. Still, Bukowsky figured he'd have a look, and stepped in through the broken window. To his dismay, he saw that all the water pipes had burst and the electrical system was in complete disarray. The previous residents had skinned a seal on the rug in between the living room and the hallway. Grease and blood had partially soaked into the floor, and various seal body parts had been left behind. There was no furniture and the kitchen had been ransacked.

Heading back to his vehicle, Bukowsky spotted what appeared to be a telephone booth along the side of the road, buried in deep snow.

What a telephone booth was doing that far out of town, he couldn't imagine. After kicking away enough snow to allow him to open the door, he reached in for the phone, lifted the receiver and was surprised to hear a dial tone. Without missing a beat, he called the bureaucrat in Ottawa, asking again about the accommodations. The bureaucrat assured him that all was in order. Bukowsky asked whether the man had ever been to Churchill. "Oh yes, I've flown over that north country plenty of times," the civil servant answered.

With the help of local tradesmen, as well as Wotton and Hickes, Bukowsky and Kearney eventually put the house in shape.

Psyched as they all were about the challenges that lay ahead of them, neither man was prepared when the polar bears started coming off the rapidly melting ice in July. To the surprise of everyone, including Wotton who had been rotating in and out of Churchill for four years, the bears just kept coming into town.

One of the first was a small bear Bukowsky found at the dump in late August. The animal appeared to be favouring its right front leg. On the advice of a veterinarian, Bukowsky decided to hold the animal for a few days before setting it free. When the bear returned and busted through the front door of the radar station the next morning, it was shot.

Wildlife specialist Roy Bukowsky uses a portable tripod and helicopter cargo net to process a bear at a leg snare site.

ARCTIC ICONS

A week later, a distressed woman, working at Fort Churchill, called to say that a polar bear was rummaging around an empty married couples quarters across the hall from her office. Not sure what to think, Wotton headed out and found the bear standing on the steps of the building. Once the bear spotted him approaching, it ran back inside. A game of hide-and-seek ensued for almost an hour before Wotton managed to shoot and kill the animal just as it poked its head out of an open window.

Then there was the bear that startled Bill and Diane Erickson one morning when it slid down the roof of their commercial greenhouse. It would be the first of nine bears to pay them a visit that fall.

Outfitters were also having more than their normal share of bear problems that summer. Steve Romanow was forced to shoot one at Camp Nanuk on September 12th, just a day before outfitter Doug Webber killed a 400-pound (181 kg) animal that could not be deterred as it ransacked his goose-hunting camp at Dymond Lake. That same day, another bear was shot at Cape Churchill after forcing two hunters to retreat to the roof of their shack.[1]

Wotton thought he had heard it all until a report came in about a bear inside Churchill's newly built and long-awaited incinerator. No amount of coaxing could get the animal out.

When Wotton ventured in to get a closer look, he saw that the bear had a nose full of porcupine quills. The wounds from the needles had badly festered, so the decision was made to put the animal down.

There were so many calls that fall that neither Bukowsky, Wotton, Kearney, nor any of the other conservation officers rotating in and out of Churchill could catch a break. Adding to their woes and adventures was their mode of transport, a Chevy Blazer with chronic front-end troubles and bald tires. More than once, the men had to pile a tranquilized polar bear into the backseat of a car with better traction in order to transport it out of town.

No one quite knew why there were so many bears around that year, although the unusually warm weather was thought to be a factor. Wotton himself wondered at the time whether the sudden increase in the population was the result of the military having pulled out. Whatever the reason, it came at some cost. By the end of that first season, a record 29 bears had been destroyed. Three of them died from apparent natural causes. A train hit one, private citizens killed nine, and departmental staff killed sixteen. Compared to other years, 1976 looked like a massacre.

Humans weren't entirely responsible. One of the bears had been killed by a pack of wolves shortly after it was darted, tagged and then released. No one foresaw the possibility that these animals would prey on a polar bear recovering from the effects of the tranquillizer.

Most times, Bukowsky felt like he was flying by the seat of his pants. Basic training had amounted to little more than Dale Cross showing him how to size up a problem bear, estimate the amount of drug needed to tranquilize it, load the dart, shoot the bear, and then mark and measure the animal after it went "down." The procedure sounded simple, and maybe even fun, on paper, but there were inherent risks at all stages for everyone involved, including the bear.

The drugs they used, Sernylan and Sparine, were also problematic. At the time, Sernylan, also known as the street drug "angel dust," was being used experimentally by veterinarians to immobilize animals. But not all bears reacted the same way, and sometimes it was very difficult to judge how an animal would respond. A few would convulse even after the application of Sparine (used to counteract the effects of Sernylan), and when they did, the officers administered artificial respiration.

One 500-pound (227kg) male that Bukowsky had caught and drugged in a snare very nearly

© Edward Struzik

tore off his arm. The bear appeared to be immobilized, but its eyes kept following him and Dale Cross, who was with him at the time. Bukowsky waited for a few minutes before walking up to the bear, and giving it a hard whack on the rear end, to see how it would react. The animal did nothing, so the two men backed up their truck so that they could put the bear into the pickup's box. Just as they began lifting, the animal bit into Bukowsky's left arm without warning, and wouldn't let go.

Cross drew his .44 magnum pistol and was about to fire a shot into the bear, when Bukowsky called him off, concerned that he might take the bullet by mistake. Bukowsky still can't forget the crazy scene that followed: "While Dale [Cross] pulled the bear by the ears one way, I pulled the other way until I managed to get free. It felt like a vice was steadily closing on my arm. Fortunately, it was extremely cold that day. So the multiple layers of clothing that I had put on to keep myself warm, saved me from serious injury."

Although Bukowsky handled many bears that first year, he did not have to shoot one until the second season on the job. He remembers the occasion all too well. Airport officials had called to complain about a bear that was hanging around the terminal, and getting awfully close to employees who were guiding planes in. This animal had a badly broken jaw, and a wound that was oozing copious amounts of pus. Bukowsky

suspected another bear had probably inflicted the damage during a fight.

Not knowing what to do when he couldn't scare the animal off, Bukowsky called the vet for some advice. The vet, seeing the sorry state of the bear, recommended that it be euthanized.

Having hunted all of his life, Bukowsky had no trouble pulling the trigger on an animal that he was going to butcher and eat. But there was something about doing it to a polar bear that made him feel very uneasy. "I don't know exactly what it was, but it felt like I was shooting another human," he recalled some years later. "I had never felt that way before. It really bothered me and it's bothered me ever since."

Even before the bear season ended in 1976, Bukowsky had already come to the conclusion that too many bears were being killed by staff, residents, and by scientists forced to defend themselves in the field. Flying the bears out to Kaskattama, which was still being done with funds from Brian Davies and the International Fund for Animal Welfare, had proved effective in keeping some, but not all of the troublemakers at bay. Like Chuck Jonkel and Dick Robertson, Bukowsky had come to the conclusion that Operation Bearlift was an extremely expensive proposition, and not a solution to the bigger problem. He and Kearney felt that another answer was needed to deal with the crisis management approach that the conservation officers had been following.

Jerry Stretch, the Anglican minister, had an idea that was gaining momentum in the pubs, and in the Legion hall he frequented. "If they won't come to church to listen to my sermons on Sundays," he liked to say, "I'll preach to them at the Legion on Thursdays." Stretch proposed fencing in problem bears to keep them out of harm's way. He claimed that it would encourage tourists to come to town. Others, like Jim Spence, who was now 75 years old, but still going strong,

insisted that the best way of dealing with the problem bears was to allow First Nations trappers like him to cull some animals.[2]

One thing everyone seemed to agree on was that Brian Davies should not be allowed to come back. The animal rights crusader had, by this time, morphed into a much different persona. His organization now boasted 80,000 members. With $1 million being raised annually, Davies was no longer begging for chump change that would barely pay for the cost of a few DC-3 flights.[3] He had a plane and helicopter that he could use to

Wildlife specialist Roy Bukowsky approaches a bear captured in a live trap in the Churchill townsite.

© Roy Bukowsky

ferry movie stars and journalists in and out of remote places. The list of celebrities supporting his cause was impressive. Along with Brigitte Bardot, there was William Shatner (*Star Trek*), Loretta Swit (*M*A*S*H**), Pamela Sue Anderson (*Dynasty*), and authors Farley Mowat and Michael Ondaatje, who all lent their names to the anti-sealing movement. Emboldened, Davies confronted the sealers on the sea ice and got himself arrested. When the Canadian government withdrew charitable tax status from the organization, he packed up and moved his office to Cape Cod.

Newfoundland seals and polar bears in Churchill, however, were no longer the exclusive foci of his attention. Davies and his colleagues at IFAW were now directing campaigns towards saving the Florida manatee; monk seals in the Mediterranean, and river otters in Thailand. An all-out bid to have leg hold traps banned in Ohio was also in the cards.

None of this endeared him to a community like Churchill, which had a long history of hunting and trapping, and which had also viewed Davies with some level of suspicion from the start. To emphasize this point, the town council passed a resolution in the fall of 1976 calling on the province of Manitoba to prevent Davies from airlifting any more bears out to Kaskattama.

During that meeting in November, council members also expressed their complete frustration at the lack of progress that was being made in solving the polar bear problem. In a letter to Manitoba Premier Ed Schreyer, they dismissed, unfairly it seems in hindsight, IFAW's relocation efforts as a failure and insisted that the provincial government find new ways to deal with the situation.

"It is the opinion of the Council of the Local Government District of Churchill that this is certainly not the solution to the Polar Bear problem in this area," Lorne Robb wrote on behalf of the councilors. "Previous experiments of this kind proved that in most cases, the bears that were transported south were back in the Churchill area within two weeks." Robb suggested that other means, such as diversionary feeding or a fenced enclosure be considered.

Harvey Bostrom, the provincial Minister of Natural Resources and Transportation Services at that time, did not react sympathetically to the Churchill letter. Feeding bears, he stated in a written response, was "considered a dangerous alternative as there is a high possibility of attracting large males to the feeding site. This would force more sub-adult males into the Churchill area. Bostrom also challenged the view that Davies' relocation efforts were a failure. "Since 1971, the International Fund for Animal Welfare had flown 53 problem bears from Churchill to the Kaskattama air strip. To our knowledge only three of these bears have returned to Churchill the same fall. In terms of removing problem bears from conflicts with humans in Churchill, the aerial transport of bears to Kaskattama is a success."

Bostrom insisted that the government had every intention of continuing to cooperate with Davies. But he did allow that he was open to suggestions if the Council had other ideas.

Bukowsky was more than happy to take on the task of figuring out what to do when given the task of finding alternative solutions. Knowing how agitated many residents were about the polar bear problem, however, he decided that some of the answers had to come from them, and not from government bureaucrats, even if members of the community's viewpoints were likely to be biased.

Like most northern towns, Churchill had its share of characters. There were the rough and tough trappers, like Joe Chambers who lived in a shack at Goose Creek with no electricity, no running water, or any of the greater comforts that urban dwellers take for granted. Chambers would just as soon have eaten from a can than from a plate. Then

there was the more refined set, such as trapper Angus MacIver who lived and dressed like a gentleman, thanks, in large part, to his wife Bernice, a former Toronto school teacher who was an avid naturalist.

In some ways, Churchill was ahead of the times. The divide between men's and women's roles in Churchill, for one, was not as great as one would expect. Sigrun Sigurdson, for example, took over the family supermarket when her husband, Fred Martin, a trapper, died in 1963. It didn't matter that she had six children to take care of at the time. She somehow managed to get a loan to renovate before buying out her brother's share in the operation. Sigrun went on to become deputy mayor and a member of the board of the Churchill Port Authority.[4]

Polar bear on the Churchill River.

© Edward Struzik

With the notable exception of the Duck Lake exiles who had a tough time integrating, the divisions between non-natives, First Nations peoples, and the Inuit were not an issue, at least not for those who had lived in the area for any length of time. This may be because "country marriages" were a common practice from the very early days of the Hudson's Bay Company's presence. White women married Chipewyan or Cree hunters in those early days, and it was not uncommon for their children to marry company employees.[5]

Children of these marriages often excelled in life. Two sons of Jenny Tootoo—George and John Hickes—went on to become speaker of the Manitoba legislature and mayor of Rankin Inlet respectively. Many others went to work with scientists who were studying beluga whales and other animals in the region.

It is not surprising, then, that the make-up of Bukowsky's committee was unique in its day.

On one side of the table was Jimmy Spence, the patriarch of the Cree community. He was an obvious choice given his experience with polar bears, and his ties with the largely aboriginal community in and around Churchill. Spence was also highly respected by members of the non-native community in Churchill who admired him for his sense of humour, and for his entrepreneurial skills.

He had started up a business ferrying tourists across the river to see Fort Prince of Wales.

Sitting next to Spence was Jack Batstone, a trapper and the son of Ed Batstone, a Newfoundlander who had come to Churchill to make a living off the land many years earlier. Although much

Sea ice near Churchill has been breaking up earlier in spring, forcing bears to spend more time fasting on land.

younger, Jack pretty much shared Spence's view of the world. He would have preferred seeing polar bears in Churchill culled and the meat fed to dogs than having them flown out. What was more, Jack wasn't shy about expressing that opinion.

On the other side of the table were Maud Mackenzie and Carol Rogers, polar opposites to Spence and Batstone as two people could be. Mackenzie was an elderly English woman who had had her own troubles with polar bears because she and her second husband, Duncan, the manager of Trans Air Airlines, lived on the outskirts of town where bears often roamed and

© Edward Struzik

caused trouble. A former naval officer, Duncan was the kind of person who would hold a DC-3 airplane for an hour or two in order to give honeymooners like Doug and Helen Webber more time to party at their reception. Maud, on the other hand, was stiff upper lip, true to her British roots, and more likely to get the plane off the ground on time, had she been in her husband's position. Maud was so imposing that even the most mischievous children called her "Mrs. Mackenzie."

Maud had grown up in the Falkland Islands before marrying her first husband, a lawyer, who eventually became attorney-general to the Last Rajah of Sarawak (which is now part

© Edward Struzik

A female and cub after finishing off a seal killed on the sea ice.

of Malaysia). Mackenzie had so many servants in those days that she could not bend down to pick up a fallen handkerchief before one of them came around to retrieve it.

No one referred to Mackenzie as Maud when she came to Churchill with Duncan in the 1950s. She hated the name Maud and insisted on being

called Carol, the name of a character in a play she once acted in during her theatre days. Carol liked to wear twinset—a matching set of cardigan and a short-sleeved pullover or jumper. As if to accentuate her frumpiness, she often wore pearls and a Liberty scarf around her neck.

By all accounts Mackenzie loved animals, so much so that she adopted an injured Great Horned Owl as a pet. She also served occasionally as the de facto veterinarian in town when treatment of an injured bird, cat, or dog was required.

Carol Rogers wanted to be a vet until her mother took her aside one day and told her that part of the job involved putting down animals. Rogers had come to Churchill from Winnipeg in 1949, shortly after her father accepted a job in construction. Just 32 years old at the time of her appointment to the committee, she shared Mackenzie's determination to find a non-lethal solution to the polar bear problem.

In addition to Bukowsky and Brian Wotton, Ollie Romanow, a Town Councilor, rounded out the committee. No one really knew where she stood on the issue, but everyone appreciated the fact that she was willing to listen to all sides.

Apart from the indigenous populations of Cree, Métis, Sayisi-Dene, and a handful of Inuit, a good number of non-aboriginal Churchillians at that time were transients—people who stayed for two or three years before moving on. Most of them did not have a big stake in the future of the town or the welfare of the bears. Recognizing this, as well as the fact that Churchillians had many good reasons not to trust the government, Bukowsky wasn't expecting the flood of replies that the committee got in writing, over the telephone, and while walking down the street. "It was amazing," he said. "Each time I went out, someone would stop me and give me a piece of their mind."

As expected, a number of people were not sympathetic to the polar bears' plight. "Would anybody please tell me what polar bears are good for anyway?" wrote one woman who had lived in Churchill most of her life. "The only thing I've heard is that they keep the seal population down. Well, big bloody deal. I would rather save the seal."

Leonore Johnson went so far as to suggest that "the sooner the bears are killed off, the safer it will be in Churchill for our children and ourselves."

"It's getting ridiculous when you can't walk out your own door morning, noon and night for fear of meeting one of them white things in your own yard," she added. "I repeat, start shooting more and more of these bears the minute the first ones are sighted up here. If anything happens to anyone in my family because of these bears, there will be hell to pay."

Bill Erickson was not nearly as extreme. But he did suggest that any bear caught moving within five or ten miles of town should be shot dead. More than one person suggested that they wouldn't hesitate to shoot a bear if the conservation officers weren't willing to do so.

Most of the letters, however, were not angry knee-jerk responses, as Bukowsky had half-expected, but long thoughtful reflections on what had happened in the past and what needed to be done.

Al and Bonnie Chartier, for example, had already recognized the economic opportunities in polar bear tourism by this time and were, like Jimmy Spence, making money seasonally ferrying nature lovers around to see both birds and bears. They were sympathetic to the idea of diversionary feeding, building a fence or a holding facility to keep problem bears from causing further trouble.

Carol Johnson suggested sending problem bears to zoos. Lillian Cloutier thought it might be worthwhile dropping off food in outlying areas to keep the bears out of town. Al Wokes, the port manager, liked the idea of building a fence, but thought it too costly. He also wondered whether the fence was supposed to keep the bears out, or people like him in. Wokes admitted to being terrified of the idea of having to shoot a bear, but even more terrified of the prospect of some person, with little or no firearm experience, having to shoot a bear in town, where a miss or non-fatal strike, might result in humans being injured or killed.

Nanette (Nan) Keeling, the head nurse at the hospital, allowed that she was also terrified of being attacked by a bear. But at the same time, she said, "I hate knowing that the real nuisance bears end up being shot. The death, as a 'solution' to the problem, seems far too harsh a measure and is somehow an embarrassing conclusion to

conversations shared with 'southern friends' and visitors interested in Churchill's polar bears." She voted, as others had, for a holding facility that would keep problem bears out of trouble until Hudson Bay froze over.

Even though she was a member of the committee, and expected to listen to all sides, Carol Mackenzie couldn't resist sending in her own letter. Hers stood out because it was so meticulous in its detail. It was neatly hand-written, single-spaced and four pages long. Mackenzie

In summer and fall, polar bears spend most of their time resting.

© Edward Struzik

would have been comfortable working with environmentalists of the 21st century. Making it clear that she was opposed to the "indiscriminate shooting" that had occurred for so many years, she insisted that the polar bear was "part of the Canadian heritage" and one that should be "conserved for the education and enjoyment of future generations." It was obvious, she insisted, that the bears were coming into town because they were attracted to the garbage that people put out into dumps and on the streets. A way needed to be found to deal with that, she insisted.

Grace Clarke, daughter of a local trapper, and wife of the manager of the Hudson's Bay Company in the 1960s, wrote what was perhaps the most powerful letter. She noted, in her analysis of the situation that the community had to come to grips with the fact that the bears were not going to change the migration routes that they had followed for centuries. Chasing bears away with explosives, she suggested, was "a waste of time." She supported the idea of finding a better way of dealing with garbage and building a holding facility for bears that got into trouble,

Two bears take a break after wrestling for more than an hour.

© Edward Struzik

then letting them loose when Hudson Bay froze over. In the final lines of her single-spaced, five page letter, she made it clear where she stood on the issue: "Churchill, in my mind, has a people problem, not one of polar bears."

That last sentiment pretty much reflected what Bukowsky had been thinking for some time. The crisis management approach wasn't working. Summing up his feelings at the Annual Meeting of Wildlife Managers and Resources Technicians the following spring, he likened the current method of managing polar bears in Churchill as the "Bated-breath approach."

"Number one: take a deep breath at the beginning of the problem period," he told his colleagues. "Number Two: cross all available fingers and toes. Number Three: hope like hell that nothing serious occurs during the problem period. Number Four: if successful, breathe a sigh of relief. If not? … We've been fortunate for the past two years," he said. "Not successful—fortunate!"

Unlike most government reports, which often take years to produce, the one that Bukowsky wrote up was done in six months. He and his colleagues wasted no time in coming up with fourteen recommendations in all.

The committee recommended, as scientists and residents had in the past, that the hunting of bears should be allowed. Not only would this relieve the social pressure on their expanding population, it was reasoned, it would supplement the income of local trappers.

Since it was clear the polar bears migrated to Cape Churchill when the temperatures dipped, the committee also recommended that problem bears be relocated in that direction rather than southeast to Kaskattama. Everyone was in favour of building a tourist industry around the bears, but no one knew how it could be done. Fencing the bears in did not make the list of recommendations.

The committee did recommend something that Bukowsky and other Churchillians had had in mind for some time. If the government could somehow lease or purchase a building at Fort Churchill, such as D-20, one of the military buildings that was going to be demolished, problem bears could be held there and later released onto the Hudson Bay ice or sent to a zoo upon request.

The reality, however, was that the government was still not focused on what was happening with polar bears in Churchill. The proposal to allow the known harvestable surplus to be hunted was still going nowhere because Manitoba officials had no interest in dealing with angry animal rights groups. If hunting was allowed, who would be eligible? Would the quota be open on an international basis or would coastal residents have priority rights? There was also the possibility that hunting would have a significant impact on the population in the long term.

There was some interest both at the local and provincial government level for a better solution to the garbage problem in Churchill. But this was also a can of worms that no one wanted to open because it would cost a lot of money.

There was, however, some sympathy for Bukowsky's polar bear jail in the summer of 1978, when the federal government was in the process of dismantling Fort Churchill. Recognizing an opportunity, Bukowsky made inquiries with the Federal Department of Public Works to see if one of the buildings could be acquired. As it turned out, the Canadian government was willing to sell D-20 for a dollar, so long as the province promised to dismantle it, remove the concrete pad, and landscape the site at the end of its useful life. The concept of the Holding Facility was not limited to a set period of time. It was a long-term solution, which would likely continue well beyond our lifetime. Therefore, it was an easy decision to make.

The Director of Wildlife bought into the idea the following year, but only with the proviso that Bukowsky get engineer-approved blueprints

with three cost estimates to him by the following Tuesday. That was just a week away.

Undeterred by the seemingly impossible deadline, Bukowsky, with the encouragement and advice of a young, highly skilled local welder, Greg Rennie, worked 24 hours a day. The first thing he did, the following Monday morning, was to blueprint his own plans at the Port of Churchill. Then he caught a flight to Thompson, booked a vehicle and headed for Winnipeg. Along the way, he stopped at three contracting companies in small towns and requested rough estimates for materials and labour. On the Tuesday, he met with the government engineers, showing them the blueprints he had produced. The only change they recommended was that he use dense rather than light concrete blocks to prevent deterioration of the concrete from bear urine. Bukowsky then took the package to the Director of Wildlife's office, only to learn that he had gone on holidays the previous day.

Unwilling to wait and let the opportunity pass, Bukowsky purchased the rebar, concrete and other building materials needed, and met with a Winnipeg fabricator to order the doors, windows, and other such like, made. Each purchase was made with a $100.00 purchase order form. Back in Churchill, Bukowsky got local contractor Merv Walkoski, to screen sand and gravel and deliver it to D-20. Walkoski and Bukowsky waited for the train to bring in the material, so they could personally see that it got to the proposed Holding Facility.

Bukowsky and his colleagues had a chance to test the facility for the first time on August 12, 1979, when a 500-pound (227 kg) male was snared on the east side of the Camp Nanuk cottage area. The bear was held at D-20 for 67 days without any apparent adverse effect, although it did drive district conservation officer Rob Dean crazy by constantly banging on the cell bars.

Once this work was completed, Bukowsky wrote his letter of resignation to the Director of Wildlife. He had hoped, by this time to have been offered permanent employment, but the folks at the Personnel Branch had been telling him for months that his term position was up and that he was out of a job. The Director had tried buying Bukowsky more time, but even he could not act on his promise of full-time work. After some thought, Bukowsky decided it was time to move on, not fully appreciating that he would soon be back.

Biologist Vicki Trim pictured. For the well-being of cubs, family groups are fed while in the holding facility.

In the past, conservation officers and scientists would use snares to deter bears such as Linda from entering Churchill.

CHAPTER FIVE

LINDA

After its successful trial run in 1981, Roy Bukowsky's polar bear jail was finally up and running in the refurbished D-20 military building. The facility had enough room for four family groups and sixteen individual bears. For conservation officers Ken John and Don Jacobs, stationed in Churchill during the early 1980s, the jail's "open for business" sign was none too soon.

Although polar bear activity over the previous five years had not been nearly as busy as it was in 1976, when 29 bears were killed, there still had been many dangerous encounters. Once again, almost everyone in Churchill had a feeling that it was only a matter of time before someone was seriously mauled or killed by polar bears.

It was just luck that saved the day on October 17, 1980, when a bear broke through the window of a house where five children were playing. Both parents had been drinking heavily. The husband had passed out on the floor, not even waking up when the glass shattered. The mother, however, was sober enough to find a gun. She fired a lethal shot into the animal's head.

Time also proved that the Polar Bear Alert program's effectiveness was limited to those residents who had phones. Gregory Chocomolin was one of many people in Churchill who didn't own one. Shortly before midnight on the evening of October 16th, 1981, Chocomolin woke up to the sound of loud banging outside his small house on the east edge of town. He looked out to see what was going on, and discovered a big polar bear, which had already broken through the glass window of his front porch door, pulling sheets of plywood off the inside door.

Fortunately for Chocomolin, he had a loaded gun nearby. Instead of the bear dropping dead, as he had hoped when he fired a shot, the bear ran off into the dark, leaving Chocomolin inside not knowing what to do.

When Ken John showed up the next morning, following up on a report of a dead bear in the area, he found Chocomolin at home, still badly shaken from the ordeal. "I got no phone to call you guys and I was scared he'd grab me if I ran away," he said. "I didn't want to just wound him either, I wanted to shoot him dead. He was at our place earlier when my wife and I were in town. I thought you guys scared it away but it came back."

It wasn't just Churchill's residents that conservation officers had to worry about this time. Hunters in outlying camps were also vulnerable because of game they stored, or left out to dry. One bear showed up at a goose camp on the Seal River during the middle of the night and smashed the bubble and both sides of the windows on a parked Bell G2 helicopter. Before being shot, the bear moved on to bang up two bush planes as well, including one in which the helicopter pilot was sleeping (he had hunkered down there the night before, after failing to find his way to the cabin in the dark).

Journalists were also becoming a challenge for the officers. Thanks to the publicity generated by Brian Davies (now no longer part of the picture in Churchill), reporters and photographers flocked to the area by the dozens. Fresh off the plane, none of them had a clue that a huff, a hiss, a pop of the jaw, or a gentle rolling back and forth signaled that the bear they were photographing up close might be about to charge.

Some, like the *National Geographic* team that came to town in 1980 to film a documentary, had no hesitation in pushing the limits to get as close to a bear as possible. The crew even had a shark cage built so that they could put one of their photographers inside at Cape

Churchill, where dozens of polar bears congregate in the fall.

And then there were the tourists. They started rolling in by the hundreds during the early 1980s to get a look at the bears at the dump, or to take advantage of the polar bear tours offered by entrepreneurs like Len Smith and Al and Bonnie Chartier.

A review of the incident reports written up since 1968 (the year of their inception), revealed that not all polar bears were alike in the manner they moved about, and/or reacted to people. Granted, there was a small, but significant, number of bears habituated to the town's dump, however, many other bears, even those whose dens were not that far from Churchill, wanted nothing whatsoever to do with people or with Churchill's garbage. Most of the bears that were hazed, or relocated never came back. Nevertheless, there was a hard coterie of problem bears that would not be deterred by any means.

The first consideration in the town's polar bear management strategy was, as it had been for some time, to ensure the safety of people and the protection of property, irrespective of what the bears were up to. While the welfare of bears was a secondary consideration prior to 1982, those bears that strayed into Churchill, Fort Churchill, Akudlik, and the Dene Village were

© Edward Struzik

simply destroyed if hazing or relocation efforts didn't deter them promptly.

As much as the tourist operators liked the idea of bears being close to town, because it made it easy for them to take their clients to see the animals, a number of local residents did not. In 1980 and 1981, both the mayor and at least one town councilor continued to press the government to allow sports hunting, which they saw as a means to make additional money on the bears, while weeding out those problem animals that threatened human life and property.

What little traction this idea might have had in the past was all but gone now. Polar bear nations were moving in a different direction. Six years after the International Agreement on Conservation of Polar Bears, signed in 1973, went into effect in 1976, the governments of Canada, Denmark, Norway, the Union of Soviet Socialist Republics, and the United States of America voted to extend it indefinitely. The agreement restricted the killing of polar bears to those scientists actively engaged in bona fide scientific research, and to aboriginal people who were taking polar bears by traditional means. Neither the Canadian Government nor the Government of Manitoba were in a position, or inclined, to back out of an agreement that had taken more than a decade to negotiate.

Ian Stirling, Steve Kearney, and other scientists had already recognized that simply marking

and capturing, measuring and weighing animals, and hazing and relocating nuisance bears wasn't going to solve all of the problems or answer many of the new emerging questions about the species. Thanks to research conducted by graduate student Paul Latour in fall of 1978

Cubs will stay with their mother for two, and occasionally three years.

and 1979, scientists knew that most of the male bears that hunkered down on the coast preferred to rest when it was hot, and then take some time to playfully wrestle when it was cold. That was about it. As explorer David Thompson had found out more than 200 years earlier, on his long walk along the coast, these animals had no interest in going anywhere near people. Nor were they keen on viciously beating each other up in the way they did when competing for a female.

No one at the time knew exactly why the

© Edward Struzik

so-called "nuisance bears" tended to be sub-adults or females with cubs. In the early 1970s, scientists believed the problem bears were so-called outcast males. The tagging programs quickly proved otherwise.

Shortly after taking over the Canadian Wildlife Service program in western Hudson Bay after Jonkel left in 1976, Ian Stirling began to suspect that the inexperience and nutritional needs of these bears might be playing a role in their aberrant behaviour. So, evidently, did food availability at the garbage dump and in town. There was also the incontrovertible fact that Churchill sat smack dab in the middle of the animals' migration path. Polar Bear Alley received its name for a reason.

© Edward Struzik

One of the bears that provided scientists and wildlife managers with insights into the minds of these animals was Linda, who was notorious for her regular visits to the town dump (Chuck Jonkel had named her in honour of a caribou biologist's wife who had fed him home-cooked meals from time to time).

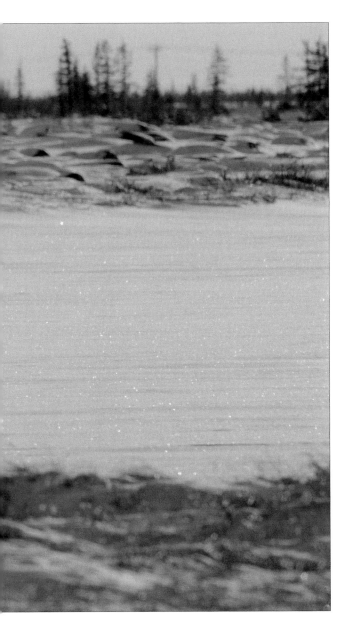

Among the hundreds of bears captured in the Churchill area up until then, Linda was, as Stirling would later say, the "most valuable polar bear known to science." Although Linda alone did not supply Stirling and his associates with all they needed to know about so-called "nuisance bears," her story demonstrated the fact that being a nuisance bear wasn't so much a matter of chance, or a choice determined by genetics, but rather the result of behaviour learned from its mother.

According to records collected by Jonkel and by Stirling, Linda was likely born in late 1964, or early 1965, somewhere in the boreal forest south of Churchill. A good guess is that she was one of two, or possibly three cubs born that year in a den that had been dug into a frozen peat bank.

Jonkel was surprised when he caught Linda feeding at the Rocket Range dump in the fall of 1966. She was alone at the age of about one and 2/3 years old, and not in the company of her mother or siblings. Like other scientists at the time, he assumed that all polar bear cubs remained with their mothers until they were at least two and a half years old. (Now we know that becoming independent at the age of one and a half was something that was unique to the polar bear population of western Hudson Bay. During the 1980s, 50 percent or more of the cubs were weaned as yearlings; but that phenomenon has now all but disappeared today.)[1]

Linda was caught again feeding at the dump during each of the next two years, and was fitted with a radio collar both times. Data from the second collar indicated that she, like other bears, except for females in maternity dens, headed north once the ice had formed on Hudson Bay in late November.

No one saw any sign of Linda again until the fall of 1972, when she showed up at the dump, this time with a single cub. That cub was caught at the same site eight times the following year when Linda was presumably back in her den on a two-year pregnancy cycle.

Linda wasn't seen again until the fall of 1976 when she showed up at the dump with triplets. That was the exceptionally busy year when 29 animals were destroyed. Overwhelmed by the number of bears wandering into town, conservation officers dispatched Linda and her cubs to Kaskattama along with 11 other animals that fall. None of Linda's family was seen again until the next year when one of her cubs showed up at the dump alone.

When Linda showed up at the dump in October 1980 with yet another family, it was obvious that cubs like hers were learning bad habits from their mothers. Linda wasn't the only female providing the data that suggested this. The mark and capture program, which had been going on now for fifteen years, was already clearly showing a similar pattern of behaviour among other family groups.[2]

Wondering whether there was an ecological advantage in bears feeding at the dump, Stirling dispatched graduate student Nick Lunn, in 1981, to find the answer.

It was an important question to be asked at the time. The town's dump had become a growing problem for wildlife managers like Kearney, even after the three dumps in the Churchill area were consolidated into one. It was now apparent that every year a number of cubs of bears, like Linda, would show up in town where the more aggressive or hungry ones posed a real threat to people's safety.

The fact that many of these bears ended up dead raised an important question for Kearney, who was getting pressure from the town council, the tourist operators, the residents, and his bosses in Thompson and Winnipeg: what, if anything, could be done to prevent bears from continuing to come into town while not reducing their value and interest as a tourist attraction?

This was a particularly tough question because tourism was not a high priority back then. Protecting people and saving the lives of polar bears was. Before 1981, bears caught at the dump, or at the incinerator, were marked and released in the same general area, mainly because the cost of moving so many of them further was prohibitively expensive.

It was not uncommon to see as many as forty bears at the dump at one time.

Nick Lunn got into polar bear science by chance in 1980, when he spotted Ian Stirling's hand-written note on the job wall at the University of Alberta. Stirling was looking for someone to work in his lab at the Canadian Wildlife Service. Initially, there was no fieldwork involved. But one thing led to another and Lunn soon found himself in Churchill observing polar bears at the dump.

Lunn's study[3] went a long way to illustrate the fact the dump was an ecological trap that lured otherwise healthy bears away from a safe environment into one which put their lives in peril. Once bears learned about the dump, they were more likely to return in subsequent years.

© Edward Struzik

Like Paul Latour's time at the polar bear tower at Cape Churchill, the protocol for this study was time-consuming. Each day, Lunn would drive to the dump to observe and record everything the bears did after they were caught, tagged, measured, and weighed. Hair dye—Lady Clairol in this case—was used to paint a number on the back of each animal so that it could be tracked.

After a little over two years of study, Lunn concluded that there was a social order that governed which bears would have access to the best garbage sites. In all but one case that he documented, Lunn discovered it was the females with cubs that dominated when they sparred with sub-adult males for position. Not surprisingly, it was these losers—driven to the perimeters of the dump—who subsequently wandered into town to investigate other potential food sources. So in a way, nuisance bears were the "outcasts," as some had originally thought, but young ones, not old.

In contrast, family groups were much more tolerant of each other. In one case, during 1983, Lunn followed with fascination the fate of two females who had a long record of visiting the dump. They got on so well that they took turns watching each other's cubs while they were all feeding on the garbage.

Lunn also found that garbage dump bears at the beginning of the off-ice season, were as physically fit as bears of the same sex and age classes captured near the coast or inland. But, unlike those bears on the coast that lost a considerable amount of weight fasting during the summer and fall months, the garbage bears would put on the pounds.

Significant as this observation might have appeared to be for females nursing cubs, or for those who were entering the next pregnancy

Polar bear walking on the rapidly melting sea ice in late June.

cycle, both Lunn and Stirling concluded that it didn't give these animals any advantage. The survival and reproductive success of the dump-feeding bears was the same as those of bears in the outlying areas. Unfortunate exceptions were those bears that ate something toxic. In one case, Lunn found a bear at the dump that appeared to have died as a result of chewing on, and swallowing, parts of a car battery.

For Steve Kearney, who was now the regional director for Manitoba Conservation, the most significant insight, from a management point of view, was the one that demonstrated that being a garbage dump bear was often the result of the behaviour cubs learned from their mothers. Nearly one third of the 207 bears captured at the dump were caught eating garbage in subsequent years. And of the 33 females that brought

© Edward Struzik

in 101 cubs to the dump, one in five of those cubs returned after being weaned. Linda may have been unique in being such an exceptionally sweet animal, but she was not alone in teaching her cubs bad, and potentially lethal, habits.

Bukowsky's jail was the tool that Kearney needed to deal with this evolving problem. Early in his term on his new job, he realized that killing bears was not the solution, More often than not, bears that came into town one year were not the same bears that showed up the next. It made no sense to kill them when there was a good chance they would not be coming back.

As promising as the new jail was in deterring bears from coming back to town, there still remained a problem with Churchill's human population, which contained many transients. Newcomers had a difficult time appreciating just how dangerous it could be living amongst so many animals. And while many of the long-time residents had learned to co-exist with polar bears, in some cases, bad habits died hard. Some residents still tied up their dogs in places where they would be easy pickings for a hungry bear. Others continued to raise chickens and rabbits, even though the outcomes were, as the pig farmer had learned years earlier, predictable. As to rabbit-raising, 1982 ended with 15 dead bunnies and one dead bear.

Journalists were another problem. Many, although not all, felt their work was more important than that of the conservation officers who were in the middle of handling a problem bear. Sometimes reporters put themselves and others in such peril that Kearney concluded a potential casualty would most likely be one of them, not a resident or a tourist (both of the latter being less likely to take unwarranted chances in the interest of a story or a photo op).

The real eye-opener for Kearney, however, was the manner in which some people responded to the opening of D-20. To his great surprise, that facility, which was closed to the public, was treated with suspicion. During the fall of 1982, some person, or possibly several persons, broke in three times. Perpetrators of the first two break-ins removed the locking pins from two of the cage doors, allowing three bears to escape. One was re-captured in town the following night. Another was found with buckshot in its rump. No one ever saw the third bear again.

Rob Dean was stationed in Churchill for two years in 1978 and 1979. As much he enjoyed the experience, he was glad to transfer out when he did. "I don't know that I had one good night of sleep during the polar bear season," he told me when I asked about his time in Churchill. "I couldn't stop thinking that someone was going to die. My worst fear was that it was going to happen on my watch."

ARCTIC ICONS

Biologist Peter Clarkson keeps a wary eye on a bear visiting the Cape Churchill's polar bear tower.

CHAPTER SIX

BAG-OF-BONES: DETECTING AND DETERRING BEARS

Ian Thorleifson was busier than he wanted to be in the fall of 1983. Although he was the wildlife technician in Churchill, Thorleifson was spending far too much time helping special officer Jim Durnin deal with an unusually large number of polar bears. The animals seemed to be everywhere that year, and farther afield than usual. In October, conservation officer Pierce Roberts had to deal with a 250-pound (113 kg) polar bear which had made it to a Cree fishing camp on Oxford Lake, some 300 kilometres inland from the coast of Hudson Bay. Although female polar bears will travel as far as 80 kilometres inland to den, bears venturing that far from the coast are an anomaly.

Dealing with problem bears was interesting work to be sure, but old hat for Thorleifson by that point in his career. When the opportunity came along to go out to Nestor 1, a summer goose camp that Canadian Wildlife Service biologist Ian Stirling was using to catch and tag polar bears along the coast, Thorleifson jumped at the chance.

It was the second week of November. Thorleifson and the pilot were to meet at the Thompson airport, 400 kilometres south of Churchill, at ten in the morning. En route to Nestor 1, they were to land at the polar bear observation tower at Cape Churchill to drop off supplies for biologist Gord Stenhouse who was conducting some polar bear deterrent experiments.

The only person in the hangar that morning was a mechanic, who was working on a plane. When Thorleifson asked which of the planes in the hangar they were to fly in, the mechanic silently pointed to a Cessna 206 parked nearby.

The Cessna 206 is a powerful, ruggedly built single-engine plane with a large cabin. It's what some bush pilots call the "sports utility vehicle" of the air. Most of the smaller Cessnas are "tail-draggers"—with two wheels under the body and one more under the back of the tail. This one, however, was on "tricycle gear"—three wheels in a triangle configuration under the front of the fuselage with the load balanced by the weight of the engine.

As best as Thorleifson could remember, a 206 had a three-blade propeller—each blade being about two and a half feet (80 cm)—long. This one had a two-blade prop instead, with three-foot blades to make up the difference. It was also a "Trainer," with two equal sets of operating gear to allow the pilot to take control from a person who was learning to fly. When Thorleifson mentioned this to the mechanic, the mechanic said it didn't make a difference.

Thinking about it, Thorleifson figured the mechanic was right, unaware that he would soon be proven wrong.

Another forty-five minutes passed, and there was still no pilot. Thorleifson was getting anxious because there are only about eight hours of daylight on the west coast of Hudson Bay in late November. If they were to get to Cape Churchill and Nestor 1, and then back to the town of Churchill before dark, they would need to get going sooner than later.

"He'll be here," the mechanic said when Thorleifson inquired once again about the pilot's whereabouts. Just then, in walked a sharply dressed young man, in his twenties. Thorleifson remembers him well because he had a city haircut and the meanest set of bloodshot eyes he had seen in a while. He didn't like the look of this.

"Been bush flying long?" Thorleifson asked.

"Just arrived from Calgary yesterday," the pilot explained. "And they threw a heck of a welcome party for me last night."

Against his better judgment, Thorleifson helped the pilot load the supplies that were to be delivered to Nestor 1 and to the polar bear tower.

Having flown the route to the Cape more times than he cared to count, Thorleifson suggested that there was no immediate need for the map the pilot was unsuccessfully looking for. That seemed to relax the pilot, so much so that his head was bobbing up and down once they reached a cruising altitude.

"Can you fly a plane?" the pilot pleaded after Thorleifson barked and snapped him back to attention.

Thorleifson's experience flying planes was extremely limited, but considering the sorry state of the pilot, he realized that their chances of getting to Cape Churchill safely were just as good with him behind the controls for a while. Besides, there was a 3,000-foot ceiling, and all that was required, he figured, was for him to see the ground.

As they headed east along the Hudson Bay coast, however, the ceiling began to drop steadily. So did the plane because Thorleifson was determined not to get lost in the clouds. By the time the pilot began stirring, the plane was no more than 300 feet above sea level. Looking out the window, the sleepy pilot nearly had a heart attack before quickly taking back the controls.

The terrain at Cape Churchill is flat and laden with shallow lakes, and sand and gravel ridges. There are no trees out there on the coast, just a few stands of willow. Visual clues are often few and far between at this time of the year, especially when the light is flat, as it was on that overcast day. Even the best of bush pilots have trouble distinguishing distances and closure rates in these conditions. Thorleifson held his breath.

All things considered, Thorleifson was impressed by how well the young pilot landed "nose up" before lowering the front end until all three wheels were rolling along the snow-covered gravel ridge. Neither one of them, however, saw the hole that a polar bear had dug about eight inches into the ground.

Shallow as it was, the hole was still deep enough to sink a tire far enough into the ground and make the extra-long blades on the propeller shave into the gravel. "Praaang" was the sound that Thorleifson recalls ringing in his ear. The plane started to vibrate before coming to a sudden stop at the tower.

From the narrow wooden deck outside the plywood hut perched 13 metres up on top of the polar bear tower, Stenhouse and contract technician Marc Cattet watched this all unfold with fascination, before climbing down to greet the new arrivals. Seeing how twisted the blade was, they knew the visitors were not going anywhere, so they invited them up for supper.

Thorleifson, however, was more intent on straightening out the blades, fearing that he might miss the semi-final Canadian Football League game between the Winnipeg Blue Bombers and the Edmonton Eskimos. A do-it-yourselfer, he went in search of a hammer in the toolkit before the pilot hopped up and down, insisting there was no way he was going to allow any amateur blacksmithing to be done on his expensive airplane.

Later that evening, they all sat down in the ten-foot by ten-foot shack, drank a glass or two of boxed wine and enjoyed the spaghetti dinner cooked up by Stenhouse.

Ian Stirling, with the help of Dale Cross, Dick Robertson, and Manitoba Hydro technicians, had the Cape Churchill tower built in 1976 so that he and students, such as Paul Latour, could observe the many polar bears that hunker down in that area during the fall. Although poorly insulated, the hut is snug, and can sleep three or four people pretty tightly. I know this because I joined Stenhouse and Cattet a few days after Thorleifson and the pilot had shown up.

Helicopter pilot Steve Miller flew me in during the third week of November on his way to Nestor 1. Miller, as most everyone who had worked with him knew, was a character—a man of calm competence, quiet enthusiasm, and understated humour. He had worked with Stirling for two years catching polar bears on the coast, and was all too familiar with the hazards of being a pilot in the sub-Arctic. Flying under 64 kilometres per hour, 12 metres above the ground in the Bell Jet Ranger that he flew at the time, Miller knew there was no room for pilot error, or time for the corrective action required in the event of engine failure, while darting back and forth across the tundra trying to get close enough for the biologist to shoot a tranquilizing dart into a polar bear.

Seasoned as he was, however, Miller was as transfixed as I was when Stenhouse recounted how

Thorleifson's saga ended. Seeing that there was no room in the tower for him and the pilot to bed down that night, Thorleifson suggested that they remove the seats from the plane and lay down some sleeping bags. The pilot was game until Stenhouse mentioned that they had counted forty-three polar bears in the vicinity earlier that day.

What followed, Stenhouse told us, was a long night constantly disrupted by the sound of gunfire. On eight different occasions, bears showed up banging on the side of the plane in an effort to get inside. Each time, Thorleifson popped open the door—sometimes banging the head of a bear—before firing off a cracker shell, or a round of bullets, in an effort to scare the bears away.

"It was surreal," Stenhouse told us. "The next morning Ian and the pilot came up for coffee before the rescue plane arrived. When we heard the sound of the plane approaching a few minutes later, the pilot, who was white as a ghost and hadn't said a word, was already putting on his parka and getting ready to climb down the ladder. He didn't say goodbye or bother to look down to see if there were any bears below, as there often are."

The first time Stenhouse came to Churchill, he was conducting research on Canada geese in the Hudson Bay lowlands. He never dreamed that he might someday be working on polar bears until one day when he found himself in the middle of a spring snow squall. Hunkered down on the treeless tundra, he realized right away that it wasn't white snow filling up his spotting scope, but a polar bear walking slowly through the nesting area, eating the eggs of the Canada geese that had scattered off in all directions.

The bear was about 30 metres away. Unwisely, Stenhouse stood up to get a better

Manitoba Conservation officer Shaun Bobier fires cracker shell to frighten off a polar bear on the outskirts of town.

look. When the bear saw him, it stood on its back legs. Stenhouse and the polar bear looked at each other for a few seconds before the bear continued on its travels.

Studying Canada geese just didn't cut it for Stenhouse after that experience. From that point on, he did all he could to find opportunities to work with Stirling, his technician Dennis Andriashek and Nick Lunn, Stirling's graduate student. When a biologist position opened up with the Government of the Northwest Territories (which was at the time responsible for the largest polar bear population in the world), Stenhouse applied and quickly accepted the offer when it was made.

Stenhouse returned to Cape Churchill in that role in 1981, thanks in large part to an informal agreement between Merlin Shoesmith, a senior official in Manitoba's Department of Natural Resources, and Jim Bourke who was Stenhouse's boss in the government of the Northwest Territories. Both men, along with Ray Schweinsberg, the senior polar bear biologist for the Northwest Territories, were interested in finding ways of detecting and deterring polar bears before it was necessary to kill them.

The declining fortunes of the polar bear had been reversed by this time, as a result of conservation measures, hunting quotas the Inuit and other indigenous groups in the Arctic world had agreed to, and to management programs pioneered by the Canadian Wildlife Service, the Northwest Territories, and the Government of Manitoba. The situation in the early 1970s had improved so much that there was room to raise hunting quotas in the Northwest Territories from 619 in 1975–76 to 648 in 1978–1979.[1]

Science and the search for oil, gas, and minerals in the North, however, brought with it a new management concern. For the first time, non-native people were showing up in the Arctic in numbers never seen before. Inexperienced and unprepared as many of them were in dealing with polar bears, conflicts inevitably arose. In 1975, three men were attacked, in three different incidents, while working in the Northwest Territories. Two were killed. The other was injured. No one knows exactly what precipitated the attacks, but, in the Beaufort Sea region, they may have resulted, in part, from a large decline in ringed seal productivity during the 1974–75 period.[2] Whatever the reason, there were a lot of hungry bears around and lot of inexperienced people as well.

More often than not, it was the polar bear that ended up being the loser, just as it had been in Churchill during the 1960s and early 1970s. The killing of problem bears in the Northwest Territories, increased from ten in 1977–78 to 34 in 1979–80 and 42 in 1982–83.

A polar bear tries to get at biologist Gordon Stenhouse at Cape Churchill.

© Edward Struzik

Rightly or wrongly, there was a genuine fear that the killing of problem bears in the 1980s could at some point result in population reductions.[3]

The idea of deterring animals before it was necessary to kill them was nothing new in those days. Vagn Flyger, the University of Maryland scientist who pioneered the art of tranquilizing polar bears, led the way in the 1950s with an experiment to relocate 1,500 white-tailed deer from the Aberdeen Proving Ground in his home state to more urban settings. Local farmers and urban gardeners, however, weren't happy with the results. The new arrivals were very rapacious in their pursuit of food.

In an effort to solve the problem, Flyger used his army engineering skills to create a minefield with M-80 firecrackers planted into the ground. The project was a tremendous success. After a few days of explosions, the deer were no longer such a nuisance. Unfortunately, a few unsuspecting people who picked up the firecrackers ended up losing a finger or two.[4]

Gary Miller, a zoologist from the University of Montana, Missoula, wasn't quite as daring when he came up to Churchill in the fall of 1978 to test commercial dog repellents, household chemicals, and more than a dozen other stimuli on polar bears and grizzly bears that had been captured and placed in a laboratory that had been built in Churchill. Miller had mixed success with Freon horns and other recorded material, but the chemicals he used were almost useless in deterring the animals from visiting baited sites.[5]

None of this surprised Ian Stirling, who had learned early on his career that some troublesome polar bears are not easily deterred. He and student Paul Latour were reminded of that fact in late October, shortly after Miller left town.

On this occasion, Stirling and Latour were both at the tower at Cape Churchill, observing polar bears with biologist Pauline Smith. When conducting this type of research, it is very helpful to be able to identify individual bears for extended periods of time. Although there were dozens of bears around, many were not marked. In the ongoing effort to dart and mark these bears, the scientists hung a bag of rancid beluga fat below the cabin so that a bear could be easily darted from one of the windows when it came in to investigate.

Usually, a drugged bear would fall asleep close to the base of the tower and the three researchers would quickly descend, tag the animal, measure

it, and paint a number on its rump for future identification. One day, however, a large male bear did not go to sleep promptly after being darted. Instead, it walked out onto the sea ice for almost a kilometre before passing out.

Canadian Wildlife Service scientist Ian Stirling arranged to have Cape Churchill's tower built in the late 1970s so that he and his students could study polar bears in the area more easily.

Stirling was well-aware that they couldn't just leave the bear where it lay; ideally, a drugged animal like this one should be put in a comfortable position to ensure it is breathing easy while it recovers. But with so many other bears around, it was dangerous to venture out on the ice on foot.

After considering the options, the trio realized they had no choice, and off they went, with

drugging bag, protective arms, and a shotgun, for firing cracker shells if necessary. Fortunately, they reached the bear without incident, but just as they were working on the animal, Stirling looked up to see a very large adult male briskly walking downwind toward them.

Stirling recognized that the bear did not know what they were, and that it was only coming to investigate. Quickly, but with firearms ready, the three of them backed up in a slow semi-circle, hoping their scent, which was very ripe after not having showered for two weeks, would identify them as human.

Normally large, fat adult polar bear males avoid humans. This bear was apparently intending to do just that. When it caught sight or scent of the three, it stood up on its hind legs the moment it came downwind and caught the human smell. It sniffed some more, and then began to walk away in the other direction.

In an effort to keep it moving, Stirling fired a cracker shell; a bad decision, it turned out. The bear was a huge male and, evidently not one used to being pushed around. Once the cracker shell exploded, the bear whirled around and began striding purposefully, head down, directly toward the trio as if to give them a lesson on manners. Things were really looking serious. Then, suddenly, the bear stopped again, stared intently, turned

around again, and began to walk slowly away, stopping periodically to turn around, peering at the three, as if to say, "Don't get any more bright ideas or you really will be in trouble!" Just like it isn't a good idea to insult the biggest guy in the bar.

Given the number of bears that congregate in the region in the fall months, Cape Churchill was the perfect place for Stenhouse and Cattet to experiment with ways of detecting and deterring polar bears.

In the weeks before I arrived on the scene, they had some help from Stirling and his technician, Dennis Andriashek, who had taken care of the first order of business with the help of Steve Miller and his helicopter. They made sure that every bear within a 15 kilometre radius of the study site was captured and marked, so that bears could later be identified when they approached the tower. Lady Clairol hair dye proved to be the best way of marking the animals because, like the advertisements on television said at the time, it didn't fade.[6]

Most of the detection and deterrent tools used by Stenhouse and Cattet that fall were in full view when I arrived at the Cape. There were shotguns, a riot gun of the variety used in Northern Ireland, pistols, flares, thunder flashes, a high-powered sound system, a microwave detection unit, and an electric fence, which had been set up on the tundra outside of the tower. The small living quarters looked to me like a munitions cache.

There was also the "shark cage" the *National Geographic* film crew had used in 1980 when they were filming a documentary on Churchill and its bears. Stenhouse had frozen this apparatus in the ground 100 metres from the tower, in the event that he or one of his colleagues was confronted by a polar bear that had somehow positioned itself between them and the ladder that goes up the tower.

Stenhouse's first step in detecting and deterring bears was to entice as many animals into camp as possible, and then experiment with any one of the detection and deterrent tools on hand.

This emaciated bear died, likely of old age or disease, three days after biologist Daryll Hedman took this photo.

© Daryll Hedman

Some days, it was all too easy, because, more often than not, the bears would hunker down around the tower at night. In the morning, at least one of them would be waiting at or near the bottom of the ladder, hoping maybe one of us would forget to look down when we descended. Deterring these bears with whatever was at hand was simple. A shot in the rump with a plastic bullet pretty much did it.

Other bears in the area, however, had little interest in coming into camp. To entice these animals, Stenhouse did as Stirling and Latour had done when they baited the animals. Instead of hanging out a chunk of rancid beluga, however, Stenhouse barbecued it, after marinating the meat and fat in a putrid mixture of horse fat.

There is no way of describing how disgusting this smelled. More than once, I gagged when it was my turn to be master of the barbecue. Worse still, there was no getting away from the odour

A polar bear attempts to pull biologist Gordon Stenhouse off a plywood plank that was designed to keep generators and equipment at the polar bear tower out of harm's way.

once the meal was done. The stench got into our skin and clothing. We had to live with it.

Once the meat was cooking, it was only a matter of time before several big white heads began popping out of the snowdrifts. Rarely did these animals have the chance to finish one of the sizzling morsels, however, because Stenhouse and Cattet were always waiting to bombard them with rubber batons or plastic bullets, shock waves, screaming flares, or the thunder flashes that they occasionally tried out.[7]

The 38 millimetre rubber batons fired at the animals with riot guns were among the most promising deterrents. In all but one case, these weapons bruised but did not injure the bears. Most of the animals that were attacked with batons didn't come back, as they often did when chased off with cracker shells.

Plastics bullets also showed some promise, but the electric fence tested was not nearly as effective as Stenhouse and Cattet had hoped. Many animals lured to the setup quickly realized that the thick pads on their paws were sufficient to insulate them from electrocution. Others suffered the pain in order to get at the bait.

That fall of 1981 was Jim Durnin's second as Special Officer for the Polar Bear Alert Program. He and Thorleifson were more than happy to test the rubber batons, plastic bullets, and other deterrent devices that the Department of Natural Resources had bought for them.[8] Although both men had reservations about the accuracy and short-range limitations of the riot gun, they were happy to report that the marked bears subjected to pain by Stenhouse at the Cape tended to be very wary when they approached a baited trap or a conservation officer in town.

Richard Goulden, the wildlife branch director, was optimistic about the possibility of using deterrents, even though one of the bears that Stenhouse and Cattet had shot with a rubber baton ended up dying. "In my opinion, this was a freak accident that was unfortunate, but should not prevent further testing of rubber bullets on deterring bears," Goulden wrote to then assistant deputy minister Dale Stewart.[9]

Promising as these methods were, one thing remained clear to all the scientists and wildlife officers who had had any experience handling polar bears. No matter how much sound and pain the bears were subjected to, some animals—albeit a very few—simply could not be deterred. Many times, these would be young skinny bears on the verge of starvation. But there were also some bears with what humans might call a "mean streak." Nothing, it seemed, could get them to back off.

"Bag-of-Bones" was one of those animals. He was in camp every day when I was there, as he had been for most of the autumn. Bones was a big, skinny bear with bloodshot eyes, and multiple scars, proving he was not one to retreat from a fight with another polar bear. "Bones" also had that "lean and hungry" look that made me think he might be "Cassius," the huge, emaciated polar bear that photographer Fred Bruemmer had written about in *Audubon Magazine,* after spending two weeks in the tower in 1981.[10]

Bag-of-Bones was far enough afield one day to allow me and Stenhouse to climb down the ladder to do some groundwork. Hunkered down on the tundra, the bear paid no notice as I took photos of Stenhouse going about his business. Chalk it up to luck, or to the "spidey-sense" that one gets when feeling watched, but when I turned around, I saw Bag-of-Bones kicking up a cloud of snow loping full speed towards us.

Stenhouse and I quickly climbed the tower ladder, taking refuge ten feet up on a plywood platform used to keep the generator and other boxes of supplies out of harm's way. This bear, however, would not be deterred by the height of our position, nor by the sound of the cracker shell that Stenhouse fired. The noise, if anything, seemed to make it angrier. Hissing and leaping up at us, the bear, at one point, dug its sharp claws into the plywood platform and started scratching. Seeing bits of wood flying in all directions, we both realized that we had to get off the platform quickly before the bear ripped it apart and pulled us down. The bear, however, wouldn't let us get to the ladder until Stenhouse fired three shots from his .44 Magnum.

****

During the week that I was at Cape Churchill, I had quickly learned that living in a small hut on top of a tower perched on a bleak spit of low-lying tundra jutting out into western Hudson Bay was a challenge. The toilet was nothing more than a green garbage bag stuffed into a pail on the open deck of the tower. The sun rose just before 9 a.m. and disappeared on the horizon well before 4 p.m. Temperatures were -20 to -30 degrees Celsius every day.

There was no relief from the storms that often blew in during the fall months, and I appreciated how Paul Latour and Dennis Andriashek, the first inhabitants, felt when the first powerful storm started blowing in during their stay. They sprawled on the floor wondering what would happen if the whole thing toppled over onto the tundra. Retreating to the ground for safety was not an option because of the multitude of hungry bears close by. They also could not call in for help. No one was going to venture out from Churchill to save them in a storm in the dark.

After that night, big storms at the Cape became known as "Hummers" because the

ARCTIC ICONS

123

cables holding the tower down vibrated so much in strong winds.

On the night we fended off the hostile advances of Bag-of-Bones, we awoke to the sound of wood creaking and the guy wires moaning. I did not know it at the time, but it was a "hummer." When the tower began swaying, I asked out loud: "What the hell is that?"

"Just a bear," said Stenhouse sleepily. "Probably Bag-of-Bones getting back at us for what happened today."

By the time we were ready to go back to Churchill on the 28th of November, Stenhouse and Cattet had spent nearly 800 hours observing bears. Nearly 200 of the animals had been subjected to some form of deterrent in the two years the scientists had worked on the project. Successful as some of the devices proved to be, Stenhouse believed there was no magical solution to handling problem bears. "When it comes right down to it, the use of deterrents is as much an art as it is a science," he said. "After three years of doing this, we're still learning how to judge the animals and the circumstances we find ourselves in."

Late that afternoon Doug Webber flew in to take Stenhouse and me back to Churchill in his Cessna 206. Webber had been living in Churchill since 1963 when he came north with the Canadian Navy. Bears were a common sight at his goose-hunting lodge at Dymond Lake and on the flights he offered to tourists who wanted to see the bears from the air. Webber was so confident of his customers sighting a polar bear that he offered a money-back-guarantee if they didn't. He'd never had to pay up, he told us that day.

Shortly after taking off, Webber circled the polar bear tower and tipped his wing towards

Cattet, who was waving at us from the platform. I counted twenty-three animals walking along the coast or lying down on the snow. Bag-of-Bones was in his familiar spot, sitting there looking up at us.

"They're beautiful animals when you see them from up here and from a safe distance," Webber said at the time. "But most people see it differently when they come into town looking for food."

As much as I tried to appreciate what Webber meant, his point didn't really sink in until midnight that day, when I saw a polar bear kill a man outside my hotel room.

© Lynn Holden

When bears wrestle in the fall months, it looks as if the battle will end in bloodshed. It rarely does.

1983: THE WORST YEAR EVER

Shortly before midnight on November 29th, 1983, 46-year-old Tommy Mutanen was rummaging through the remnants of the Churchill Hotel, which had burnt to the ground a week before. It was snowing at the time, and a cold wind was blowing in from Hudson Bay. Mutanen made his way on hands and knees to a freezer still filled with meat. After filling up his coat pockets, he headed back to the street where a polar bear confronted him. Mutanen was lame in one leg. With food in his pocket and a slab of lard smeared on his coat, he never had a chance.

The bear knocked him to the ground with a single swat, and dragged him by his head next door to the Arctic Trading Post. There, the animal gave the struggling man a shake, tearing a chunk of scalp off his head. Still alive, Mutanen was then dragged across the street in front of the Arctic Inn, where biologist Gord Stenhouse and I had checked in earlier that evening.

I was in a deep sleep when I heard the screaming outside my main floor window. Initially, I thought it was just a couple of drunks getting into a fight on their way home from a bar. But when the screaming persisted, I got up and pulled the curtains back to see what was going on. For a brief few seconds, I didn't know what I was seeing. Seven or eight people had surrounded the polar bear. They were throwing snowballs and other paraphernalia, trying to make it to let go of its victim. It looked too much like a bad dream to be real. But once I got hold of

my senses, I raced down the hallway and banged on Stenhouse's door, knowing that he had a gun in his room.

By the time Gord and I arrived on the scene, it was too late to do anything. Shots were being fired and we both dove to the ground. Mike Reimer, who happened to be pilot Doug Webber's son-in-law, had already put two bullets into the animal. The bear was lying in the snow, breathing its last. Beside it, Mutanen was face down in a pool of his own blood. One of the bystanders turned him over to administer CPR. For a time, that was enough to bring Mutanen back to life. He died, however, about an hour after an ambulance transported him to hospital. Doctors could not stop the bleeding in time to save him.

In the hour that followed, I sat in an RCMP truck hoping to piece together a story for the newspaper I was working for at the time. To

my surprise, Constable Dennis Strongquill[1] was more than happy to have the company. Not much older than I was, he had grown up in Barrows, Manitoba on the Saskatchewan border, a First Nations community so small that the government of Manitoba hadn't officially designated it to be a community (that happened in 1984).[2] Strongquill had been just two years on the force. He confessed that he enjoyed working in Churchill, but not at this

When the temperatures begin to cool off in the fall, polar bears become much more active.

© Robert and Carolyn Buchanan

time of the year. There were just too many polar bears around for his liking. That may have been the reason why he didn't mind me tagging along when the senior officer radioed in to suggest that he look around for any other evidence that might help piece together what had happened.

With Strongquill lighting the way with his flashlight, we found part of Mutanen's scalp in a blood-stained pile of snow near the burnt out hotel. From there, we followed the drag marks to the front of the Arctic Inn. Conservation officers Brian Ogilvie and Irwin Schellenberg had removed the dead animal by this time, but the pool of blood the polar bear had died in was still there, soaked into the snow.

"I can handle black bears, no problem," Strongquill told me that night. "But this is why polar bears freak me out."

Bears were everywhere that fall, just as they were in 1976. In record numbers, they were breaking into houses, hunting camps and stores, terrorizing people on the streets and in outlying camps.

Conservation officers responded to 227 calls between late September and the first week of December—three times more than they did the year before, and almost eight times more than they did in 1980. In ongoing attempts to frighten off the animals, they used up their entire supply of 1,500 cracker shells. Roy Bukowksy's polar bear jail was so full at times that nineteen polar bears had to be flown out by helicopter to make room for other more troublesome animals. By the time the bears were finally gone, eighteen animals were dead and three others had been shipped off to zoos. It was, as wildlife technician Ian Thorleifson would later recall, "the worst year ever" in the history of the fifteen year effort to keep bears and people in Churchill safely apart.

Everyone associated with the Polar Bear Alert Program knew that a year like this would occur. They had seen it coming in 1976 when 29 bears died. The only surprise to veterans like Steve Kearney was that it took as long as this for another nightmare season to unfold.

A family of polar bears heads out into Hudson Bay after feeding on a beluga whale carcass that had washed up on shore.

The first sign of trouble came in early August when two Americans shot and killed a polar bear on the Seal River, north of town. James Goodman and Boyd Tuve were canoeing, and looking for a place to camp, when they spotted the animal sitting about 30 yards away watching them. When the bear started circling, the men got out of their canoe, loaded the shotgun and climbed up to the safety of a large rock.

From this seemingly secure vantage point, they watched with equal amounts of horror and fascination as the bear began rummaging through the canoe, trying unsuccessfully to tear open the Duluth bag that contained their tent and clothing. When the animal turned its attention on them, they yelled and fired a warning shot, without effect.

Weighing perhaps 400 pounds, the bear was not a particularly big animal. But then again, it was as big as the average male grizzly gets in the Canadian Rockies. When the animal stood up and put its paws on the rock in an attempt to lift itself onto the platform supporting the two men, Tuve knew they were in serious danger. Once again, the animal didn't flinch when they yelled; it was absolutely fearless. With only two shells left, Tuve wasn't about to waste another shot. So when the bear tried lifting itself up a second time with more success, Tuve pulled the trigger, killing the animal instantly.

As it turned out, Strongquill was on duty when the men came in to report what had happened. He had no reason to believe that they had done anything wrong, so he sent them on their way.

Thorleifson wasn't altogether surprised when he read Strongquill's report. The ice in Hudson Bay had melted early that year. As a result, many of the bears that he, Steve Kearney, and scientists Ian Stirling and Malcolm Ramsay were catching and tagging along the coast were not nearly as fat as they would normally be in years when the ice allowed them more time to hunt seals. One notable exception was a 1,500 pound monster Ramsay and Kearney caught and tagged at Cape Tatnam to the south, near the Ontario border, in July. It was the biggest bear seen by scientists working in western Hudson Bay up until then.

One bear was so desperate for something to eat that it did all it could to get at some geese being raised in a pen just outside of town. Terrorized, the geese somehow got their heads caught in the holes of the chain-link that fenced them in. One by one, the bear decapitated each one of them.

By the end of October, many of the bears in the region were as skinny as anyone had ever seen them. One 21-year-old bear that had been caught and tagged in late July of 1982, for example, weighed 441 kilograms. When it was captured again in November of 1983, it had lost more than half its weight. The animal was so physically wasted that the conservation officer who examined it wondered whether it would have lived another day.

Another bear was so desperate to eat something that it leaped onto a Russian ship that was loading grain at the port. The Russian sailors scattered in all directions before a harbour crew was able to frighten the animal off. Then there was the animal that tried to break through the door of Doug Webber's Dymond Lake Goose-hunting camp. The employee on duty at the time could not scare it off by firing several warning shots. When the bear began ripping up the outdoor freezer, he shot it dead.

The bears weren't entirely to blame for the trouble they caused that fall. John Bilenduke, who thought he could raise 400 chickens in his backyard, didn't bother contacting the Polar Bear Alert team when a hungry bear came along to get an easy meal. Instead, he shot it, proclaiming later that there were too many bears in the region anyway.

The tipping point came at midnight of September 29th when a polar bear broke into the home of trainman Elias Hill, who was in the railroad house at the time. Making a hasty exit, Hill ran outside to get his gun from the tool shed. Inside he crouched down in the dark, listening to the sound of his house being trashed. Hearing the sound of an approaching train in the distance, Hill made a dash for the tracks, only to hear the heavy footsteps of the bear coming up behind him. Hill turned just in time to shoot the bear before it overtook him.[3]

Based on past experience, wildlife managers knew that the situation was bound to get worse as the bears became more active in October and November. And it did. Reinforcement officers were so busy that Thorleifson was compelled to spend most of his time assisting them instead of tending to his duties as regional wildlife technician.

The tragedies that followed that fall may well have been averted had the deep freeze, which arrived in mid-November, remained. But just as the bears were moving onto the ice, a warm south wind blew in, forcing the starving animals to come back onto land. No one in Churchill had ever encountered such Chinook-like conditions at that time of the year.

"The ice melted completely," Thorleifson recalled. "The number of bears we saw along the coast in the days that followed was amazing. During a 14-mile drive one day, I counted fifty bears. Eight bears were shot by local people in self-defence that year. The Polar Bear Alert crew was handling as many as fifteen bears a day. Many of the animals we handled were no more than walking skeletons."

Polar bears came in droves to feed on fermenting grain waste they discovered at an old dumpsite. Many of them got drunk.

For Roy Bukowsky, the warm weather had been a blessing of sorts, at least at the time. Following his departure from Manitoba Conservation, he partnered up with Len Smith, the man who invented the Tundra Buggy—an all-terrain vehicle that he put together with parts from an army surplus, four-wheel drive dump truck, the differential from a front end loader and windows and seats from an old school bus.[4] The big bus was a hit with a *National Geographic* film crew that got to go for a test drive three years earlier.

Smith and Bukowsky had hoped to build on that success with Anne Fadiman, a reporter from *Life Magazine*, who was in town the second week of November to do a story on the polar bears of Churchill. The cold snap would have sent her home without much to write. But the return of the animals gave them a chance to take her out to the coast.

The trip included Dan Guravich and Fred Bruemmer, photographers who had helped put Churchill on the map with their books and magazine articles. Fred Truel, businessman and amateur photographer from Minnesota was there as well.

Everything went smoothly for the first week until Truel spotted an Ivory gull on the coast. The bird is rare in the Arctic, and almost never seen in this part of the world. In an effort to get this

ARCTIC ICONS

135

once-in-a-lifetime photo, Truel and Bruemmer took up positions by the driver's seat, which happened to be lower to the ground than any of the other windows.

With no bears in sight, Treul put his arm out the window to adjust his lens. "That's when we heard this sickening crunch," recalls Bukowsky. "We didn't know it at the time, but a big skinny bear had been hiding under the buggy waiting for an opportunity for something like this. We had a gun, but I knew that I had to act fast. So I grabbed Truel by the shoulder and punched the bear in the jaw as hard as I could. Still, it wouldn't

© Edward Struzik

let go. So I kept on punching until it tried to bite me. That gave me enough time to pull Truel in."

Having been a tank commander during the Second World War, Guravich was comfortable enough to step in and cut away Truel's blood-stained parka in order to inspect the damage

done to his arm. The wound was extremely deep, but fortunately no arteries had been severed. So he bandaged Truel up as best as he could while Len Smith called the RCMP on the radio telephone for help.

Almost nothing but bad luck followed. With a blizzard moving in, it was too dangerous to send out a Twin Otter, or even a helicopter, to take Truel to hospital. With no other options, Smith and Bukowsky decided to use a track machine and haul him out in the big Tundra Buggy.

"The ride out was a nightmare," recalls Bukowsky. "Visibility was near zero and we had to use a compass to find our way in the dark to the rendezvous point where another track vehicle was supposed to be waiting with a doctor. It was slow-going out there on the tundra. To make matters worse, all that bouncing around kept opening up Truel's wounds. Then, the windshield wipers broke and the housing on the sliding roof collapsed. We had to stand up in order to see where we were going. Just when we could see the lights of the vehicle waiting for us in the distance, the buggy crashed through the ice. We spent nearly an hour trying to haul it out, but failed. So we all piled into the tracking machine."

By the time Truel got to the hospital, he had lost nearly a third of his blood supply. Doctors told him that he would have died had he stayed out there on the tundra or been delayed any longer coming out. He was lucky to be alive.

Steve Kearney was the regional wildlife manager stationed in Thompson in the fall of 1983. He had, however, been working with Stirling and Ramsay that summer, capturing and tagging bears. Like Thorleifson, he was not surprised by what had occurred, given the overall big picture. "Having worked on the program since 1976, and having lived in Churchill for a couple of years, it was always my personal belief that it wasn't a question of 'if' but rather 'when' the next serious injury or fatality would occur," he told me. "This was the moment we were all dreading."

There was, of course, nothing he or his managers in Manitoba Conservation could have done to prevent the attack on Truel. It was, in its own way, just one of those things that inevitably happen when tourists don't have their guards up. But the news of Mutanen's death was different. When conservation officer Irwin Schellenberg called and told him what had happened, Kearney immediately advised Rich Goulden, the Wildlife Branch Director in Winnipeg and Harvey Boyle, the Regional Manager responsible for the Polar Bear Alert team in Thompson. They decided to have Kearney and Barry Chalmers, the chief conservation resources officer, fly to Churchill at daybreak.

The two men almost didn't make it. Freezing rain nearly forced the pilot of their small plane to turn back as they approached the runway, not that it would have mattered. There wasn't a lot that Kearney could do given the fact that this was a fatality, and that the RCMP had the lead in the investigation. So it was decided that Kearney would field calls that were pouring in from newspaper, radio and television reporters from all over the world.

In Churchill, where schools were closed until arrangements could be made to bus children from pick-up spots near their homes, residents were clearly upset by what had happened, just as they were when Paulosie Meeko was killed by a bear in 1968. The chicken farmer, who was also the president of the Churchill Wildlife Association, wanted more bears shot.

"There are simply too many bears around," John Bilenduke told me and other journalists the next day. "The animals are killers. We have a right to protect ourselves and our property."[5]

Others, however, called for calm and common sense. "The bears were here before the people were," mayor-elect Mark Ingebrigtson, noted the same day. "They are a fact of life like car accidents are a fact of life in Winnipeg or Edmonton. People are going to have to learn to adapt and keep their guard up."

"We have bears in town from July to early November," Pat Penwarden told Richard Cleroux of *The Globe and Mail*. "They [the bears] should have left by now. It's only because the ice hasn't formed. As soon as it does, they'll be gone. Most people realize they shouldn't be walking the streets alone at night when there are bears around. In the city, you have muggers. Up here, you have bears."[6]

As it turned out, it would be another ten days before there would be enough ice on Hudson Bay to allow the bears to clear out. In that time, three more animals had to be put down. One of them reminded me of "Bag-of-Bones," the bear that had haunted us at the polar bear tower at Cape Churchill. In his report, Thorleifson described the dead animal as just that: "a decrepit bag of bones." On a scale of one to five, he rated the animal's fat content as a "one," which means that he was already close to death's door when he tranquilized it. "Specific cause of death was not determined," Thorleifson wrote at the time. "I would hazard a guess that he just gave up."

Tour guide Kevin Burke gets a surprise when he sticks his head of the window of a tundra buggy.

© Edward Struzik

THE BUSINESS OF BEARS

No one in Churchill knew quite what to expect when word came out that *Life Magazine* would be publishing Anne Fadiman's polar bear article in the February issue of 1984. There was little reason to think that it would be a booster for the town's future prospects given all that had happened the previous fall. Tommy Mutanen had lost his life and tourist Fred Truel had come awfully close to suffering the same fate. A record number of bears had died and Fadiman had left town badly shaken.

The article, however, was a long thoughtful story, sandwiched handsomely in between features on the Shroud of Turin and the 20th anniversary of the Beatles' arrival in America. Fadiman did not blame anyone for the polar bear maulings: Truel is quoted as thanking Bukowsky for saving his life and saying that he bore no grudge against the bears. He even promised to return to see the animals the next year. Tommy Mutanen's death, tragic as it was, was not overly dramatized. Nor was the unfortunate need to kill so many bears that fall.

It was Len Smith, however, who was the star of the article. Readers learned that when Smith returned to retrieve the Tundra Buggy that broke through the ice, he found it had been trashed by polar bears. They had smashed windows and ripped up the seats. Instead of cursing, Smith surveyed the scene impassively and then, very quietly, began to whistle "Chariots of Fire," as he proceeded to clean up the mess. Fadiman ended her story with Smith driving the tundra buggy back to Churchill, stopping along the way to watch a family of bears pass by in a snowstorm—homage, Fadiman suggested, to the animals Smith considered to be "the most beautiful in the world."

Len Smith deservedly received credit for the business boom that followed publication of Fadiman's story and other major media reports that followed. Within a few short years, the number of visitors travelling to Churchill soared from 3,000 or 4,000 to between 10,000 and 14,000.

No one saw this coming in 1950 when the Canadian Travel Bureau promoted tourism in the region with the film, *North to Hudson Bay*, which made no mention of polar bears whatsoever. It wasn't an oversight. To most of the outside world, there was no link between polar bears and Churchill. "There are no luxury hotels, but there are Indians and colourful Mounties to attract the camera enthusiast," *The New York Times* opined in a travel article promoting a $140 train trip from Winnipeg to Churchill in 1958. "Visitors may be lucky enough to see rockets and meteorological missiles being fired into the air from their launching pads near the seaport."[1]

The first time that anyone even hinted that the polar bears of Churchill could be a tourist draw occurred in 1969, when the Hudson's Bay Company offered an "Up-Up Away Churchill," prize that included a round trip flight to the community. In an ad the company posted in the *Winnipeg Free Press*, it stated that staff at the Hudson's Bay Company store in Churchill would take the winners on a tour of the Northern Museum at the Roman Catholic Mission, the rocket base, and historic Fort Prince of Wales. Winners were promised the chance of seeing an Arctic fox and/or a polar bear.[2]

As best as anyone can remember, the idea that locals could actually make money on polar bears got its start in 1972 when two American journalists arrived in Churchill looking for an opportunity to see and take pictures of the animals. No one knew why, or even how the town got onto their radar; although the publicity generated by Operation Bearlift in 1971 may most likely have been the reason. When the journalists asked conservation officer Brian Wotton whether anyone could take them out onto the tundra,

Wotton scratched his head for a while before suggesting that Al Chartier might be the only person crazy enough to do it.

Chartier had come to Churchill in the fall of 1963 by way of the military. Like his friend, Doug Webber, who had come up around the same time with the Canadian Navy, Chartier immediately fell in love with the town and its people, as well as with Bonnie Batstone, the daughter of a local trapper. When the army pulled out in 1964–65, Chartier stayed on to make a new life with his young bride. Together, they set up a sporting goods store in 1968 and a guiding/outfitting business two years later.

A jack-of-all-trades, Chartier was also a transportation and logistics specialist, ferrying in mail, people, equipment, and supplies for the likes of biologists Fred Cooke, Bob Jefferies, and Rocky Rockwell who were studying snow geese at La Perouse Bay, east of Churchill. For that purpose, Chartier had access to a small track vehicle, which he used to give the Americans what they came for.

"We got about halfway out to Knight's Hill where I used to see a lot of bears during my time in the military," Chartier recalls. "But there wasn't a single bear around. On our way back, the machine broke down and we ended up walking five miles to get back. I felt bad about that so I suggested that they might have more luck if they came back later in the fall when there were sure to be more bears in the area."

No one was more surprised than Chartier when the two men took him up on the offer, and returned with money to pay for the trip. This time, Chartier put them in the back of an old military dump truck he had stripped down to the frame. To make the photographers as comfortable as possible, he placed two old car seats onto a plywood platform and then wrapped the poorly dressed men in sleeping bags. There wasn't a person in Churchill who didn't get a chuckle when they saw that first polar bear safari leaving town that day.

"I was scared shitless that we would break down or have problems with the bears," Chartier recalled more than 30 years later. "I didn't really know what to expect. But they ended up having a great time, even though it was cold as hell."

This wasn't the first tourism venture ever launched in Churchill. Jimmy Spence and John Hickes, the son of an Inuit mother and Scottish father, had been running a modest trade ferrying people by boat to and from Fort Prince of Wales on an ad hoc basis. And in 1967, Doug Webber, with the help of three Chipewyan men from Tadoule Lake and three Cree men from Churchill, got things going when they set up a

© Lynn Holden

canvas-covered Quonset goose-hunting hut on Dymond Lake 30 kilometres north of town.

But Chartier's trip to the tundra that fall represented the birth of a unique enterprise, one that would eventually put Churchill on the world map. Response to the article that the photographers published in the United States may not have generated the interest that followed the *National Geographic* documentary or the *Life Magazine* article that Fadiman would write years later; it did, however, have Al and Bonnie, and a handful of other people who got in on the action, hopping, answering calls from people who wanted to come and see the bears, the beluga whales, and the vast array of birds that pass through or nest along the tundra and treeline.[3] The Chartiers eventually became so busy they begged Doug Webber to keep his single engine plane in town during the fall months so he could give tourists an aerial view of the polar bears.

One of those tourists was Dan Guravich, a freelance photographer from Greenville, Mississippi, who arrived in Churchill in 1976 with a plan to photograph birds before leaving with the idea of writing a magazine article on polar bears. Guravich hardly fit the profile of an outdoor photographer shooting polar bears in the wild. A former commander with the Calgary Tanks in the Canadian Armed Forces, he was more than 50 years old.

Guravich's passion for polar bears, however, got its start legitimately in 1969 when he was hired as the official photographer to record Humble Oil's historic transit of the Northwest Passage on the S.S. *Manhattan*. The trip, which was made at the height of the oil boom in Alaska, was meant to be a signal that Arctic oil and gas could, and would soon be coming south. Guravich saw his first polar bear in the wild on that journey. The animal, he recalled years later, was peeling off the fat of a freshly killed seal on the sea ice in Viscount Melville Sound. Unperturbed by the sight of the giant icebreaker heading towards it, the bear turned its back on Guravich and the dozens of other excited observers who were on deck. Then, as if to signal its indifference to all of them, the bear defecated.

Guravich was never quite the same photographer after that. The sight of that first polar bear, and the several others he saw in the weeks that followed, was a life-changing experience. From that point on, he was determined to make his living as a nature photographer.

It wasn't easy doing that in the state of Mississippi, better known for producing Elvis Presley, Kermit the Frog, Coca-Cola and the much gentler Teddy Bear. So Guravich decided to switch gears and geography, turning his attention to Churchill, which was becoming a popular destination spot for serious bird and polar bear watchers.

By all accounts, Guravich was generous and a good soul. But he could also be prickly and taciturn, probably not unusual for a former tank commander. That might have been the reason why he and Chartier didn't see eye to eye when they first met. As a result, Guravich ended up hiring Boris Oszurkiewcz to take him out to photograph bears in the single-track vehicle that Oszurkiewcz had acquired and run for a short while before packing in the business.

Response to the article that Guravich and writer Jack Wiley produced for the *Smithsonian Magazine* in the February issue of 1978 was so positive that Guravich decided to follow it up with a book. This time, he approached Len Smith, the local Shell gas station owner, with the idea of building something bigger and better to get him and his camera equipment out onto the tundra for several days.

Like Chartier, Doug Webber, and Merv Walkoski, who later helped Bukowsky build the polar bear jail, Smith was a mechanical genius, and genuinely interested when Guravich pitched him the idea. With a crankcase from a gravel truck, an engine from a snowplough, differentials from a front-end loader, seats from an old school bus, and sixty-six-inch crop-spraying tires, Smith assembled what initially became known as the Tundra Bus before it morphed into the trademark "Tundra Buggy."

The business of polar bear tours began in earnest in the early 1980s.

The all-terrain vehicle may not have provided Guravich with the smoothest of rides, but it gave him another idea. Why not offer larger, well-heeled groups of southerners the opportunity to see polar bears in the wild?

Victor Emanuel, the owner of Texas-based Nature Tours Company was initially sceptical when Guravich pitched the idea to him in 1979. Bird-watching was the bread and butter of his three-year-old company. But when the Canadian Department of Tourism stepped in with an offer to support a promotional tour to Churchill in the fall of 1980, Emanuel decided to give it a try. He was amazed by how well the tour went, and by how many people signed up for future trips.

It didn't hurt that author Peter Matthiessen and a film crew for the popular CBS *Sunday Morning News* show agreed to come along for the ride. Charles Kuralt was the host of the CBS program and a serious celebrity in journalism, thanks in part to a documentary in which he and a television crew joined adventurer Ralph Plaisted in his attempt to reach the North Pole by snowmobile in 1967. Matthiessen was, in his own way, just as famous. Along with George Plimpton, Thomas Guinsberg and a handful of others, he founded the *Paris Review* literary magazine in 1953. His books on natural history included the highly acclaimed *Wildlife in America*, which was one of the most widely read books in environmental literature at the time.

With the airing of the CBS documentary, publication of Matthiessen's magazine article, and the publicity that Brian Davies and the International Fund for Animal Welfare had already generated, media interest in Churchill's bears mushroomed. CBC's *Fifth Estate* television news program showed up in 1981, a year before Guravich and colleague Richard C. Davids' book *Lords of the Arctic*, became a bestseller. That same year, *National Geographic* aired a one-hour show, hosted by actor E. G. Marshall and narrated by actor and Academy Award winner Jason Robards.

Looking back on it now, Bonnie Chartier acknowledges that no one in Churchill really knew much about the tourism industry until *National Geographic* aired that program. Up until then, the business of ferrying people around was done on an ad hoc basis, usually by locals in response to requests from film crews and professional photographers.

It was, however, multicultural in a unique way, with non-natives working with Cree, Chipewyan, Métis, and Inuit entrepreneurs. Recognizing an opportunity when they saw one after watching the *National Geographic* show, they all got together at the Chamber of Commerce level to see how they could turn this publicity into a successful economic venture.

"Not all of us saw eye to eye on some things, but we did see an opportunity to save the town, which had fallen on hard times when the military pulled out," says Bonnie Chartier. "Johnny Hickes had a brochure made up for Nanuk Lodge. Doug Webber got one made up for Dymond Lake Lodge. Len Smith put one together. And so did me and Al and a bunch of others. Each one of us contributed about $500 so that Penny Rawlings (Arctic Trading Company) could mail the flyers out."

This is exactly what Roy Bukowsky and members of the town's polar bear committee had envisioned in 1976 when they drew up a plan for polar bear management in Churchill. The hope back then was that the polar bear would no longer be viewed as a great white rat that ate garbage, but as a remarkably beautiful predator that could, if managed well, save an increasingly impoverished town.

Inspiring as these business opportunities were, the rapid growth of tourism created a number of unexpected challenges for conservation officers like Ken John, Don Jacobs, special officer Jim Durnin, and wildlife technician Ian Thorleifson, who were all stationed in Churchill during the early 1980s. Notable among them was the death of Tommy Mutanen in 1983. That, and the mauling of Fred Truel the same year, made everyone realize that such a tragedy could, and was likely to, happen again.

Adding to that concern was the issue of baiting bears. By the time the *Life Magazine*

article was published, there were four operators—all locally based—using 18 vehicles to ferry tourists around. On principle, some of the guides were opposed to the idea of using bait to lure in animals. But others saw no harm in it so long as it was kept to a minimum, and so long as tourists and film crews didn't mind. Guravich, who acted as a guide for the Tundra Buggy tours, was one of them. He never hid the fact that he routinely used a can of sardines to get bears to come close to one of the off-road vehicles. "I don't just bait them. I feed them and I make no secret of it," he told Bob Lowery of the *Winnipeg Free Press.* "People come to see bears. If I don't feed them, there won't be many around to see."[4]

On this issue, Don Jacobs found himself agreeing with John Bilenduke who was a constant thorn in his side. Bilenduke predicted that bear-baiting would result in someone being mauled, or a bear being killed. Jacobs never had any doubt that he would be proven right. He just didn't know when.

Jacobs got his answer in the fall of 1984, when both major Canadian television networks—CBC and CTV—were in town, along with dozens of newspaper, magazine, radio journalists, and documentary filmmakers.

One of them was Ron Shanin, who happened to come from the same town as Victor

Emanuel. Shanin was, for a short period of time, the "Crocodile Hunter" (Steve Irwin) of the 1980s. Like Irwin, he was more than happy to get up close and personal with the wild animals he filmed and photographed. In a 98 minute documentary, *African Safari,* which he produced in 1968, Shanin is shown capturing two of the deadliest snakes in Central Africa with his bare hands. In another scene, a lion pounces on him before it is shot.

And just like Irwin, until a stingray fatally stabbed him in 2006, Shanin always came out alive. But two crew members associated with the filming of *African Safari* weren't so lucky. One died from pneumonia; the other from a gunshot wound.

When Shanin showed up unannounced in Churchill in the fall of 1984, he set up a three-by-four-foot cage, then smeared it with sardines. Shanin sat in that cage for six hours a day over a four-day period while a photographer and Florida journalist Sandy Huff, waited nearby in a van.

Two bears—a male and a female, marked with the letters 'CV,' approached the cage

© Lynn Holden

on the second and the third day. "I reached out and touched the male's nose," Shanin told freelancer Huff. "Its first reaction was surprise—obviously it had never been close to a human. But the bear was a carnivore, and I was a warm-blooded animal—food. The foxes around kept constant eye contact [on the bears] while the two bears put their heads down and tried to push my cage over," he added. "I shouted and talked to them, but nothing fazes bears—they do not realize that man is a dangerous predator."[5]

By all accounts, CV was a gentle soul of a bear who delighted tourists with the nonchalant manner in which she approached off-road vehicles. Shanin, however, evidently misjudged her determination to get at him and the can of sardines he had inside the cage. At one point, CV knocked the cage over, rolling it at least ten times over a period of 25 minutes before it finally came to a stop 135 feet away.

"It was terrifying," said Shanin. "She hit it so hard I had to pull my extremities away. Each time she hit the cage, I had about three seconds to get up on my knees and try to position the pillow I had brought so I wouldn't hit the angle irons inside. Her claws hit my boots. They are needle sharp and, up close, I could see they were black at the base, striped in between and like needles at the tips … Her goal was clearly to break the cage and claw through the two camera openings. They are four inches wide, big enough for a bear to get its foot in about 12 inches."

After nearly a half hour of this, the animal backed off long enough for Shanin to get out of the cage and into the van. He was then taken to hospital where he was X-rayed and treated for extreme bruising. Shanin later told Huff that his biggest concern wasn't his injuries but the possibility that the photographer in the van might have been laughing too hard to get steady film shots of what had transpired.

"I'd do it again," he said, noting that he planned to come back the following year. "After all life is too short. I'd like to say that I was rolled over by a polar bear."[6]

The story did not end there. A few days later, a group of local men drove out to the area with the intention of hunting ptarmigan. When CV showed up at their campfire, they shot the animal dead, claiming CV charged at them without warning.

News of CV's death spread quickly. One tourist from California was so upset, she sent an angry letter to Don Jacobs calling for

© Lynn Holden

something to be done. "That bear was not a rogue," she wrote. "It had not been in town, was on a preserve, and had entertained us for two days—if not for her, we might not have had pictures at all. I feel we have contributed to her death by supplying her with sardine bait so she could stay around our buggy, but we liked that bear and did not tease her, nor attempt to

© Lynn Holden

be physically close to her. All seventeen of us paying tourists felt very badly when told the circumstances of her death … It seems to me that responsible townspeople should know what effect an incident like this can have on their economy."[7]

Jacobs couldn't disagree and said so in a report that he wrote for his superiors:

"I feel that bear-baiting is a serious problem that should be looked at carefully. To say that a bear can be baited into a steel mesh cage for four days and teased to the point that the bear is biting and hitting the cage with a human in it, and then to say this will have no effect on that bear's behaviour is pure nonsense. I believe that this is conditioning the bear to hate humans and also to relate humans with food. Furthermore, the bear will lose his fear of man as nothing was done to stop the bear from doing this … There is nothing wrong with people looking and taking pictures of bears in a safe and natural manner. We should take steps to correct this problem. This should be stopped."[8]

Jacobs' report did not surprise Steve Kearney when he reviewed it that winter. Following the death of Tommy Mutanen in 1983, he and Richard Goulden had decided to begin seriously evaluating all the data collected since 1967, when Chuck Jonkel began tagging polar bears.

Kearney was confident the Polar Bear Alert program was working, but he also realized that new and innovative solutions needed to be considered now that there were thousands of people, and probably many more in the future, coming north to see polar bears. Churchill was no longer just a grain port and abandoned military base, it was now the "Polar Bear Capital of the World."

Wayde Roberts was stationed in Churchill from 1997–2000.

ARCTIC ICONS

CHAPTER NINE

THE SCIENCE OF BEARS

In spring of 1982, Ian Stirling and his colleagues at the Canadian Wildlife Service caught and tagged 19 polar bear families on the sea ice and in the denning areas of western Hudson Bay. Adult females were given a unique number so they could be tracked to see how well their cubs survived, and how old they were when weaned. After several years of tracking these and many other animals, Stirling was able to confirm what he had long suspected. The female polar bears of Churchill were unique in that over 40 percent of them bred every two years rather than the norm of three years in most populations, and occasionally four years in more northerly areas where biological productivity tends to be low.

Remarkably, the cubs, which were weaned after only about eighteen months with their mothers, had similar survival rates to those cubs that were not weaned until a year later in polar bear populations elsewhere. Churchill area bears typically produced one or two, and occasionally three cubs. That same spring, the late Malcolm Ramsay, Stirling's graduate student at the time, caught an extremely rare set of quadruplets along the banks of Hoot Creek in the main denning area south of Churchill.

There were other reasons to be optimistic about the future of these bears, even though they spent an extraordinarily long period of time fasting on land. The adult male that was caught by Steve Kearney and Ramsay at Cape Tatnam near the Ontario border in 1982 weighed in at 1,540 pounds. It was not only the largest specimen caught in western Hudson Bay up until then, but one of the largest found anywhere in the world. Clearly, there were enough seals out there to sustain most of the bears through the long fasting season.

Science and techniques for polar bear study had come a long way since the 1960s when Dick Harington used dog teams to search for and sometimes punch holes through the roofs of maternity dens so that he could poke a tranquilizing dart into the animal with a harpoon stick. During the 1960s, scientists did not understand the relative importance of each of the species of marine mammals comprising the diet of polar bears in the wild. They did not know how long the bears fasted, or how they managed to survive in temperatures that could dip to -50 degrees Celsius in winter, and rise to 25 degrees Celsius in summer. How a polar bear could swim for several kilometres in open water and then climb back onto the ice in sub-zero temperatures, apparently without any ill effects, was a complete mystery.

The natural history of polar bears in western Hudson Bay was so sketchy that Chuck Jonkel had to rely on reports from local Cree trappers such as Jimmy Spence to find out where exactly the polar bears of the region denned. His documentation of an enormous denning area south of Churchill in 1970 proved eventually to be one of the largest in the world, outside of Wrangel Island in Siberia.

These large knowledge gaps, however, were beginning to be filled in by the early 1980s, thanks in large part to the research that had been done on the western coast of Hudson Bay by Stirling, Chuck Jonkel, and Nils Øritsland, a Norwegian scientist who pushed the limits of polar bear science in ways that were almost unimaginable.

Data from the recovery of tagged animals by Stirling and his colleagues, and by Inuit and First Nations hunters, for example, eventually confirmed that the polar bears of Churchill represented part of a distinct group of animals with a high degree of fidelity to western Hudson Bay. By this time as well, Stirling, his students, and his colleagues had also begun to map smaller den sites, both to the north and south of the main denning area. They knew, by then, that

ringed seals represented 95 percent of the bears' diet, and that most problem bears tended to be young males.

What's more, they had proof that garbage dump bears were more likely to be destroyed as problem animals than those bears that had not become familiar with refuse sites. And they knew that garbage dump bears that had been tagged and tracked were more likely to be harvested by Inuit hunters in Nunavut. What they didn't know was why most male garbage bears did not come back to the dump once they matured, and why some sub-adults and females accompanied by cubs did.

I was in the field twice with Stirling: once while he was capturing and tagging polar bears in the Beaufort Sea, and on another occasion when he, Wendy Calvert, and graduate student Becky Sjare were conducting research on polar bears and walrus at Dundas Island in the High Arctic.

The trip to Dundas in the spring of 1989 pretty much confirmed everything that I had learned and heard about Stirling outside of our many conversations. The man was a prolific scientist not just because he was blessed with a sharp mind, but because he was patient, stubbornly tenacious and always looking at the big picture. Stirling wasn't just interested in studying polar bears, he was interested in their interrelationships with seals, walrus, belugas, and with sea ice and polynyas, those bodies of water in the Arctic that remain open year-round.

Stirling's research at Dundas Island exemplified that ethos. He had come upon the polynya there by chance in the spring of 1979 when he was doing a helicopter survey in the region. Snow still covered the ground, and, as expected, there was no sign that the winter ice was about to melt. Heading north from Lancaster Sound towards Baillie-Hamilton Island, Stirling spied a cloud of mist in the distance, a cloud that signalled open water. Not only

Norwegian biologist Nils Øritsland was pilloried in the press for trying to determine what might happen if polar bears were caught up in an Arctic oil spill.

© Thor S. Larsen, Norsk

was he surprised to find so much open water there, he was impressed by the preponderance of wildlife in the area. Tracks of polar bears dotted the sea ice and there were both seals and walrus in abundance.

With its vertical cliffs, inhospitable terrain, and the exposure to fog, which tends to build over open water in the Arctic, Dundas Island is not a place that most scientists would choose to conduct research. But at the top of an imposing

Two young bears sense that a bigger, older male is approaching.

90-metre-high cliff, routinely pounded by gale force winds and blinding blizzards, Stirling envisioned a small hut, from which he and his colleagues could watch polar bears and walrus interacting.

Stirling had a thing for precipitous vantage points like this one. Most times it worked out, as it did at the polar bear tower at Cape Churchill in western Hudson Bay, and at Caswall Tower[1] on Devon Island where he and his colleagues observed polar bears hunting seals in the spring and early summer months. The one time it didn't was in the spring of 1975 when student Paul Latour and biologist Lorraine Allison spotted only one bear after sitting in an unheated hut at the top of Nelson Head on Banks Island for a month.

Even at Dundas Island, scientists often went weeks without seeing a polar bear, although ultimately, their patience was rewarded. During nine seasons, they not only observed polar bears successfully preying on seals, they also found evidence of polar bears attacking and wounding three walrus and killing seven others. This was indisputable proof that, given the right circumstances, a 600-pound bear can, on occasion, kill a 300- to 400-pound walrus.

For Stirling, the road to Churchill began on the opposite side of the globe in the 1960s, when he was conducting studies on Antarctica's Weddell seals, the ecological equivalent of the Arctic's ringed seal, though several times larger. International concern for the plight of the polar bear was high at that time, and just as Environment Canada recruited Chuck Jonkel to come to Canada in 1966, the department offered Stirling the opportunity to come back home to conduct population studies on polar bears, and their ecological relationships with seals, in the Beaufort Sea four years later.

Based initially in Ottawa, Stirling worked with Jonkel in Churchill for two seasons until he moved his family to Edmonton where the Canadian Wildlife Service's regional office had the responsibility for research in the western Canadian Arctic. It was an especially fortuitous fit. Ward Stevens, the research manager for mammals at the time, was old school, the kind of boss who encouraged his scientists to think and act on their own judgment. While that did not sit well with some scientists who preferred to have direction, it suited Stirling perfectly.

Funding, however, was limited, even in those early days. While the Canadian Wildlife Service provided a very modest amount of seed money annually, logistical support came by way of Polar Continental Shelf Project, a lean and mean operation which provided scientists with grants of Twin Otter and helicopter time, and accommodations in Resolute and Tuktoyaktuk, if they were required. Funding from the Natural Sciences and Engineering Research Council was just enough to pay for the cost of students and equipment.

Money was so tight that on more than one occasion, Stirling complained that he felt like an organ grinder standing at the corner with a monkey on his shoulder and a cup in his hand.

With that cup in hand, Stirling was successful in getting money from several non-government sources such as the energy industry and the World Wildlife Fund of Canada, which was looking for more effective ways of investing in wildlife conservation.

Monte Hummel, president of the WWF at the time, vividly recalls his first meeting with Stirling in Churchill in 1981. The two men were walking along the coast just before the tide came in. Hummel spotted mussels in the tidal pools and suggested that they collect some for dinner. While Stirling didn't object, he did emphasize the importance of frequently looking around while in polar bear country. Otherwise, he advised, it might be too late to do anything about a bear that might sneak up. Just as Stirling ended this lecture, the two men turned around only to find a polar bear between them and their truck.

"The tide was coming in, but somehow we managed to get back to the truck without incident," Hummel recalls. "Instead of driving back and counting ourselves lucky, as I had expected, Ian took the opportunity to dart and mark the bear. I learned then that he never let go of a chance to further his research. And I also learned that our investment in his research was

On the long walk out to Hudson Bay from the denning grounds, a female will stop at night to dig a hole in the snow so her cubs can rest and take shelter.

not going to go wasted."

The list of research projects Stirling pursued in those early years was an exceptionally long one. From 1971 to 1979 he worked in the Beaufort Sea conducting population ecology studies of polar bears, and ringed seal ecology studies with Tom Smith, a Fisheries and Oceans scientist who was well on his way to becoming one of the world's foremost authorities on small whale and seal populations in the Arctic. To that end, Stirling and Smith did a series of studies on ringed seal breeding habitats in the eastern Beaufort Sea, then later in the High Arctic and southeastern Baffin Island.

From 1974 to 1979, Stirling's group conducted aerial surveys of ringed seals in the Beaufort Sea to better understand their importance to polar bears.

During that time, he expanded the work he was doing out of Resolute to include population studies of polar bears in Barrow Strait and Lancaster Sound, in response to the then proposed Arctic Islands Pipeline. And then from 1975 to 1979, he conducted the first population study of polar bears in the Labrador Sea.

One of the key results of those studies was evidence of significant fluctuations in the productivity and survival of ringed seals. That productivity, Stirling surmised, had to have had an enormous effect on the survival and reproduction of polar bears or, in some years, a marked reduction in both parameters.

These conclusions convinced Stirling of the importance of maintaining a long-term study of the population ecology of polar bears. He was convinced that sound management of the species would be dependent on an understanding of the natural variability of their ecosystem, and the frequency and scale of such variability.

Busy as Stirling was in those early years, he didn't think twice about taking over the research in western Hudson Bay in 1976 when Jonkel left the Canadian Wildlife Service to take a job at the University of Montana in Missoula. Not only did Churchill provide Stirling accessibility to a great number of bears, it provided him with a more cost-effective means of deploying graduate students such as Paul Latour, Malcolm Ramsay, Nick Lunn, Mark Cattet, Andrew Derocher, and Evan Richardson to study polar bear behaviour, population dynamics, reproduction, den sites, and the value of the supplementary feeding that occurred at the garbage dump.

Stirling's arrival in Churchill was a watershed moment for polar bear science in the region, as well as for wildlife specialists like the late Dick Robertson, Steve Kearney, and Daryll

Hedman. For several decades, they successfully used the research results from his group to help frame management and policy decisions for their bosses in the Manitoba government.

Another watershed moment in the study of polar bears was the arrival of the late Nils Øritsland, who came to Churchill in 1971. In the world of large carnivore biology, there was no one quite like Øritsland. Tall,

handsome, extremely athletic, and disarmingly charming, he was blessed with a sense of humour that was both understated and wickedly funny.

Øritsland had come by way of Churchill via the Halmaneøya in Svalbard archipelago where he spent a year on the uninhabited island with well-known Norwegian polar bear scientist Thor Larsen. One of their goals was to determine how much energy a polar bear loses and gains in its natural environment. Another was to map den sites in Kong Karls Land, travelling only on skis—not an easy task with one of the largest and most dangerous predators in the world. Nevertheless, Øritsland and Larsen persevered. One orphaned cub became so accustomed to their presence that it followed Øritsland around pretty much everywhere he went. Øritsland

In winter, spring, and early summer, polar bears constantly wander the west coast of Hudson Bay searching for seals on the sea ice.

© Edward Struzik

called the cub "Douglas" for a short time until a closer examination of the animal revealed its feminine features. His colleagues never let him forget this misnomer.

Øritsland came to the University of Guelph as a Postdoctoral Fellow and turned his talents and attention to Churchill in 1971, primarily because the region promised access to a large number of bears, and to a vacant military building that he could use for experiments in polar bear physiology. Conservation officers also offered a helping hand by turning over problem bears that might otherwise have been destroyed.

Øritsland was just 31 years old at the time. An innovative thinker, he was always coming up with ideas that no one had ever previously contemplated. Even his admirers were surprised though, when he and University of Guelph graduate student, the late Robin Best, built a cage big enough to put a makeshift treadmill and a breathing chamber inside so that they could measure the amount of oxygen and carbon dioxide a bear breathed while resting and walking at different speeds.

Biologist Brian Knudsen couldn't believe it when he first saw how the captive bears had taken to the machine. Knudsen had come to Churchill in the 1960s as one of Chuck Jonkel's field assistants. Under the supervision of John

Craighead, the legendary grizzly bear biologist from the University of Montana in Missoula, Knudsen subsequently spent 13 months conducting his own polar bear research on North Twin Island before doing some freelance work, helping to capture problem bears for Manitoba Conservation, and for Øritsland's physiology experiments.

"The bears clearly enjoyed being on the treadmill so long as it was going fast enough," he told me when I caught up with him in the summer of 2012. "One bear I saw was so anxious to get on the machine in the morning that it pounded on the treadmill as if it was demanding that Robin Best switch it on. That bear was particular about the speed the treadmill went. It would growl if it went too slow or get off the machine if it went too fast."

Øritsland confirmed this observation, which led to the realization that there is an optimal speed that maximizes energetic efficiency of movement for bears of different sizes.

Øritsland, Best, and later, Ricki Hurst were also able to measure thermoregulation through transmitters which were surgically implanted into the bears' abdomen. Through these experiments, the scientists discovered, among many other things, that the opening and contracting of certain blood vessels connected to a thick layer of outside fat, helped polar bears deal with the problem of overheating in summer and keeping warm during the coldest days of winter.

This research also explained why it is that polar bears prefer to hunt by lying or waiting rather than by actively stalking their prey. Unlike most animals, polar bears use twice as much energy walking or running.

Years later, this insight triggered a "eureka" moment for Ian Stirling and Nick Lunn. It explained why it was, and still is true, that a hungry polar bear will walk through a colony of flightless snow geese on the coast of western Hudson Bay in summertime, rather than chase them down and eat them. Using the results from Øritsland's treadmill studies, Lunn was able to calculate that in order to add calories to its diet, a polar bear must be able to catch a snow goose in only 12 seconds. Otherwise, it spends more energy than it gets in return.[2]

Almost everything we know about temperature regulation, digestive efficiency, the cost of walking, and metabolic rates, comes from the research that Øritsland and his students did during the 1970s.

Polar bear leaping from one small ice floe to another during the spring melt.

© Edward Struzik

Like Stirling, Øritsland managed to do this all on a shoestring budget. Field assistant Ricki Hurst recalls how he and graduate student Paul Watts were so low on funds in the summer of 1976 that they offered a local pilot half a cow, which had been stored in their freezer, to pay for the cost of a flight to the denning area. There in the forest, the two men spent a month camped out, walking along lakesides, searching for dens in the permafrost embankments. Technologically, it was as primitive as science gets. Whenever they found a den, for example, they tossed a stick in to see if there was a bear inside. Fortunately, Nicki, the husky that accompanied them, had a knack, if needed, for running in and flushing out the bear without getting mauled.

Not all went according to plan, however. Øritsland's research in Churchill was cut short in 1980 after he and his colleagues were given permission to catch four polar bears and expose them to fouling their fur with crude oil when they passed through a water tank to determine what the consequences might be for animals if they were subjected to a real life spill in the Arctic. The negative public fallout from the tragic and unexpected events that followed contributed to Øritsland's decision to return to the University of Oslo in Norway. He never came back.

The idea of oiling bears to determine how they might react to a spill was nothing new. It had been bandied around since the early 1970s when scientists were conducting similar experiments on seals. But given the "likelihood of an oil spill" in the Arctic at the time and the "total lack of knowledge" about how it would affect bears, the International Union on the Conservation of Nature's polar bear specialist group passed a resolution in 1979 supporting what Øritsland proposed to do.[3]

While this research may have seemed cruel at the time, the reasons were altruistic. The fall of the Shah of Iran the year before had precipitated an energy crisis. To make up for the energy shortfall, oil and gas companies began searching for new reserves in the Arctic, thanks in large part to the National Energy Program, which often paid for the entire cost of their exploration through generous incentives.

Industry and government were determined to see energy development take place in the Arctic, and their proponents vastly outnumbered Øritsland, who was sceptical about the claim that there would be no threat to polar bears and Arctic marine mammals.[4]

Scientific research being done in Churchill and in Alaska at the time suggested otherwise. Observations made in those studies clearly demonstrated that polar bears were not averse to consuming antifreeze, used hydraulic fluid, and even parts of a lead-acid battery in garbage dumps, possibly because of the presence of attractive aromatic smells. Arctic exploration during the early 1970s also demonstrated that oil production activities occurred along the spring and fall migration paths of these animals. Should a spill occur, there were valid reasons to believe that polar bears would be in harm's way.[5]

No one involved in the oiling experiments thought the bears would suffer serious consequences. Canadian government biologist Bryan Kemper said as much a year earlier when he told *Canadian Press* that "no bears will die and those used will undergo minimal discomfort."[6]

Presumably, the Canadian Council of Animal Care felt the same way. Its inspectors assessed Øritsland's facility in February 1979 before giving the experiment the green light.

In the initial phase of the $80,000 study, funded by the Canadian government, three of the four problem bears made available for the project were ushered through a passageway that led to a small pool containing 7,000 litres of seawater covered with one centimetre of crude oil. Once the animals emerged from the water, they immediately began to groom themselves, licking

Biologist Chuck Jonkel (right) was the first scientist to study polar bears on the west coast of Hudson Bay.

the oil off their fur, just as they would do with blood and fat after killing and eating a seal.

Ricki Hurst insists that neither he nor anyone else involved in the experiment thought that this behaviour would occur as quickly and obsessively as it did. "It was a shock," he said. "They were determined to remove the oil from their fur. And there was nothing I could do at the time to stop them."

Canadian government officials ran for cover when Brian Ransom, Manitoba's Minister of Natural Resources, announced, in a press release,

that two of the experimental bears had died. Although the Manitoba government had not designed or funded the project, its approval had been required for use of the four Churchill bears in the study. Responding to questions in the legislature from Jay Cowan, Churchill's representative in the Manitoba legislature, the next day, Ransom insisted that the intent of the project was not to see the bears die or suffer, as had been suggested. The experiments, he insisted, were worthwhile, unfortunate as the ending may have been.

"The study has shown to this point that the potential impact of a spill is considerably greater

Canadian Wildlife Service scientist Chuck Jonkel took over the job of studying polar bears when Dick Harington left to restart a career in paleontology.

© Fred Bruemmer

than they [the scientists] had originally anticipated," said Ransom. "One must realize that the bears were not immersed in oil, as, perhaps the public perception is, but immersed in water which had an oil slick upon it."[7]

In the days that followed, Merlin Shoesmith, head of wildlife research in Manitoba at the time, tried his best to explain the science and the value of the experiments, but without success. Both the media and a handful of environmental groups would have none of it. "If we hear of these experiments again, they are going to be done over our dead bodies," warned Greenpeace founder Patrick Moore.[8]

Greenpeace had, by this time, eclipsed the International Fund for Animal Welfare as one of the more radical and daring environmental organizations in Canada. Like Brian Davies, Moore had a way with words that made policy makers cringe, and newspaper editors excited. Throughout various interviews, Moore described the polar bear experiment as "Frankensteinish" and "a travesty of science."[9]

No one, it seemed, could be convinced otherwise, even when Bill Pruitt, an eminent scientist from the University of Manitoba, weighed in on the subject. The editorial board of the *Toronto Star* tore a strip off Pruitt when he suggested that media coverage of the story was over-the-top and sometimes nonsensical.

Newspaper subscribers were similarly incensed by what had happened to the bears. "Appalled" and "disgusted," were typical of the words *Globe and Mail* readers used. Subscribers to the *Toronto Star* were even more worked up. The editorial page of that newspaper ran as many as six letters of protest a day over a period of more than a week. One reader demanded that Ø!ritsland be prosecuted. Others described the experiment as "diabolical," "sadistic," and "barbaric."[10]

At the height of the frenzy, Øritsland tried to calm things down by holding a press conference. But all that did was get the media and the public worked up even more. Following the press conference, one journalist cornered Ricki Hurst and likened him to Charles Manson, the notorious mass murderer.

For his part, Øritsland took all of this on the chin. But when Barbara Frum, the popular host of the CBC radio program *As It Happens*, went after him relentlessly on her popular evening show one night, he managed to silence her by pointing out that none of this would have been necessary had humankind not been so dependent on cars, trucks, and everything else that requires oil.

For perhaps the first time, many people in Churchill found themselves in agreement with Toronto media's coverage of the story. Carol Mackenzie, the 70-year-old woman who had worked hard to get her community to learn to live with polar bears, circulated a petition calling on Manitoba premier Sterling Lyon to ban further tests such as this one.[11] Sensing which way the wind was blowing, Lyon did just that.

Although the oiling experiments pretty much put an end to Øritsland's research in Churchill, they ended the debate about polar bears and oil. From that point on, no one in industry or government suggested that a spill in the Arctic would not be catastrophic for these animals.

Bad as the fallout was, Ian Stirling was able to carry on with a variety of ecologically oriented projects, thanks in large part to the late Richard (Rich) Goulden, Merlin Shoesmith, and Steve Kearney who valued the science too much to shut it down. For that he was grateful.

"The folks in Manitoba Conservation were able to recognize the importance of the oil work and the value of having someone of the quality of Nils Øritsland involved, so to a fair degree, they just rode it [the controversy] out," Stirling recalls. "A while later, they were actually willing to help me get some more physiological work done there but, for other reasons, it didn't work out in the end. As head of the Polar Bear Technical Committee around that time, I spent a lot of time talking to people about the importance of that work. I have no idea if it had any effect. However, I was always very impressed with the quality of managers

that Manitoba had for a couple of decades. They were good at deflecting flack and staying with the important stuff, as far as polar bears were concerned anyway."[12]

Good as they were in deflecting flack, Kearney and his colleagues could not ignore the public backlash that followed the maulings that occurred in the fall of 1983. It was, at times, as intense as the media maulings that followed the oiling experiments.

In the months following that nightmare season, Kearney was assigned the task of reviewing every aspect of the Polar Bear Alert Program in hopes that new strategies could be used to ensure the safety of humans and the welfare of polar bears. Questionnaires were sent out to every adult in Churchill. Residents and businesspeople were asked if they felt the bear problem was serious, whether they were concerned about human safety, and whether they had had any serious encounters with polar bears, or had suffered property damage as a result of polar bears.

Residents were also asked whether they thought the handling of polar bears for scientific study and for management purposes was causing Churchill's bears to lose their fear of man.

The results were yet another reminder of how much more still needed to be done to win back the confidence of the public. A little over half of Churchill's population indicated that they had, at one time or another, a dangerous encounter with a polar bear or experienced property damage. The respondents overwhelmingly expressed the view that not enough was being done to make their town safe. A majority believed that the handling of bears was causing them to be less afraid of humans. In short, they sent a message to Manitoba Conservation calling on them to be much more aggressive in keeping bears out of town.

Kearney believed that the answers would have been different had the questions been asked before the Tommy Mutanen and Fred Truel maulings. He said as much to Richard Goulden, director of Manitoba's Wildlife Branch. Conservation officers stationed in Churchill, he insisted, were doing a good job, and D-20, combined with the new protocols for dealing with problem bears, had dramatically improved the Churchill bear versus human situation. Kearney firmly believed that being more aggressive with polar bears would only result in more animals being killed or, alternatively, sent off to zoos.

Polar Bear Alert Program
REPORT BEAR SIGHTINGS
204-675-2327 (BEAR)
Manitoba

© Edward Struzik

Nevertheless, both he and Goulden appreciated that a fresh management plan was needed to reassure the public that they would be safe.

The new plan that was put in place in January 1985, dictated that polar bears showing up at the dump would be trapped and locked up in D-20, the polar bear holding facility, for a few weeks, or until the ice on Hudson Bay froze over. The baiting of bears was prohibited.[13]

Control zones were also created. This meant that bears caught within Churchill proper would be actively deterred, captured and/or destroyed, if they were three-time repeat offenders and should no zoos agree to take them.[14]

Polar bears will sometimes pair up in summer and fall to keep each other company during the long fasting season.

Locals Jack Batstone and Louis "Louie" Voisey were hired to bolster the presence of the Polar Bear Alert Program. This not only provided the alert team with extra manpower, it also established continuity in a system which had been undermined by the fact that conservation officers were constantly rotating in and out of town.[15] More importantly, recruiting two local residents sent a message to the community that its involvement was important.

Most people in town were supportive of the new regulations.[16] Several tourism operators, however, complained when they learned that bears would no longer be allowed to feed on garbage at the dump.

Their complaints were not unfounded. Sixty-six bears were caught and removed in 1985; fifty-six of them were taken from the dump where tourists flocked when they could not afford one of the more expensive tundra trips.[17]

The late Dan Guravich was especially unhappy. "My people go out on the Tundra Buggies and we go 15 to 20 miles out along the coast of Hudson Bay," he told *Winnipeg Free Press* reporter, Doug Speirs. "We see bears out there. But there are hundreds and hundreds of people coming to Churchill to see polar bears at the dump. I'm upset because a lot of people are going to come to Churchill and not see any bears. That part of the tourist business could be destroyed and it's unnecessary. Dump bears are happy, lethargic bears who come to the dump twice a day … I don't think they ever come to town once they latch onto that food source."[18]

Neither Kearney nor Goulden were willing to back down. "There's no point waiting for a bear to become a problem bear," Kearney told Speirs. "It's not unusual for a dump bear to wander into town. A lot don't, but some do, especially the young bears."

As vociferous as some of the complaining was, and continued to be, the Polar Bear Alert team received an unexpected pat on the back in December 1985. Nearly ninety per cent of those residents responding to a new survey said they were satisfied with the program. Only five pecent claimed there was no improvement from previous years. To top it off, the town council congratulated Don Jacobs and the Polar Bear Alert team for a job well done. Councilor John Bilenduke, often a thorn in the team's side, co-signed the letter.

Scientist Ian Stirling (right) has been studying polar bears for more than 35 years.

CHAPTER TEN

HOW TO RESCUE A DROWNING POLAR BEAR

In the summer of 1984, the Manitoba Government supplied conservation officers in Churchill with their first dart guns. Prior to this time, these guns were only used by wildlife staff in the capturing and tagging of animals.

The dart gun was a new tool to be used when dealing with problem bears that could not be deterred with rubber batons, honking horns and/or cracker shells. Don Jacobs, the supervising wildlife officer in Churchill, was new on the job. He was so busy that summer, he had already fired a hundred tranquilizer darts before he was able to take the course at the University of Saskatchewan to show him how to use one.[1]

The first call to the Polar Bear Alert line came in on May 2, and the calls kept coming, and coming, in July and August, usually on the weekends. Jacobs began using D-20 on July 29th, months earlier than what would be considered normal.

The good news was that an alarm system had been installed at D-20 to deter whoever it was in town that was breaking into the jail and releasing bears. Wire meshes were also installed on both of the large entry doors so that officers

could look and make sure that no animal was on the loose. Previously, a few bears had figured out how to butt out of their compounds.

The bad news was the lights in D-20 were not always working. Sometimes they would flicker on and off, and sometimes they would go out completely. Not only did this light show freak out the bears, it was a little unnerving for whomever was guarding the bears at the time. There was always the chance an agitated bear could force its way out.

To add to the nightmares of that summer, another person was mauled in August. Sonny Voisey was out hunting with friends when he went out for a walk on his own and was attacked by a 900-pound polar bear. He tried to play dead, but as he later told the RCMP, "the bear did not fall for that old trick."[2] Fortunately for him, his companions arrived soon enough to save him from what would have been a certain death. The bear had no chance in this case. Twenty shots were fired. Seven struck the bear and killed it.

Sorting through the story with the RCMP proved to be a bit of a challenge for Jacobs. The hunters admitted that they had been drinking, and no one was able to explain why Voisey went for a walk on the coast when there were fresh tracks in the area. It was also not entirely clear why the bear attacked. Voisey, according to one of his rescuers was "cranky" when they got to him and "asking for water and whiskey." The bear had bitten him on the legs and the buttocks. Voisey was bleeding profusely,[3] and was in no mood or condition to talk.

Nothing, however, prepared Jacobs for what occurred on an afternoon in mid-October when he and conservation officer Rick Tease darted a big 800-pound animal with Lars Øivind Knutsen standing by. The 25-year-old Norwegian was there to do a study on how different drugs, including this one, affected the metabolism of bears.

In this case, the bear did not go down as expected. Instead, the animal raced off and jumped into the frigid waters of Hudson Bay, just as many bears do instinctively when they are being hazed, or when a drug fails to take full effect.

Believing there was nothing they could do, Jacobs and Tease stood by, figuring that was the end of the animal. They both felt terrible. Knutsen, however, had no intention of standing by and watching the animal drown. He threw off his boots, jumped into the frigid ocean and swam after the bear. "Rick and I looked at each other and we both agreed: 'That kid is going to die,'" Jacobs recalls. "Neither one of us was going to take off our boots and pull down our pants to save him, especially with a big bear out there..."

Knutsen was ten metres from shore when he finally grabbed the bear by the leg just as the animal was going under. "Its head had fallen down and its nose was submerged," he told me in a long email recounting the experience. "Air bubbles were coming out of its nose and to the surface. But it was breathing steadily."

Although Knutsen was sure that the bear was aware of his presence, he felt confident that the drug had kicked in sufficiently to prevent it from turning on him. He admitted, however, that it was difficult swimming back with a big water-soaked animal whose consciousness was fading fast. Knutsen says he wasn't sure he was going to make it. Had it not been for Jacobs and Tease standing on shore to give him a helping hand, Knutsen doubts that he would have been able to pull the bear all the way in and turn it over.

"We spent about 30 minutes pumping water out of its lungs," Knutsen recalled. "Honestly,

none of us thought that the bear was going to live, but the next day, it seemed to be okay."

Dealing with polar bears was, and still can still be, adventuresome. Ian Stirling and his crew, for example, have been involved in two helicopter crashes, two fixed wing crashes, two helicopter engine failures and more narrow escapes than he'd care to talk about.

Up until the late 1980s, the process of drugging bears also presented some serious challenges, as Jacobs could attest. Occasionally, a bear would go into convulsions or stop breathing when drugs like Sernalyn, or a combination of Ketamine and Rompun were used. In this case, artificial respiration was required to stabilize the animal.[4] Most times, it worked, but sometimes it didn't.

That's why Knutsen, a student with Thor Larsen in Norway, was brought in to do the study that he was doing under Stirling's supervision. The good news was that the scientists had a lot of success with the drug Yohimbine as an antidote to counter the effects of Rompun and Ketamine. Some of the bears given the Yohimbine were back on their feet minutes after it was administered.

There was, however, one notable exception. Biologist Malcolm Ramsay, Canadian Wildlife Service veterinarian Eric Broughton, and helicopter pilot Steve Miller were with Stirling in Churchill as he was testing the Yohimbine drug on an animal. Not knowing how the bear would react, Stirling watched cautiously from a distance after he injected a small amount of the drug into a vein beneath the bear's tongue. After waiting several minutes, they prodded the bear to see if it was recovering. There was no response.

Stirling knelt down and pulled the bear's tongue, as he would normally do while determining how deeply tranquilized the animal might be. Again, there was no response. A few minutes later, Stirling tried again assuming that nothing would happen. But this time he made the mistake of reaching into the bear's mouth from the front instead of the side (the latter procedure being normal practice in order to avoid the possibility of the bear's sharp front teeth clamping down). Just as Stirling grabbed its tongue, the bear's jaws snapped tight, piercing the sides of Stirling's thumb and forefinger, just missing the bone. The antidote was working. As the bear's eyes became more alert and focused, Stirling knew he was in serious trouble. Eric Broughton tried to pry the bear's mouth open but to no success. Only when he slapped the bear on the nose, did the bear loosen its grip long enough to allow Stirling to pull his hand out.

Incidents such as this one became the stuff of legend in Churchill, whose residents were learning to live with polar bears in some very unique ways.

Recognizing the danger of walking to work at night during the polar bear season, Gary Doer, president of the Manitoba Government Employees Union, negotiated a "polar bear clause" in the union's government contract, ensuring that government employees in Churchill would still be paid if the danger of a polar bear attack prevented them from going to work. The genius of Doer's negotiating skill was not lost on the public; Doer eventually became Premier of the Province.

Conservation officers, of course, were not part of that package; the danger of going to work each day in Churchill was just part of the job. Conservation officer Laury Brouzes was reminded of this in November 1993 when he, special officer Pat Cronin, Jack Batstone and Donald Spence headed out to D-20 to check on four animals in detention. Although bears regularly figured out how to get out of their cages, on this occasion, the night before the four bear conservationists arrived, another bear had managed to break in, attracted by a freezer full of seal meat. The bear was so intent on getting to the food, that he batted the freezer around the room before driving it through an interior wall.

Brouzes and his colleagues had no idea the bear was there because a powerful gale had blown D-20's outside door closed. Once the officers recovered from the shock of seeing this trespasser, gorging itself on seal, they darted the offender and put it behind bars.

Churchill lore contains many polar bears tales like this. Len Smith recalled a time when he was out hunting ducks on one of the lakes outside of town. His dog retrieved the first duck, and to Smith's surprise, a polar bear came out of the willows on the other side of the lake to grab the next. Smith kept hunting, while his dog and the bear took turns retrieving the ducks.

Dwight Allen was born in Churchill in 1960. He worked at the port and a number of other jobs before going into the tourism business in 1987. Allen thought he had seen and heard pretty much every polar bear story there was to tell. But the one that still boggles Allen's mind is the one where a polar bear showed up at his cabin. It was fall. There was a skiff of snow on the ground and a thin sheet of ice on the lake. The animal dug up a duck decoy that it had chewed up the previous summer. Allen watched with fascination as the

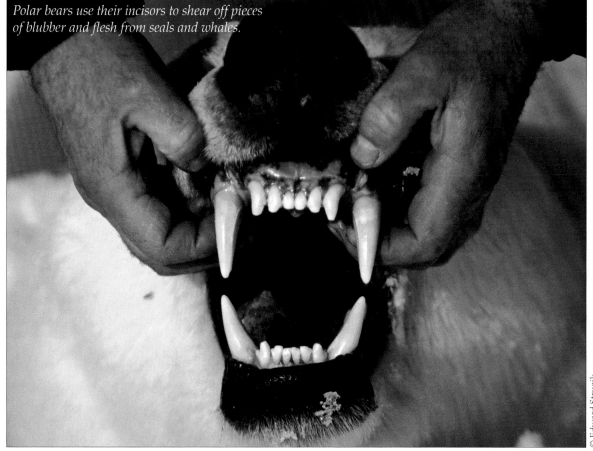

Polar bears use their incisors to shear off pieces of blubber and flesh from seals and whales.

bear walked over to the lake and punched a big hole in the ice, just as a bear might do when it is busting into a seal lair. Once the pool of water was big enough for the bear's liking, the bear carefully put the decoy down into the water and watched as it floated off. It was like a child playing in a wading pool.

Over the years, Allen has spent a great deal of time filming bears and putting the footage on YouTube. One of the shots he hoped to get was of a bear walking into town, just as conservation officers were coming in to intercept it. Allen got his chance on the night of October 1, 2006, when X17286, a three-year-old (which had been caught 11 times in its short life), returned. On this night, conservation officers Shaun Bobier and Syd McGregor were called out five times. Each time, they found no sign of the bear.

Standing by with his camera on one of those occasions, Allen saw why. Once the bear heard the sound of the conservation truck approaching, the bear lay down in the snow, put its paw on its nose and waited until the truck disappeared. Then, once the truck had driven by, the bear got back up and continued on with its business in town.

Pat Cronin, the special officer who was stationed in Churchill in 1993, insists that some animals could tell the difference between a conservation officer's truck and one of similar size and shape driven by a local resident. "Repeat offenders knew what was coming," he says. "They were smart. If they didn't run when they saw the truck coming, they sure did once we opened the door."

None of this surprises Stirling. The bears also quickly learned to recognize the truck he had rented for his fall work in Churchill. Once the bears learned that they could be immobilized by a tranquilizer dart fired from Stirling's truck, they simply moved away when it approached. It became so difficult to get close enough to some of the cleverer bears that Stirling had to borrow an unfamiliar vehicle from a friend in order to get close enough to them.

Nick Lunn saw a similar thing happen when he was doing his study on bears at the town dump during 1981 and 1982. "I swear the bears knew when it was dinner time," he noted. "Ten minutes before the garbage truck showed up, they'd wake up from their sleep and start walking to the dump. I have no idea how they figured it out. I can only guess that they must have heard the trucks coming from quite a distance."

Lunn never felt seriously threatened by the bears he studied at the dump. But, in later years, there were times while he was catching bears along the coast when he had a few heart-stopping, or head-scratching, moments.

One bear—X19173—was caught and captured three times in 2004, 2005, and 2007. This big male was so aggressive that it turned and jumped up at the helicopter during the immobilization process. Each time, Lunn scribbled a note describing its behaviour. And, each time, he wondered what might happen if the bear encountered humans on land. Another four years would pass before he found a frightening answer to that question.

Lunn followed in the footsteps of Ian Stirling by continuing with the denning surveys his mentor had begun in the 1970s. Federal funding was tight during the 1990s, so when Manitoba Conservation offered to share in some of the costs, an arrangement was made to work together on the project. Howard Buffett, son of Warren Buffett, the second richest man in the world, came on the trip in the spring of 1999, hoping to get photos of females emerging from the dens with their cubs. Conservation officer Wayde Roberts was there when they immobilized a female with a cub of the year (COY)—a bear that is in its first year of life.

Resource management technician Jack Batstone attempting to drive off a polar bear that is heading into town.

© Edward Struzik

Conservation officer Wayde Roberts tries to retrieve a polar bear cub that has climbed a tree.

© Howard Buffett

The COY, Roberts recalls, turned out to be a real scrapper. It took off up the riverbank on the Owl River, southeast of Churchill, inland from the Hudson Bay coast. Roberts chased the little guy and eventually caught up. The bear, however, wanted nothing to do with him and climbed to the top of a black spruce tree.

Roberts had to rope and wrestle the cub down from the tree and return it to his mother. Unbeknownst to Roberts, Buffett captured the scene on film, and left a copy of it in Roberts' mailbox before leaving town. It remains one of the very few pictures taken of a polar bear up in a tree.

One incident that still amazes most everyone in Churchill occurred in the fall of 1992. *National Geographic* photographer Norbert Rosing, was taking pictures of bears congregating around breeder Brian Ladoon's dogs at Mile 5, 15 kilometres outside of town. Ladoon had about 40 huskies, and all but one of them went crazy as a bear approached, likely because polar bears sometimes killed and ate them when there was no dog food around. One husky, however, a dog named Hudson, stood its ground and began wagging its tail as the big polar bear continued approaching. According to Rosing, the two "put aside their ancestral animus," and gently touched noses, apparently trying to make friends.

When another large polar bear arrived and began walking towards Barren, one of Ladoon's other huskies, the dog rolled onto its back, wagging its tail. The animals started playing "like two roughhousing kids." No one had ever seen anything like it. These gentle games continued for ten days straight.

Remarkable as that story was, no one seriously bought into the idea polar bears were big cuddly animals that would rather play than kill. That's why Daryll Hedman acted fast and aggressively when a polar bear wandered into the town of Sundance in the fall of 1990. Hedman was the conservation officer at the time.

Polar bears are sometimes attracted to the many sled dogs that are found in and around Churchill. In rare cases, the polar bear befriends them.

© Edward Struzik

This was not an entirely new ball game for Hedman. He had been up to Churchill three times before to help out with the patrols. But polar bears almost never come so far south, so there was no protocol in place in Sundance, as there was in Churchill, to deal with a polar bear such as this one. Nothing, it seemed—not cracker shells or the sound of a shotgun—could scare it away. "I even got a helicopter at one point to try to get it to leave town."

Out of options, Hedman called his manager in Thompson to see what he should do. His manager told him to shoot it and he did.

"And that's when the shit hit the fan," he recalls. "Every mother in town, including my wife, Sherry, wanted to crucify me. A meeting was called at the hockey rink and I tried to explain why I did what I had done, but there was no way, they wouldn't listen. I tried asking how they would have felt if that bear had come after one of their children walking home from school. But again, they weren't interested. I had just killed a cuddly white bear and they wanted me to pay for it."

One month to the day passed and the unthinkable happened. Another polar bear showed up in Sundance. This time, Hedman got on the phone and announced that there was no way he was going to kill this animal. So helicopter pilot Steve Miller was brought in with conservation officer Gary Friesen who put a dart in the bear so they could fly and release it on the coast.

The drama, however, continued as the sleeping bear began to stir in the back seat of the chopper just as they took off. This wasn't the first time a tranquilized polar bear began to wake up in a helicopter during flight. But like the others, it had a happy ending.

Hedman had a similar experience a few years later when he was looking for a polar bear reported to be skulking around near the tiny whistlestop town of Pikwitonei.

Some 100 people lived in the town, most of them trappers, fishermen, or railway workers. Hedman heard that one trapper, a man by the name of Lloyd Hanson, even had a polar bear for a pet. Hedman was working for Cam Elliott out of the regional office in Thompson at the time. He had already listened to a lot of polar bear tall tales by then, and figured that this was just another. But when people insisted that it was true, Hedman went out to see for himself.

Hedman spent several hours sitting on top of a beaver house, before coming to the conclusion that this was all a practical joke. Then, just as he was about to pack the whole thing in and go home, a big COY came strolling along. Hedman fired a dart at the roly-poly polar bear, but missed. Refusing to give up, he set a couple of snares and went to bed. The next day he and Hanson were surprised to find the COY had been caught. When the helicopter arrived later that day, Hedman put a dart into the bear, before loading it into the back seat. Hedman had never given a drug to a COY before, and it was apparent on the flight to the Hudson Bay coast that his tranquilizer dose was not enough. By the time the pilot was preparing to land, the bear was sitting up in the back seat, looking out the window just like a paying customer.

Hedman redeemed himself a few years later, after he became the wildlife specialist for the department. He was working with Wayde Roberts on a plan to unite orphaned cubs with a surrogate family. Up until this time, all baby bears that had lost their mothers were either sent to zoos or euthanized.

One of these cubs being held in D-20, however, would not eat anything offered to it until a surrogate family could be found. A frustrated Hedman called JoAnne Simerson, a senior keeper at the San Diego Zoo, who had been working with Polar Bears International. She suggested that he try using polar bear breast milk.

"Well, how the hell do I do that?" Hedman asked.

Conservation officers remove a tranquilized polar bear from the polar bear jail in Churchill.

© Edward Struzik

"With a breast pump," she suggested.

Sherry Hedman didn't know what to think when her husband phoned to ask where he might find a breast pump. Once she got to the bottom of the story, Sherry suggested that Darryl call their daughter, Mandy, who had just given birth to a baby.

To this day, Hedman lays claim to the fact that he is the only person in Manitoba Conservation who has successfully used a government purchase order to obtain a breast pump.

Stories like this were media gems, and reporters constantly searched these tidbits out whenever they came to town. This drove conservation officers like Wayde Roberts, Pat Cronin, Geoff Smith, and Laury Brouzes crazy. Dealing with dozens of journalists and filmmakers during the frenetic six-week period was not only tiresome; it ate into valuable time.

Most journalists were polite and respectful when read the ground rules. Some, however, thought their job was more important and that they could do as they pleased. Brouzes and his colleagues did what they could to accommodate those who wanted to see them at work. But he drew the line when a reporter for *The Globe*, an American-based supermarket tabloid similar to the *National Enquirer*, came into town in Fall 1993, looking for a story. When the reporter asked if she could see a jailed bear being airlifted out of town, Brouzes was exasperated. He told her she would have to pay for the helicopter flight.

To his surprise, she agreed. That got Brouzes thinking that other journalists and filmmakers might be willing to pay for similar experiences. As it turned out, they were. The next year, four different outfits paid for the cost of the airlifts.

The practice, which is common now, does not always go over well with some local residents who see it as catering to the rich and famous. It doesn't matter to them that hundreds of thousands of taxpayers' dollars are being saved. They think it a pitiful sight when hundreds of tourists are bussed in to watch a tranquilized animal being carted out of D-20 and then loaded unceremoniously into a helicopter net.

A problem polar bear that is about to be slung out of town by helicopter.

ARCTIC ICONS

187

CHAPTER ELEVEN

"THE SUAREZ SEVEN": CHURCHILL'S BEARS IN ZOOS

On the afternoon of March 3, 1981, Dennis Andriashek and Malcolm Ramsay were tagging female polar bears and their newborn cubs along Kelsey Creek, in a denning area southeast of Churchill. Around 3 p.m. that afternoon, the two scientists spotted a small polar bear all alone, ploughing through deep snow. The COY, a cub less than a year old, was about a half-kilometre away from the tracks of a female bear and her two cubs, all of which were heading northeast to Hudson Bay.

After searching unsuccessfully for signs of another polar bear family closer by, Andriashek and Ramsay made the decision to catch the COY and unite it with the bears heading northeast. There was no way of telling just then whether the animals were related, but Andriashek and Ramsay were willing to take the chance. Leaving the young bear behind would have resulted in its certain death. Uniting it with another family, even if it turned out not to be a family member, might at least demonstrate whether a female was willing to take care of a cub to which she was not the natural mother. It was a question that polar bear biologists had not been able to answer up until then.

The two men darted the COY and loaded it into their helicopter. Shortly after lifting off with the tranquilized cub on board, the helicopter developed severe engine problems, requiring an immediate return to Churchill. It was too dangerous to try and find the family of bears.

Back in town, when it became clear that the engine problem would not be fixed quickly, Andriashek called Richard Goulden in Winnipeg, and Steve Kearney in Thompson, to discuss what might be done. Given the bear's age and the fact that it was unwilling to take food and water, there were really only two options. She could either be euthanized humanely, or sent to a zoo. She would not survive if released on her own.

Neither Goulden nor Kearney had given much thought to the idea of sending a bear to a zoo up until then, because it was not common practice.

Although a home for this bear was found at the Assiniboine Zoo in Winnipeg, the fact remained that most zoos at the time were not interested in animals that were more than a year old, especially if they had a history of problems.

Something, however, had to done about establishing a formal zoo policy when Churchill's zero tolerance rule came into effect in Fall 1984 (a year after Tommy Mutanen and Fred Truel were mauled): bears caught within a new control zone were to be captured, or pursued and removed. Although polar bears had previously been tolerated in the dump, they also were not exempt under the new rules.

"'Remove from the population' was a phrase that sent chills up our spines," recalls Ian Thorleifson, who began working as the wildlife specialist for the Government of Manitoba in 1981. "Nevertheless, we compiled a list of bears that had been a problem in the past, or expected to raise problem offspring in the future, based on their history of association with the dump, or town, or other human habitations … If we captured any of these repeat offenders, we were directed not to allow them to return to the wild. We just needed to do our jobs, but there were options. My preference was to find a zoo that would take them."

Thorleifson addressed the challenge of finding homes for older bears by suggesting that zoos should not be given cubs if said zoos were not willing to include some older bears as part of the package. Realizing that there was nothing to lose, Goulden and Kearney agreed to give this new plan a try.

The bargaining tool worked. In just a few short years, twenty bears were struck off the list of animals to be permanently removed from the population in and around Churchill. New zoo homes were found for each one of them.

From the outset, officials with the Wildlife Branch made it clear that any zoo receiving bears from Churchill had to be certified by the Canadian Association of Zoological Parks and Aquariums—or certified by a sister organization elsewhere in the world. The quality of a zoo's facilities and the ethics of zoo operators were also taken into consideration.

All this was well and good in principle, but more often than not, it left something to be desired in practice.

No one, however, knew this in the fall of 1984 when the first bears were shipped off to Montreal, where an animal trader had made arrangements to sell them to zoos in Mexico and Scotland. In this case, an 11-year-old female and her cub, and two three-year-old males with a history of causing trouble in town were included in this consignment.

Lars Knutsen, the Norwegian student who had saved the drowning polar bear earlier that year, volunteered to come along with Thorleifson on the DC-3 flight from Churchill to Mirabel, Montreal's new airport, to deliver the animals.

It had been largely an uneventful trip until the aircraft landed in Montreal. Looking out the window as the plane began taxiing towards a warehouse at Mirabel, Thorleifson and Knutsen could see RCMP vehicles with lights flashing. Several sharpshooters were also standing by with high-powered rifles. Neither one of them realized just then that these officers were present to ensure that the bears were secure.

Young polar bear caught in one of a number of culvert traps that are set up along the town's perimeters.

On the tarmac, a forklift was on hand when the plane's cargo door was opened. The Spanish-speaking forklift operator, however, had not been briefed about what it was that he was unloading. Once the first cage was lowered to ground, the man jumped off the forklift and ran over to see what was inside.

Bug-eyed, the man recoiled from the cage, and ran away, swinging his arms wildly, leaving his supervisor to take over the controls. Glancing into one end of a cage, the supervisor turned to Thorleifson and asked: "Why are they all white?"

The following day, a reception was held in the hangar. As Thorleifson and invited guests sipped wine and ate canapés alongside the captive bears, animal rights activists showed up, protesting loudly. Thorleifson tried to explain that the bears would have to be euthanized if they did not find new homes in a zoo, but the protestors weren't listening. Security guards eventually escorted them away.

Although the Manitoba Conservation's "no tolerance" rule was reasonably clear, it was not always easy deciding which bears would be

Suarez Circus. Several problem bears that were shipped out of Churchill ended up in circuses and zoos. Many were abused and lived in squalid conditions.

© Dan Guravich

selected for deportation. Linda, for one, may have been a prime candidate, but given her gentle disposition, not to mention her notorious reputation, no one really wanted to see her go.

She and her cubs had become habitual visitors to the dump since she was first caught in 1966 at the Rocket Range. While Linda herself never caused any trouble, some of the 18 cubs she produced did when they were old enough to be on their own. At least two were shot when they could not be deterred from causing problems.

Entering her senior years in the summer of 1985, Linda hadn't changed her ways. She and her cubs were among the first to be incarcerated when the D-20 holding facility had been officially opened two years earlier. Even then, time spent in jail didn't stop her and her cubs from reoffending. Determined to see that Linda would not get into trouble again, Jim Durnin, the special officer stationed in Churchill, tried to give her a last chance when she and her yearlings showed up in Fall 1983. He locked them up that winter with a good supply of fresh seal meat, and kept them there until well into February of 1984, two months longer than normal.

Ian Stirling made it a policy of not giving polar bears human names as some scientists do. He was loath to become attached to an individual animal because of concerns that it might influence his or his students' objectivity. But even he was reluctant to see Linda sent to a zoo. Over the years, she and her cubs had supplied him and his team with so much scientific data that Stirling felt it would be nice if Linda could live the rest of her life in the wild, especially since she was likely going to produce only one more litter. That, however, was no longer an option when Linda returned to the dump again in the summer of 1985 with another cub in tow. This time, authorities finally decided that she had to go.

Thorleifson had heard through the grapevine that the Albuquerque Zoo in New Mexico was looking for a polar bear to be the centrepiece for a new exhibit. When he phoned Ingrid Schmidt, the zoo's director, to inquire, she casually informed Thorleifson that a pair of polar bears would cost the zoo $30,000 if the zoo bought one from an animal dealer.

Sensing an opportunity, Thorleifson offered a cheaper option. "I told her that if she was willing to take an older bear— one of the ones we wanted removed—and pay all expenses, we would supply three bears for free as they became available. I already had Linda and her COY."

To his surprise, Schmidt accepted. The zoo quickly modified its housing plans to accommodate an older single female, and Manitoba Conservation agreed to keep Linda and her cub, Chilly, a male, in the D-20 Holding Facility until the zoo was ready for them.

By April 1986, when the Albuquerque Zoo was finally equipped to receive the bears, Linda and her cub were loaded onto a train to Thompson, then shipped by truck to Emerson where they cleared Customs at the Manitoba–North Dakota border point. A long trip to Albuquerque followed, but Linda and Chilly arrived safely.

The following September, Thorleifson and his colleagues made good on the promise to send a third bear to the zoo. This one was a 40-kilogram orphan cub that had been found alone at the dump. When asked this time how the zoo wanted to handle transportation, Albuquerque officials answered with a question:

"Could you deliver the bear in a Lear executive jet?"

As it turned out, Tom Lang, publisher of the *Albuquerque Journal*, was bankrolling the polar bear exhibit. He was willing to send his executive jet up to Churchill to pick up the cub.

Once the jet landed in Churchill, Thorleifson immobilized the young bear in D-20 before carrying her onto the aircraft and placing her in a

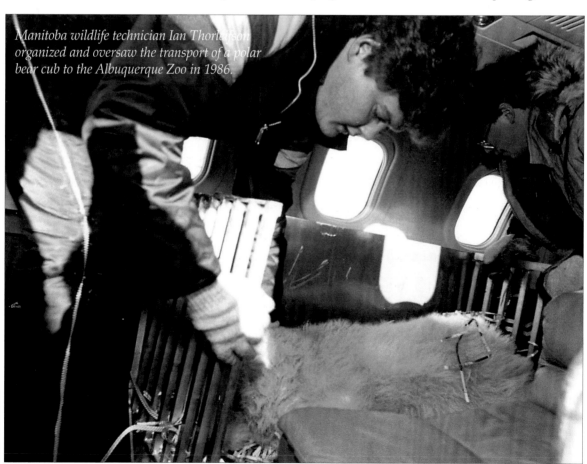

Manitoba wildlife technician Ian Thorleifson organized and oversaw the transport of a polar bear cub to the Albuquerque Zoo in 1986.

© Ian Thorleifson

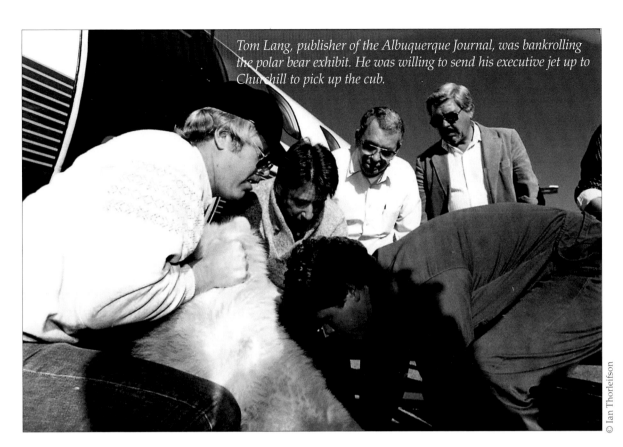

Tom Lang, publisher of the Albuquerque Journal, was bankrolling the polar bear exhibit. He was willing to send his executive jet up to Churchill to pick up the cub.

© Ian Thorleifson

small cage that had been specially built for this occasion. On the tarmac in Albuquerque, Thorleifson immobilized the bear once again before unbolting the cage and carrying the animal off in his arms. At the bottom of the stairs, he handed the bear over to Lang, who was so tickled by the remarkable offering that he had a picture of it put on the front page of the *Albuquerque Journal* the next day.

Media interest in polar bears had been high since the mid-1960s when the world suddenly came to appreciate just how threatened the animal was in many parts of the circumpolar world. Brian Davies kept that interest alive in the 1970s with Operation Bearlift.

In the years that followed, the animal developed a certain cachet that made it even more appealing than the lion or the tiger. Coca-Cola, for example, began using an animated polar bear in one of the company's most popular advertising symbols.[1] People who knew little about the animal in the wild were enchanted by the television commercial wherein a polar bear drinking a bottle of Coke admired the Northern Lights. The public loved the commercial where polar bears played with penguins, ludicrous as that scenario may have been. Although the science was often wrong, Coca-Cola did so well with this line of advertising that it went on to produce dozens of gift items with polar bears pasted on them. A 128-page book, *Coca-Cola Collectible Polar Bears*,[2] was written to pay homage to this strange union between polar bears and a company that specializes in making soft drinks.

A Mercedes dealer in Scotland also saw a commercial opportunity when the Edinburgh Zoo went looking for a bear in Canada in 1984. He offered to pay all expenses in order to get one of those four bears to Scotland.

Being the only captive polar bear in the United Kingdom at the time, Mercedes, as she came to be called, became a perpetual media star. British newspapers constantly reported on her well-being, the arrival of a male partner, her two births, and her move to bigger and better surroundings after animal rights activists highlighted the poor state of her holding facility.

Not all zoo stories, however, ended as well for Churchill's polar bears as they did for Linda and Mercedes.

Kenny, a three-year-old male shipped out in 1986, ended up performing in the State Circus of the German Democratic Republic. Under the care of the legendary trainer Ursula Bottcher, the so-called "Baroness of Bears," Kenny and several

© Edward Struzik

other captive polar bears became a worldwide sensation. They travelled the world performing acts like the Kiss of Death, where Bottcher would lean down with sugar or meat in her mouth so that it appeared as if her lips were touching those of Alaska, her favourite polar bear, when it tried to retrieve the treat.[3]

The polar bears were not always cooperative. An animal knocked down Bottcher at least three times during her career. On one occasion, a circus performer saw Bottcher emerge from a cage with blood pouring from her leg. "I said, 'What happened, are you okay?'" he asked. "Miss Ursula answered: 'It was just Neptune, he was playing with me,' I said, 'Playing with you, are you sure?' She answered, 'My dear, if he was not playing with me, we would not be having this conversation.'"[4]

Pathetic as circus life was for Alaska, Kenny, and the other polar bears in the act, it only got worse when the German show was shut down in the early 1990s due to financial problems. Bottcher did her best to find the animals decent homes, and for a while she had the media on her side. But because she had little say in the matter, a number of the bears ended up in Mexico with the Suarez Brothers Circus.

Among the seven bears that were sent to Mexico, there was Kenny, a bear named Barle, and at least one other animal from Churchill.

There, and on circus tours to the Caribbean and southern United States, the bears were poorly fed and often whipped into submission.

Winnipeg Free Press photographer Ken Gigliotti was one of the first to raise concerns about the plight of these animals. He came upon the show by chance in March 1996, when he was vacationing in Cozumel. Gigliotti was appalled to see the animals being forced into cages where they were compelled to walk upright, slip down slides and give the trainer a playful hug.

"One of the bears didn't want to go into the ring and he was jabbed by the handler in the rear ribs," Giglotti reported in an article that ran on the front page of the *Winnipeg Free Press*. "He really cranked that bear."[5]

Curious, Gigliotti asked a zoo staff member about the origin of the animals. He was genuinely surprised to discover that three of them had come from his home province.

Manitoba Conservation officials were clearly caught off guard when the news broke. Gordon Graham, legislative specialist with the Manitoba Wildlife Branch, assured the *Winnipeg Free Press* that the department wasn't interested in seeing Churchill bears ending up in circuses. But he also admitted that little could be done to right the wrongs of the past. "We always felt that we were dealing with reputable people," he said. "But things change … and there is no legal obligation for them to tell us anything."[6]

Following the *Winnipeg Free Press* report, which received worldwide attention, officials with Zoocheck Canada and the Winnipeg Humane Society demanded a meeting with the Manitoba government.

Having dealt with Brian Davies and the International Fund for Animal Welfare and Patrick Moore of Greenpeace in the past, Manitoba Conservation officials had their antennae up when Rob Laidlaw of Zoocheck, and Vicki Burns of the Winnipeg Humane Society eventually came calling in the fall of 1996. Officials in attendance were quick to accept the fact that the current system of sending Churchill bears to zoos had serious flaws. They agreed to the suggestion that an advisory committee be established to oversee the future export of Churchill's bears to zoos.

Comprised of two representatives from the Wildlife Branch, two officials from the Assiniboine Park Zoo, one from the Winnipeg Humane Society, and one non-affiliated person, the Polar Bear Facility Standards Advisory Committee seemed like a sensible answer to the problems that had arisen. Laidlaw, however, was not asked to be on the committee, and complained loudly. He claimed that the Winnipeg Zoo directors were in a conflict of interest and had no business being on the committee.

Undeterred by the snub, Laidlaw continued with some independent sleuthing.

Through letters and access-to-information requests, as well as reports from other animal rights organizations from around the world, he discovered in due course even more examples of Churchill bears suffering in zoos.[7]

The April 1997 report Zoocheck produced was another publicity nightmare for the Manitoba government.

Zoocheck was founded in 1984 by Rob Laidlaw after he stopped by a roadside zoo in rural Ontario a few years earlier and reportedly saw firsthand the appalling conditions some captive animals were living in. In relatively short order, Laidlaw and his organization were making headlines by focusing attention on poorly-run zoos in Ontario, in addition to highlighting the dolphins that were being held in captivity at West Edmonton Mall in Edmonton.

It described how one female polar bear sent to Japan's Aso Bear Park was forced to dance daily.

"The worst enclosures at Aso are the underground chambers," Zoocheck stated, citing a 1991 study by the World Society for the Protection of Animals. "From these dungeons, the sound of bears roaring and throwing their bodies against metal doors could be heard throughout the park. Each chamber is less than one metre wide and two metres long. They [the two polar bears at Aso] share a bare cement compound only eight metres square, including a pool. When the huge male was not sleeping or swimming, he was pacing the tiny cement platform. The female rubbed the right side of her neck on the bars of a cage at the back of the enclosure. She continued this stereotypic behaviour hour after hour."

Zoocheck's description of how a bear was faring at The Dublin Zoo was almost as bad.

"The polar bears are a pair of extraordinary contrasts," a veterinarian and animal behaviour specialist stated in Zoocheck's report. "The female was lying in exactly the same position, without movement, on both the Friday and the Saturday. The male was engaged in constant swimming … one could see that this was a complex display of stereotypic behaviour with every movement, twist and turn of the head and eyes identical to the cycle before… An adjacent mother with her children was overhead patiently explaining to them that this animal had gone mad after years in captivity and that was why he was doing the same thing over and over again…"

"Those bears should never have come here," former Dublin Zookeeper Brendan Price was quoted as saying in the Zoocheck report. "It's been a miserable life for those bears. It's about time things changed. If they don't, the zoo should be prosecuted for cruelty."

The controversy over zoos and Churchill's bears did not end with the Zoocheck report.

Pressure to do even more continued when the plight of the Suarez Seven was highlighted in a videotape that People for the Ethical Treatment of Animals (PETA) made four years later in the summer of 2001. The video described how the bears were repeatedly hit, jabbed, and whipped in the face, sides, and hindquarters to force them to do tricks. It described holding facilities that were nothing short of deplorable.

At one point in the controversy, PETA went to Ian Stirling to get his opinion on the situation. Stirling is by no means an animal rights activist, but when he saw the holding conditions, how the bears were being treated, and how the bears were behaving in the circumstances, he did not hesitate to say that they were horrible. Zoo officials from the United States came to similar conclusions when PETA sent them the video as well. Officials from the Baltimore Zoo were so disgusted that they offered to take some of the animals.

That same summer, the Puerto Rican Department of Natural Resources filed animal-cruelty charges against the circus for keeping the polar bears in filthy cages in extreme heat. "These poor things are suffering horribly," Howard White, Humane Society spokesman told the *Philadelphia Inquirer*. "They've lost something like 30 or 40 percent of their body mass. They have mange."[8]

Two females say hello while the cub looks on.

The plight of the bears struck a chord with executives of Coca-Cola. On August 22, 2001, just a day after the company received a copy of the PETA videotape, Coca-Cola withdrew its sponsorship of the Suarez Brothers Circus.

Celebrities such as British actor Ewan McGregor, who was playing the role of Obi Wan Kenobi in the *Star Wars* prequels, chimed in on the issue when U.S. officials refused to do anything about the animals. So did Canadian folk singer Sarah McLachlan. "It is heartbreaking to see these beautiful bears, regarded in Canada as national treasures, belittled and mistreated by the owners of a traveling show," McLachlan stated in letter she sent to the U.S. Department of Agriculture in August 2001.

McLachlan's involvement may not have come as a surprise, considering the fact that there was no end of Hollywood stars and musicians willing to lend their names to the animal rights movement. But even animal rights proponents were caught off guard when the fate of the so-called Suarez Seven captured the sympathetic attention of the Manitoba government and members of Congress.

Manitoba Conservation Minister Oscar Lathlin told *The Globe and Mail* that summer that he had written a letter to U.S. authorities calling on them to take action to ensure the welfare of Churchill's former bears.

"We are writing them to ensure the needs of polar bears are being met, and if not, we're asking [authorities]…to seize them and put them somewhere where they will be treated humanely."[9]

U.S. Rep George Miller, a Democrat from California, was highly critical of the U.S. Fish and Wildlife Service and the U.S. Department of Agriculture for approving permits "which allow the Suarez Circus to keep these huge and powerful animals in transient facilities without access to water and cool air." In a press release, he stated that "it is disturbing that two federal agencies responsible for protecting polar bears would allow arctic animals to be held in tropical climates."

On November 9, 2001, 16 Senators and 55 House members turned up the heat by demanding speedy federal action to rescue the polar bears. In a letter on the "serious matter," the 16 senators cited a report that the bears sometimes endured temperatures as high as 110 degrees "without a way to deal with the heat." They asked for "immediate steps" that, if necessary, included "seizing the polar bears for safe and proper keeping."[10]

The political uproar and a lawsuit filed by PETA eventually produced some results. In March 2002, U.S. officials seized Alaska, Bottcher's favourite polar bear, on the basis that the circus had presented fraudulent papers to demonstrate that she had not been born in the wild. The big bear was sent to the Maryland Zoo—overweight, weakly-muscled, and stone deaf. Zoo keepers there weren't even sure if she could swim in the pool they had built.[11]

To the chagrin of animal rights activists, the Department of Agriculture and the U.S. Fish and Wildlife Service were still unwilling to do anything about the other animals. One sensational news story led to another, before Congressman Earl Blumenauer of Oregon and 38 of his colleagues in the House of Representatives resolved the matter by introducing *The Polar Bear Protection Act*. The purpose of the bill, according to Blumenauer, was "to make sure that the other six bears are not forgotten and that polar bears will not suffer like this in the future. The bottom line is that the circus is just not an appropriate place for a polar bear," said Congressman Blumenauer. "We have the power to stop this outrage, end the cruelty and prohibit future mistreatment of these amazing animals."

The *Act* did what its proponents had hoped it would do. Six months after the *Act* was introduced, the six remaining members of the Suarez Seven were seized, put on FedEx planes, and sent to various zoos in the United States. One of the bears was in such bad shape, however, that it died en route to the Memphis Zoo. Kenny and another animal named Boris, however, made it to the Point Defiance Zoo outside of Tacoma, Washington. Barle found a home in Detroit. It took months to nurse these animals back to health.

Throughout this long controversy, members of the Polar Bear Alert Program in Churchill and

Thompson had been watching with frustration as the press pilloried them in public. None of the team members had dreamed that any of the problem bears they handled would end up in such unseemly surroundings.

Many of them realized that it was going to be increasingly difficult to find homes for bears in zoos in the future. In the hopes of finding a viable alternative for orphaned cubs, Wayde Roberts proposed the idea of finding surrogate females.

Even then, no one knew with certainty whether this would work. The chance that Malcolm Ramsay and Dennis Andriashek had in 1991 was lost when engine troubles forced them to abandon their plan to reunite that COY with another family in the wild.

In 1979, Churchill Conservation officer Rob Dean was given custody of this orphan cub. It was among the first of many polar bears that ended up in zoos.

© Rob Dean

There was, however, some evidence to suggest that this kind of surrogacy occasionally happens in the wild. In the spring of 1994, for example, biologist Mitch Taylor captured an 11-year-old female with two COYs in the High Arctic. When he caught up with the COYs a year later, they were travelling with another female. Around the same time, Malcolm Ramsay and Marc Cattet caught a female just as she was emerging from a maternity den in the Churchill area with a pair of three-month-old cubs. When conservation officers captured and relocated her from Churchill the following October, she had a third cub in tow.

No one knows how this occurs in the wild. Scientists, however, had evidence to suggest that the longer females are away from their dens, the more likely they are to discriminate between their own and any introduced orphaned cub by smell.[12]

In an effort to disguise this smell, Wayde Roberts and Daryll Hedman decided, on the advice of a wildlife biologist they consulted, to use Vick's VapoRub on the nose, heads, and backs of those bears they hoped to bring together.

The first opportunity to try this out came when an eight-month-old cub was captured in a culvert trap at the Flats near Churchill on September 11, 2001—the same day terrorists hijacked and flew two planes into New York City's World Trade Center. Roberts and Hedman held the COY in D-20 for two weeks before a female travelling with another similarly aged cub was captured.

All three animals were tranquilized so that the Vick's VapoRub could be applied. The animals were then transported out of town. When they woke up, it appeared they had accepted each other.

Helicopter pilot Steve Miller spotted the trio travelling together three days later. There was, however, no way of telling for sure whether the bond held. The orphaned cub did not show up the following year, or any subsequent year.

Daryll Hedman tried four more times to unite orphaned cubs with females that fall after Roberts moved on to another posting. None of them, however, were successful.

Frustrations for the Polar Bear Alert team reached a peak that same fall when Ewan McGregor showed up with a BBC *Nature* film crew to do a documentary on the Churchill bears. Most everyone in the Wildlife Branch thought that he would target them in a wider campaign to save polar bears from zoos.

Suspicious as everyone was, almost all stops were pulled to make sure McGregor got the full story.

Wayde Roberts was brought back for several days to demonstrate to McGregor how problem polar bears were handled. Roberts allowed McGregor and the film crew to be involved in the hands-on day-to-day activity of the program. Several bears were captured, handled and transported to D-20. The only thing McGregor and the film crew didn't get to do was to go inside the bear holding facility. There was a standing order that no media were allowed inside.

McGregor was apparently impressed. At the end of his visit, he and Roberts went out and drank a couple of bottles of wine and talked

© Edward Struzik

about their lives. McGregor introduced Roberts to his girlfriend, and told him that they were going to get married in the same castle in which the singer Madonna tied the knot. Before departing, McGregor left Roberts three autographed *Star Wars* movie posters for Roberts' three sons, Ryan, Tyler, and Christian.

Roberts was unimpressed until his wife Joanne told him later that McGregor had starred in the film.

The media was evidently as impressed as McGregor was. A number of newspapers reviewed the *Nature* documentary that ran on television stations in Great Britain, Canada, and the United States in April of 2002. London's *Daily Mirror* previewed the show, declaring that "Ewan McGregor is clearly fortunate to have been picked as the man to lead this documentary about the great care being taken to preserve polar bears in the frozen wastes of northern Canada."[13]

****

After Wayde Roberts moved on to become director of the Northwest Region of Manitoba Conservation, Hedman assumed sole responsibility for the adoption program. Kim Daley, working with Born Free Society, was also involved. But as time went by, there just were not enough orphaned bears to make the program work. It was costly, and efforts to unite orphaned cubs with surrogate families failed, for the most part, to produce positive outcomes. Hedman finally made up his mind to pull the plug on the adoption program after he, Donald Spence and a helicopter pilot were nearly pulled out of the sky by a female polar bear they were trying to dart for surrogacy purposes.

"She turned, jumped, and whacked the helicopter," Hedman recalls. "We were that close to the ground. I figured then that this just wasn't worth dying for. The adoption program was not working. It was time to end it. And we did."[14]

In the summer of 2002, Manitoba legislators introduced their own version of the *Polar Bear Protection Act*. Enacted into law on January 1, 2003, the bill stated that "every effort should be made to keep polar bears in their natural habitat." The act demanded that, in the event when it is appropriate to remove a polar bear from the wild, the facility that the bear is destined for must meet the highest standards for animal care and that follow-ups on the welfare of the bears be made.

Linda, as this bear was called, was such a gentle animal that she allowed people to feed her.

© Fred Bruemmer

Linda's image lived on for years in newspaper articles and in a Sierra Club Christmas card sent out to prospective zoo donors in the 1980s. When she died at the age of 35 in 1999, Linda was one of the oldest bears ever held in captivity. In a unique tribute to her contribution to polar bear science, Ian Stirling and other members of the Polar Bear Technical Committee held a wake for her in 2001.

As far as zoo experiences go, Linda's daughter Ulu also fared reasonably well. When Ulu turned 32 in 2012, officials at the San Francisco zoo brought in 10 tonnes of snow to celebrate. Videos and pictures of Ulu rolling around in the snow were aired on national television networks, and on the front pages of many major newspapers from around the world.[15]

Two polar bears wrestle playfully.

A female will travel with her cubs for up to two years or more.

Chapter Twelve

Pinatubo Bears

In Fall 2009, Kevin Burke was in a Tundra Buggy guiding a group of tourists along the coast of Hudson Bay when he spotted six polar bears in the distance. The animals were particularly animated, and Burke did not know what to make of the small female among them, which kept bluff-charging a much bigger male in a stand of willows. Once the Tundra Buggy moved up close, however, Burke quickly discovered what the commotion was all about.

"First, I saw the pool of blood on the icy pond. Then I saw a male bear with something in its mouth. And then, when it turned towards us, I realized, 'oh oh that's the head of a cub.' The mother in this case was desperately trying to save her cub while the rest of the bears were trying to get in on the action. It was all over by that point. There was almost nothing left of the cub when we got there."[1]

Burke had guided and worked with polar bear scientists in the field for more than twenty years. He had seen and heard of cannibalism incidents, although, like some Inuit hunters on Hudson Bay's west coast, he did not think this particular act of cannibalism was especially extraordinary.

Scientists Ian Stirling and Andrew Derocher, however, suspected that this incident, like seven other acts of cannibalism recorded that year, may have been yet another more alarming sign that climate change was taking its toll on the bears of western Hudson Bay, and on bears in other regions of the Arctic.

Neither researcher could recall a year like it. "To get eight in one year is really dramatic, especially when the bears came off the ice this year in fairly good shape," Stirling told me a few weeks after the end of Churchill's 2009 polar bear season. "It was a long winter and they had that extra time to hunt seals and put on weight before the ice went out. But it apparently wasn't enough to sustain all of them until freeze-up, which was particularly late."

"Cannibalism events such as these aren't proof that climate change is the cause," Stirling said. "But they are consistent with what you might expect when polar bears exhaust their fat reserves and become hungry. They don't just lie down and die quietly."[2]

The 2009 season was not the first time scientists had made a link between climate change and polar bears. The possibility that a warming world would negatively impact the animals of western and southern Hudson Bay had been a topic of scientific discussion during the 1980s, when I was working as a field correspondent for *Equinox Magazine*. "End of Arctic" was a story I worked on for nearly four years before it graced the cover of the magazine's November/December issue in 1992.

In the fall of 2009, a group of tourists witnessed this act of cannibalism on the west coast of Hudson Bay.

"The decline of polar bears we are seeing in western Hudson Bay does not represent a short term fluctuation," Stirling told me back then. "The decline has been on a downward trend for so long that it suggests that something negative may be happening with the entire ecosystem."

The prospect of a warming western Hudson Bay was highlighted in 1986 when Canadian Climate Centre scientist David Etkin and others suggested that a single degree rise in temperature would advance the breakup of sea ice in the region by about a week.

Two years later, Stirling and Derocher used that projection, as well as their own data, to describe what the logical consequences would be for polar bears if the ice-free season lasted longer than the typical four months. Both scientists suggested that a longer ice-free season could result in declining body condition, lower reproductive rates, reduced cub survival, den collapses, and an increase in conflicts with humans.

The projection was based on more than mathematical models and knowledge of how bears hunt and what they eat. Stirling had seen firsthand what the situation would look like in western Hudson Bay, should the climate regime be dramatically reversed (as it was in the fall and winter of 1991–92). In that case, a single episode—the eruption of Mt. Pinatubo in the Philippines in 1990—temporarily halted the greenhouse-warming trend that was already very noticeable in the Arctic. For a short time, volcanic ash and the emission of aerosol gases disrupted the transmission of solar radiation to the Earth's surface. This triggered a change in the Arctic Oscillation, the climatic pattern that influences weather in this part of the world.

During the fall of 1992, Stirling found polar bears on shore to be much fatter than they were the year before, and a good deal heftier than normally expected. The cubs also did well, so well, in fact, that Stirling nicknamed them the "Pinatubo Bears." It was clear to him then that a few extra weeks of being able to feed on seals had benefited the animals. Thus, it was not a stretch for both Stirling and Derocher to suggest that the reverse trend would be debilitating.

Like many people at the time, some conservation officers had doubts about global warming, and those who did not were not entirely certain how global warming might affect bears of the region. Until the mid-1990s, the problem bear season was, with a few exceptions, limited to the fall months—from September until the occurrence of the mid-November freeze-up. Many of the bears the officers observed coming off the ice in July were in such good shape that their body fat literally rolled when they ran. It was hard to believe that these animals could end up starving.

By 1996, however, scientists and conservation officers began to see a new trend emerging. Not only was the ice breaking up earlier than usual, the officers were handling more bears, and the data confirmed what they suspected. Between 1983 and 1995, the average number of bears captured, and the number of polar bear occurrences reported in Churchill each year, ranged between 46.2 and 115.5. Between 1996 and 2003, those numbers shot up to 113.8 and 199.2 respectively.[3]

I had seen the changes being manifested in other ways as well when the editors at *Equinox* once again sent me to Churchill in the summer of 1997. I was there with Gerald McKeating, Regional Director General of the Canadian Wildlife Service, Bob Jefferies, a University of Toronto botanist, and Rocky Rockwell of the American Museum of Natural History. These men weren't so much interested in what climate change was doing to the sea ice as they were in what it was doing to the land. In 1969, when Al Chartier was ferrying Jefferies and Rockwell out

Polar bears occasionally catch and kill seals in open water as this female did while travelling on the west coast of Hudson Bay with her cubs.

to La Perouse Bay, there were just 2,500 nesting pairs of snow geese in the area. By the time I arrived, that number had exceeded 50,000. The birds were literally eating themselves out of house and home, and turning the lush salt marshes into an alkaline wasteland. Flying over the tundra, the scene looked as if it had been napalmed.[4] Jefferies and Rockwell had hoped that the polar bears, which were common in this part of Wapusk National Park during the summer, might control the situation by feeding on goose eggs. With few exceptions, that did not happen. Ian Stirling and Nick Lunn had been right in their explanation as to why polar bears tend to casually walk through massive goose colonies instead of running the birds down and eating them. If the bears can't catch a goose in twelve seconds, the energy they burn is not worth the meal.

The situation did not improve on land, or on the ice, in the years that followed. Nightmarish as Churchill's 1983 polar bear field season had been, 2003 was even worse. And it could have ended just as disastrously, had Steve Kearney and his colleagues not learned the lessons, and made the changes implemented in 1985.

Virtually every statistic recorded in 2003 was off the charts. Operating and manpower costs were up dramatically. More than $250,000 was spent dealing with bears in 2003 compared to $70,000 a decade earlier. Damage reports were 600 percent higher than they were in 1991.[5]

In all, Richard Romaniuk and his fellow conservation officers filed a record 347 reports. They were so busy that Jack Batstone, who was, at the time, on an ongoing seasonal contract with the government, was asked to come in a week earlier than he would in a normal polar bear season. Daryll Hedman, the regional wildlife manager, and Steve Danyluk, the chief Conservation Officer, pitched in by flying in from Thompson to give a helping hand. Hearing how crazy the situation was in Churchill, Dan Shewchuk, the director of wildlife in Nunavut, called in to see whether his staff could help. Even Sheila McGillivary, the district clerk, was called into action. In addition to her role of fielding polar bear reports and complaints, as well as calls from the media, she mixed the drugs, and cleaned the drug equipment that was needed to immobilize problem bears.

A total of 176 bears was handled in 2003, 34 more than the previous record set in 2001.[6] Had Romaniuk and the other conservation officers not been forced to ration their supply of tranquilizers, they would have easily handled 200 animals or more. Approximately 50 percent of the district's budget was spent on airlifting 147 animals north of town in the ongoing effort to deal with problem bears.[7] Because the D-20 jail was often full, some of the problem bears had to be relocated immediately. On two occasions, culvert traps containing these bears had to be chained to

D-20's walls because weather wouldn't permit the bears being airlifted out of town.

"I still have bad dreams about that time," Romaniuk told me several years later. "We got our first report of a bear at the dump some time towards the end of May. The bears just kept coming after that. It was unbelievable. We had complaints about bears all through the summer and we rang in the New Year with confirmed sightings of bears near town. I thought they'd never leave."

There was one statistic that stood out from all the rest, and the one of which Romaniuk and his colleagues are most proud. In spite of the record number of problem bears, an acute shortage of tranquilizers, serious problems with vehicles, a break-in at the polar bear jail, and scores of media inquiries, only four bears died in 2003. Only one of those deaths was due to the conservation officers.[8]

The protection of polar bears and people in western Hudson Bay had come a long way since 1983 and 1984 when three people were mauled, and dozens of bears shot. Regulatory and management changes made in 1985 addressed a number of issues which had dogged the Polar Bear Control and Alert programs in the 1970s and early 1980s. The establishment of Wapusk National Park in 1996 also helped, especially

A grizzly bear with a freshly killed polar bear cub in Wapusk National Park, in the summer of 2013. Until about 15 years ago, grizzlies were unheard of in Manitoba.

© Bruce Bremner

when Cam Elliott, a former Manitoba Conservation biologist was appointed as superintendent. The creation of Wapusk ensured that the majority of denning areas would be protected, and that Parks Canada would offer a helping hand in research, education and some management issues. The passing of the *Polar Bear Protection Act* in 2002 was also important, as it formally addressed the challenges associated with dealing with problem bears and provided guidelines for sending them to zoos.

No one in Churchill during the fall and winter of 2003–04, however, believed that these measures were good enough. Stirling, Derocher, and Nick Lunn predicted the situation was only going to get worse in 2004.

With more than 75 years of experience between them, the scientists compiled a synthesis of existing studies, summing up what had been learned about the natural history and ecology of polar bears. Sea ice loss was not only going to be bad news for polar bears, they warned, it was going to be bad news for those people living in polar bear country.[9] As if to underscore that warning, a student researcher was knocked down and bitten, but not seriously hurt, by a polar bear in Wapusk National Park on November 18, 2004.[10]

Steve Kearney and Steve Danyluk, while reviewing prospects for the future that year,

decided to call a meeting to review every aspect of the Polar Bear Alert Program and determine what improvements could be made.

Syd McGregor, who had replaced Pat Cronin that fall, was present at the meeting, as were Kearney, Hedman, Romaniuk, and Danyluk. Virtually every option was put on the table, no matter how outlandish some of them might have seemed. There was talk of reversing the policy of removing bears from the dump, and allowing the dump to act as a kind of holding area for problem bears that might otherwise find their way into town. The idea of keeping bears in D-20 for longer than 30 days was also brought up. Serious consideration was also given to the prospect of euthanizing animals with a long-term history of causing trouble in town.[11]

There were also the ongoing issues with D-20. Earlier, bears had managed to bust out of their cages, but in 2003 the Polar Bear Alert Team recorded its first actual D-20 jail break, ostensibly because the building was in such bad shape. Acoustical issues also needed to be addressed, as the sound of adult bears hissing, clicking, and banging on bars freaked out the young COYs. More than once, Conservation officers found themselves inside the jail alongside a bear that had somehow gotten free, or, in Laury Brouzes' case, alongside a bear that had broken in.[12]

The committee realized that significant funding was required to deal with these issues. The committee also felt it was time to resolve the issue of Brian Ladoon's Husky kennel, which, since the late 1970s, had long been a major vector for hungry polar bears looking for dogs, or dog food, to eat. Much to the embarrassment of some Manitoba Conservation officials, Ladoon had planted his kennel on Crown land with a permit in those early years. Later, he even charged people to see those bears attracted to his site.

In the end, the Polar Bear Alert Team recognized that the dump could not be counted on as a holding area because of the likely prospect it would finally be closed down in 2005, as had been envisioned for several years. The team also concluded that it was premature to extend the incarceration time for problem bears. What Churchill needed, the committee realized, was more manpower and more money.

Much to their delight, money was forthcoming over the next four years to improve D-20. In 2005,

Some polar bears are successful in catching seals in open water, as this trio did near Churchill in the summer of 2012.

© Edward Struzik

the province spent $130,000 to repair the roof of the building. Another $225,000 was allocated the following year to pay for the construction of new cells and the installation of a cooling system for bears being held in warmer weather. The electrical system was upgraded in 2008.

Following a series of negotiations between the province, the town of Churchill, and the Canadian government, the dump was officially closed down in 2005, as planned. The closing did what the town and conservation officers hoped it would do. In 2006, Syd McGregor, Shaun Bobier, and their colleagues handled just 62 bears. While that number was slightly up from 2005, both officers figured that they would have handled well over 100 animals had they still been required to deal with bears at the dump.

The storing of garbage in L5, an old military complex on the outskirts of town, however, created some unforeseen problems because there was still no funding in place to ship said garbage out by rail to Thompson. Even worse,

Coming off the ice in July, polar bears are usually fat—as these three are—after spending the spring gorging on seals.

© Edward Struzik

Thompson's landfill was running out of room. The smell of refuse piling up was so strong that people could detect it from two miles away on a warm day. The bears evidently did too. Those bears that came looking for something to eat soon discovered that the walls of the old military building were so rotten that they could push their way through them.

On one occasion, a female and her two cubs forced their way into the building. They were only driven away after a town employee used his truck to chase them out.[13] On another occasion, Bobier and Jack Batstone were faced with the unnerving challenge of finding a renegade bear which had broken in and then disappeared into the building's dark recesses. "Once they got into the garbage, it was difficult getting them out," Bobier told me when he took me on a tour of the site in November 2006. "We darted three bears inside the building that first year, and trapped or free ranged another 18 outside. We realized that it was quickly growing into a safety issue."

Fortunately for the conservation officers, the town was willing to cooperate. Metal cladding was put up around the exterior of the building, and plans were made to secure the area.

By this point, the relationship between the town council and the Polar Bear Alert Program was as good as it had ever been. In 2004, Churchill's mayor and councilors voted to build a statue and monument to honour those conservation officers who had served in the Polar Bear Alert Program.

Mike Spence was very active in dealing with the Polar Bear Alert Program. He was constantly drumming up publicity for the town's bears and the tourism trade. Apparently Manitoba Premier Gary Doer noticed, because, beginning in 2005, he made it a tradition of travelling to Churchill to impress and entertain dignitaries and businessmen who might be interested in investing in the province. Among those Doer brought along with him were Prime Minister Stephen Harper, the U.S. and Russian ambassadors, several of the country's premiers, Paul and Andre Desmarais of Power Corp, and Janet Napolitano, the Governor of Arizona.

Adding to the interest was the fact that the polar bear had become an international icon for climate change, thanks to a *TIME* magazine special issue on the subject, printed in April 2006. "Be Worried, Be Very Worried" stated the headline on a cover depicting a polar bear standing on a melting ice floe.[14]

News on the scientific front continued to worsen, much of it coming from research that Stirling and his colleagues had been doing on polar bears in western Hudson Bay. Pregnant polar bear females had lost, on average, 50 kilograms of body fat between 1980 and 2007. This resulted in smaller litter sizes, with fewer cubs maturing into adults. The occasional triplets that the scientists had been used to seeing during the 1980s were now extremely rare. Not one of the females they observed leaving dens had four cubs with them.

The overall polar bear population had also declined from around 1,200 in 1987 to 935 in 2004—a 22 percent decrease. If sea ice continued to recede, as climatologists were predicting, there was not much hope for the polar bears of western Hudson Bay in the long term, unless greenhouse warming was halted somehow, and reversed.

But it was not just the bears of western Hudson Bay facing an uncertain future. There was evidence to suggest that several other polar bear populations, including the one shared by both the U.S. and Canada in the Beaufort Sea area, were also on the decline. Summer 2007 drove that point home. Up until that time, some scientists were still skeptical that the climate system keeping the Arctic Ocean cold and its ice frozen for much of the year could unravel as rapidly as climatologists like NASA's Josefino Comiso were suggesting. In 2007, the ice retreated so far beyond all expectations that most experts were shocked by what they saw in the satellite imagery. Across the Arctic as a whole, the meltdown was where climatologists expected it would be by 2030. What really made the big melt of 2007 an eye-popping experience

was the absence of ice in areas where it almost never melts. The so-called "mortuary" of old ice which normally chokes McClintock Channel in the High Arctic, for example, was almost all gone. What's more, Viscount Melville Sound, the so-called "birthplace" of a great deal of new Arctic ice, was down to half its normal summer cover. "The ice is no longer growing or getting old," John Falkingham, chief forecaster for the Canadian Ice Service, told me that fall. "Ten years from now," he said, "we may look back on 2007 and say that was the year we passed the tipping point."[15]

Like the Canadian Government, the Bush Administration in the United States showed little interest in addressing the issue of climate change and polar bears. But Bush's administration was backed up against a legal wall in 2008 when the United States' Center for Biological Diversity, Greenpeace, and the Natural Resources Defense Council successfully went to the courts to secure protection for the polar bear under the *Endangered Species Act*.

Interior Secretary Dirk Kempthorne responded by appointing a blue ribbon panel of 19 scientists to advise him on the issue. The panel, which was led by U.S. Geological Survey scientist Steve Amstrup, represented some of the best, the brightest, and the most experienced scientists in the field of climate change and polar bear biology. Team members were selected from twelve organizations, including the U.S. Geological Survey, Woods Hole Oceanographic Institute, the U.S. Fish and Wildlife Service, the Canadian Wildlife Service, the Wildlife Conservation Society, the Ontario government and several American universities. Two of the scientists—Amstrup and Ian Stirling—had more than 60 years of field experience between them and more than 400 scientific papers published.

In the report, the scientists concluded that two-thirds of the world's polar bears, including those in western Hudson Bay, Alaska, and most of Canada's western Arctic, would be gone by 2050. The only ones remaining, the scientists warned, would be those inhabiting the High Arctic regions of Canada and western Greenland.

Keeping in mind the U.S. administration's stand on climate change, no one knew what to expect from Kempthorne. However, a few days after personally thanking the scientists for their report, he announced the United States would list the polar bear as a "threatened" species.

In the summer heat, many polar bears spend considerable time in water to cool off.

"My hope is that the projections from these models are wrong, and that sea ice does not recede further," Kempthorne said. "But the best science available to me currently says that this is not likely to happen in the next 45 years."[16]

There was an expectation in some quarters that Canada would do something similar the following year when the Committee on the Status on Endangered Wildlife in Canada (COSEWIC) was scheduled to issue its update on polar bears. Much to the chagrin of Ian Stirling, and every other member on the International Union for the Conservation of Nature's (IUCN) Polar Bear Specialist Group, the authors of the COSEWIC report recommended remaining with the status quo, listing the polar bear as merely vulnerable, not threatened, as the IUCN had done in 2008.[17]

The fact that climate change was not even mentioned as a threat in the first draft of the COSEWIC report should not have come as a surprise to anyone. Co-author, biologist Mitch Taylor, was openly skeptical of climate change and stated his position publicly when he submitted his comments to the U.S. Fish and Wildlife Service while that organization was assessing the status of the polar bear.

The COSEWIC report gave Canadian Environment Minister Jim Prentice the excuse he needed to support the decision not to follow in the footsteps of the Bush Administration.

The bear's summer habitat on the west coast of Hudson Bay is much different than the sea ice they are accustomed to living in for most of the year.

ARCTIC ICONS

225

Instead, Prentice called a meeting of scientists, conservation groups, and Inuit leaders to discuss the issue at a round table in Winnipeg in early 2009. Although the $115,000 cost of the gathering did not result in either a united direction or a momentum to tackle difficult issues, the meeting did give the Inuit a voice on a subject that they felt was being ignored. Nevertheless, when Environment Minister John Baird replaced Prentice, it was clear that nothing was going to be done by the federal government to help the polar bears of western Hudson Bay.

The Manitoba government, however, took a very different approach. Polar bears were listed as a threatened species under Manitoba's *Endangered Species Act* in 2008, due to concerns of the potential impact of climate change on polar bear habitat and polar bears. A year later, Premier Greg Selinger flew to the climate change talks in

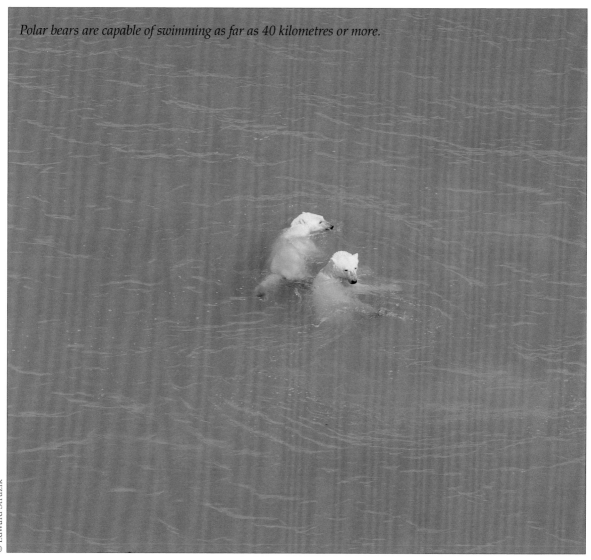

Polar bears are capable of swimming as far as 40 kilometres or more.

© Edward Struzik

Copenhagen, armed with a number of new initiatives for polar bear conservation in northern Manitoba.

One of them was a plan to protect 259,530 hectares of land in the Kaskatamagan Wildlife Management Area, home to the western Hudson Bay sub-population of polar bears from July to November, and to caribou during the summer.

"One of the key protected areas in the North is an area of polar-bear habitat," Selinger said. "They will have their natural environment protected for the future … Their population has been declining over the last several years. We want to ensure that they survive and thrive."[18]

Selinger also announced $31 million in funding for a new polar bear rescue shelter and polar bear exhibit to be constructed at Winnipeg's Assiniboine Park Zoo. Billed as the first of its kind in North America, the polar bear centre was seen as a way of conducting and coordinating polar bear rescue research, conservation and public education initiatives.

"As the home of Churchill, the world's polar bear capital, there is no better place than Manitoba to host this centre of research and education on the impact climate change is having on our polar bears," Selinger said.[19]

Selinger may not have appreciated it at the time, but the climate change story in Churchill was going to heat up faster than he might have expected, and the upcoming news was not going to be good.

Polar bears wrestling in the snow.

© Edward Struzik

CHAPTER THIRTEEN

POLAR BEAR ALLIES

I am standing on the coast of Hudson Bay watching two polar bears cautiously approaching each other on the sea ice. Robert Buchanan, a big bear of a man, who heads up Polar Bears International, the non-profit organization dedicated to the worldwide conservation of the great white wanderer, is animated.

He is telling me about the organization's webcam that allows people down south to see polar bears outside of Churchill in their natural habitat. He is expounding on the student leadership program, the field lectures, the office and library in Winnipeg, the International Centre for Polar Bear Conservation in Winnipeg, and all of the other good things that he and his well-heeled, but unpaid, colleagues from Canada and the United States are selflessly promoting. He wants the world to care about polar bears and the Arctic. But, most of all, he wants the world to care, and to do something, about anthropogenic climate warming.

Just before the two bears meet head to head, they stand up and do a little dance around each other. With his back to the bears, Buchanan keeps on talking. I try, but can't concentrate on what he is telling me. The bears are now locked up like two Sumo wrestlers.

Seeing that he does not have my full attention, Buchanan takes a sideways step and blocks my view. I am no longer listening. On my toes, I look over Buchanan's shoulder and see that one of the bears has stepped back. It takes a wild swing and slaps the other animal on the side of the head.

Buchanan turns, but only for a moment. He won't give up talking. The bear that has been hit is on its keister. His attacker pounces. Now both bears are swinging like a couple of well-matched boxers in the final moments of a fight. It's incredible that no blood has been spilled. In vying for the right to mate with a female, male bears sometimes get badly injured in a fight like this one. But for some reason, that no one clearly understands, there seems to be a set of rules in place at this time of year wherein one bear seriously hurting another is prohibited.

A few feet away, John Gunter, director of Frontiers North, the Tundra Buggy Adventure tour company that ferried Buchanan and me out here together, is smiling as this scene unfolds. He's seen Buchanan on the pulpit promoting the cause of polar bear conservation many times before and evidently enjoys it. He's also appreciative of the show the bears are putting on because he knows the tourists in another Tundra Buggy coming our way are going to go home happy.

In the long, economically troubled history of Churchill, Polar Bears International (PBI), has provided a much needed boost for the town's fortunes. Thanks largely to PBI, a steady stream of celebrities and Hollywood actors have been coming into Churchill to catch a glimpse of the bears in their

While watching its mother interact with other bears, a cub learns which other bears are safe and which ones to avoid.

© Robert and Carolyn Buchanan

natural habitat. These celebrity visits, which remind the world that Churchill is "The Polar Bear Capital of the World," help keep the tourists coming.

Buchanan came up with the idea of regrouping and forming PBI when it became clear that Polar Bears Alive, the small organization that he, photographer Dan Guravich, Bob Wilson, and others had created in 1992, in an effort to get people to care about bears, was too narrowly focused to gain the broader public support it needed.

Polar Bears Alive began in much the same way, on a Tundra Buggy at Cape Churchill. Outside, two male polar bears sparred in the snow, testing their strength in mock battles. As Buchanan, Guravich, and a band of fellow polar bear enthusiasts sipped snotch—scotch poured over snow—and watched the males do battle, someone came up with the idea of creating a non-profit group to focus on the needs of polar bears.

Buchanan was proud of what Polar Bears Alive had accomplished with Guravich as its de facto leader. But that organization was not as science-friendly back then as PBI is today, or as cognizant of what the Inuit and First Nations think about polar bears. When Guravich died, Buchanan's vision for the future was a much broader one than that which was originally framed back in 1992. Buchanan wanted the world to not only understand the natural history of polar bears but, more importantly, the vital nature of arctic ecosystems. He wanted to inspire individuals to take urgent action to reduce greenhouse gas emissions in order to conserve polar bears and countless other species worldwide. PBI, Buchanan hoped, would be an organization governed by the top polar bear scientists, and one which supported research, education, and stewardship of the planet. By saving the polar bear, Buchanan reasoned back then, you can save so many other species that are not as charismatic or even those species which are not charismatic at all.

In his ongoing efforts to do what he had set out to since PBI was established in 1999, Buchanan did indeed recruit polar bear scientists such as Ian Stirling, Steven Amstrup, Andrew Derocher, and Tom S. Smith to guide his organization on the scientific issues. He has worked with Daryll Hedman and members of the Polar Bear Alert team in Manitoba to wow and educate students, singers, actors and philanthropists, all of whom have been brought in to see the bears. In a similar way to what Brian Davies and the International Fund for Animal Welfare did more than 40 years ago, Buchanan's organization routinely pays for the cost of relocating some bears, as well as the cost of other equipment the Polar Bear Alert team has need of. However, unlike IFAW, the focus of PBI on the global problem of anthropogenic warming of the climate is much more broadly based.

Marshall McLuhan, the man who once proposed that the medium, not necessarily the content that it carries, is most important, would have been proud. Buchanan does not come from the world of biology as the World Wildlife Fund's polar bear experts Geoff York and Peter Ewins do. His background is in sales and marketing. Buchanan spent decades with Seagram's, selling high-priced whiskies and Scotches, some with names that he himself invented. But through the efforts of PBI, not to mention collaborative work with WWF and the Centre for Biological Diversity, Buchanan has helped frame the plight of polar bears of western Hudson Bay in a context that might otherwise have been lost on the media.

As a result, Churchill bears are no longer portrayed as they were in the 1982 *National Geographic* documentary—dangerous predators that once compelled mothers in Churchill to walk down the street with a rifle in one hand and the handle of a baby buggy in the other. Neither are the bears viewed as the kings of the Arctic Dan Guravich and Fred Bruemmer portrayed them as in their books. Nowadays, polar bears are iconic symbols illustrating how humans are warming the Earth's climate to dangerous levels.

It's an astounding achievement, given the media's earlier treatment of both the town of Churchill and polar bears in the days when the Polar Bear Control Program was founded in 1968. Back then, Canadian newspapers such as *The Globe and Mail* had little sympathy for the polar bear situation on the west coast of Hudson Bay.

Part of this attitude had to do with Brian Davies' anti-sealing campaign, which tarnished Canada's reputation abroad. The editorial board of *The Globe and Mail* responded to Davies' plan to airlift polar bears out of Churchill with cynicism that bordered on contempt. One editorialist called it a "phony bear crusade," one that would create "a hostile and unjustified impression overseas of Canadians as people indifferent to animal welfare and conservation." The editorialist also suggested that it was probably best to dispatch these problem bears in more lethal ways:

"The Churchill scavengers are believed to be male rogues driven from their normal bear community, and that they are so addicted to garbage that they will probably come back to Churchill, no matter how far away you bear-lift them, just as fast as their grubby paws will carry them. And ... obviously, since the females will have nothing to do with them, they are of no use to the future generations of polar bears."[1]

The Globe and Mail insisted that, contrary to public perception, there was no need for conservation measures in Churchill because the western Hudson Bay population was "thriving," and, according to some, "getting too big for its own good."

A polar bear circles an equipment cage at the polar bear tower at Cape Churchill.

© Edward Struzik

Polar bear looks in at the author who is inside the equipment cage at the polar bear tower.

© Edward Struzik

"If nice old ladies in Tooting Bec and school kids in Birmingham [England] want to give a few pence in the fond belief that they are saving a few deadbeat bears, it's all the same to Churchill. Just so long as you get them off our back..." the editorial stated glibly.

The Globe and Mail's editorial board was clearly agitated about this issue. In another editorial printed that same month, the paper referred to Churchill's problem bears as "Southern louts," possibly because they are among the southernmost population of polar bears in the world. The writer agreed with demands from some people in Churchill to thin out the population by simply going out and killing them. "Churchill obviously has polar bears the way some other towns have motorcycle gangs, and it has set about curing this malady in the most practical manner."[2]

Unlike other newspapers in Canada, *The Globe and Mail* did at least spend a great deal of money covering Operation Bearlift. Reporter Martin O'Malley was sent up to Churchill for several days to cover the event. Like his editorial board members, O'Malley was somewhat contemptuous of what Davies was doing and how Fleet Street journalists were buying into Davies' message. Three women in Churchill were apparently so upset with O'Malley's coverage that they "harangued" him when he was at the airport waiting for a plane to fly him back to Toronto. A Fleet Street journalist standing by at the time spat in his face for good measure.[3]

Like polar bears, the town of Churchill had a tough time getting respect from the Canadian media during the 1970s and early 1980s. Although nearly 14,000 tourists visited Churchill in 1984,[4] many newspapers, including *The Globe and Mail*, kept suggesting that there was no economic reason for the town to continue. It was as if Churchill was a rundown port town and nothing else.

"Churchill has existed for years by subsidy, as it prepares to digest the further $14-million allocation (for the grain port) by the federal government. Questions are being raised. *How much more? How much longer? Does this make sense?* In the determined picture, it runs counter to the advice of the task force,[5] which counselled that Churchill be returned to the polar bear ... What is to be said of Churchill's survival? In truth, not a great deal of substance."[6]

The editorial followed newspaper reports which suggested that the port of Churchill might have outlived its usefulness. Government critics wanted to know why $14 million was being invested in the facility in 1986 when just the year before, the director of the Canadian Wheat Board was contemplating the possibility of no grain moving through Hudson Bay.[7]

Speculation at the time was that the Conservative government of Prime Minister Brian Mulroney wanted the town of Churchill to die. Citing unnamed government sources, *Globe and Mail* reporter Ross Howard gave his readers the impression that there was nothing worth saving in Churchill. "Churchill is an old Canadian problem, a one industry town supported by years of government subsidy. By Conservative [Party] thinking, it should be allowed to die or kept alive by less surreptitious costly methods."[8]

This kind of publicity drove many people in Churchill crazy. So did reports that suggested the town was constantly in conflict with polar bears. In that respect, some residents were to blame. Shortly after Sonny Voisey was mauled in 1984, an elected Churchill official suggested that residents should be allowed to go out and shoot a few bears. "We don't want to look like barbarians running around shooting, but we're trying to protect our right to freedom of movement," said Councillor John Bilenduke who had been championing the idea of a sports hunt for years, without success.[9]

Buried in the coverage were those people in Churchill who recognized how polar bear tourism had breathed new life into the local economy. "I'm not opposed to some form of control but I am opposed to people being armed and shooting them," said

Jack O'Connor, president of the Churchill Chamber of Commerce. "The bears are a tourist attraction, no doubt… Who wants to visit a town where people are running around with guns?"[10]

"They are the Kings of the North," O'Connor told the same reporter the next day. "They are afraid of nothing, even a locomotive. And they are our lifeblood as far as tourism goes."

No matter how much some residents and businessmen tried, they could not shake off the outside world's belief that they were in constant battle with bears. One 1989 headline in *The Wall Street Journal* suggested that the animals are often out of control: "They Menace Manitobans, Tear up the Town Dump, But Tourists Bear Cash."

In the article that followed, the staff reporter suggested that the arrival of the polar bears each year is a "nerve-wracking" experience for residents. "One night in 1984," he wrote (about the mauling that actually took place in 1983), "an unlucky resident, scavenging in a burned out hotel on Churchill's main street, ran into a polar bear on a similar mission. The bear," he noted incorrectly, "ate the man."[11]

Adding fuel to the fire, an unnamed Churchill businessman was quoted as suggesting that the best thing that could happen to tourism in Churchill was "for someone to be eaten every few years."[12]

The article, however, did give equal space to scientist Ian Stirling and to Doug Webber who was, by then, mayor of Churchill. Both Webber and Stirling pointed out that polar bear tourism had saved the town.[13]

Canadian newspapers were in some ways out of step with the rest of the western world's media. *The New York Times*, for example, had been championing the cause of polar bear conservation since 1965 when it printed an article in its weekly magazine: "Are the Days of the Arctic King Running out?"[14] That piece, and others which followed, presented the polar bear as a powerful, beautiful, and intelligent animal that was on the brink of extinction because of technological innovations that made hunting it so easy. When a *New York Times* reporter came to town in 1992, he noted how Churchill "is doing all it can to keep [conflict with humans] to a minimum, both for safety and economic reasons." The writer described the Polar Bear Alert Program and the steps that conservation officers take to make sure that people are safe and that bears are not destroyed.[15]

During the late 1970s, Fred Bruemmer, Dan Guravich, Manitoba's Robert Taylor, along with a handful of other writers and photographers, paved the way for more sympathetic coverage of Churchill's bears in magazines such as the *Smithsonian, Audubon, National Geographic* and

Canadian Geographic. The willingness of wildlife technicians like Dale Cross, and conservation officers like Ken John, Rob Dean, and others to entertain and talk to reporters and photographers was essential for those reports to get published. So was the research and public awareness work being done by Chuck Jonkel, Ian Stirling, Malcolm Ramsay, Nick Lunn, Andrew Derocher, and others.

The tagging, blood work, tissue sampling, and denning and population surveys logged in the 1960s, 1970s, and early 1980s provided reporters, photographers, and documentary producers with new angles to the story of Churchill's polar bears.

One of the most important research findings was the discovery of PCBs (polychlorinated biphenyls), dioxins and other man-made toxins in the liver and tissues of polar bears. "I think it's of grave concern," Ray Schweinsberg, a Northwest Territories biologist said in May 1985, when Canadian Wildlife Service chemist Ross Norstrum presented the results at a conference in Yellowknife. "The question that has to be asked

A polar bear stops in the middle of a fight to see what the author is up to.

© Edward Struzik

is this: if polar bears are getting this from eating seals, then what are people up here getting from eating seals and what are people down south getting from eating cattle, and other animals and fish?"[16]

The discovery of PCBs in polar bear livers, and the coverage that followed, led to a new genre of polar bear stories arising out of Churchill. From that point on, it wasn't just daily newspapers, travel section writers, and natural history magazines that were interested. Science magazines were also paying attention.

In 1989, *New Scientist*, a highly respected British magazine with a worldwide following in the scientific community, ran a cover story and an eight page spread on the research being done on polar bears in Churchill and other parts of the Arctic. That article elevated the profile of the town, the Polar Bear Alert Program and the scientists who worked in western Hudson Bay to a new level.

"No one knows the precise reasons for such congregations of polar bears in Churchill," writer and scientist Caroline Pond noted, "But the migration of polar bears to Cape Churchill provides scientists, and, increasingly, tourists with the best opportunity to watch their varied and often amusing behaviour in comfort. A former rocket range a few kilometres from Churchill has been converted into the Northern Studies Centre for scientists and students."[17]

No one had seen it coming, nor was it ever intended, but the scientific research and the handling of bears by the Polar Bear Alert team quickly became an important part of a tourist's visit to Churchill. Soon, Robert Buchanan and other members of PBI were bringing in scientists such as Ian Stirling, Steven Amstrup, and Andrew Derocher to speak to tourists on the studies being undertaken. The Polar Bear Alert team, in the meantime, began experimenting with the idea of allowing tourists to watch them as they processed the animals. "This goes over really well with the tourists," Richard Romaniuk noted in his annual report for 2003. "As well, flying bears out of D-20 was another big tourist attraction this year."

This new profile of Churchill's polar bears in the first part of the 20th century was not lost on the man who had negotiated the so-called "polar bear clause" for Manitoba employees in 1989—Gary Doer was elected premier of the province a decade later. Then, beginning in 2004, when Doer brought the Russian Ambassador to Churchill, he, his cabinet ministers and, at one point in time, the Canadian Prime Minister, often came to Churchill to entertain themselves. High profile guests such as the American ambassador, the governor of Arizona, several Canadian Premiers, and powerful businessmen accompanied Doer to Churchill as well.

The situation, however, became a little more complicated when the issue of climate change entered the discussions in a serious way. Since it was first elected in 2006, Prime Minister Stephen Harper's government has been cool about doing anything about climate change. And because organizations like the World Wildlife Fund, Polar Bears International, the Centre for Biological Diversity, and other groups made the polar bear a symbol for the dangers associated with a warming world, the Conservative government has been especially diligent in its efforts to muzzle federal government scientists to ensure they could not talk about polar bears in a climate change context.

Ian Stirling was able to carry on with the media in semi-retirement so long as he identified himself as an adjunct professor at the University of Alberta. But Nick Lunn, who had taken over Stirling's position leading the polar bear project for Environment Canada and the Canadian Wildlife Service has been, like most other scientists in government, severely restricted in what he can say, if he is allowed to say anything. The days when the media could call and speak directly with scientists like Lunn vanished after the Harper Government came to power. All media inquiries about polar bears

If sea ice continues to retreat in western Hudson Bay, this population could be in trouble.

© Edward Struzik

are now vetted by "communications" people whose job it is to blunt discussion about climate change and polar bears.

That's when Polar Bears International stepped in as an important player. The PBI website has become not only an important resource for students, teachers, and the general public, it is also a tool the media can use to connect with polar bear and climate change scientists. Robert Buchanan has also become a cheerleader of sorts, patting Premier Doer and his successor Greg Selinger (2009) on the back for raising the profile of polar bear conservation in a way that neither the government of Canada, the Yukon, the Northwest Territories, Nunavut, or northern Quebec has ever done.

In what may be its biggest challenge in the future, Buchanan and Polar Bears International are trying to convince politicians, the public, and the media that zoos have an important role in polar bear conservation. PBI is also trying to convince key zoos in North America, and eventually the world, to evolve from entertainment venues into places of education and conservation.

PBI has made some strides in this direction with its funding of a study to learn how to solve the problem of stereotypical behaviour in zoo bears. Through Steve Amstrup, PBI's chief scientist, the organization has been trying to demonstrate how zoos can play an important

role in educating the public about threats to the polar bears' existence. PBI is also working to inspire people to do something about reducing greenhouse gas emissions,[18] and by lobbying Congressmen in Washington, PBI is trying to get U.S. officials to loosen regulations which restrict the importation of polar bears to American zoos.

"Canada understands that they have a crisis on their hands," Buchanan told a small group of Congressional staffers in February 2012. With slides of a polar bear family sitting on an ice floe hundreds of kilometres from shore, he noted how Canada had three options:

"One, you can watch 'em die.

Two, you can shoot 'em in the head.

Three, you can move the species and help it survive."[19]

Like it or not, the day may soon come when members of the Polar Bear Alert team are shipping many more problem bears to zoos, albeit under significantly improved situations and more stringent rules.

As anyone in politics knows, it is difficult to sustain the media interest in one subject. But when I was in Churchill talking to Buchanan that same year, and touring around with Shaun Bobier, a member of the Polar Bear Alert team, media interest was as high as it has ever been. In town that fall were the ABC News show *Nightline,* CBC's *Country Canada, National Geographic, 60 Minutes Australia,* RDF Television from England, *Le Figaro* from France and 20 other newspapers, television stations, and documentary crews. It got so busy at times that Bobier had to turn down some interview requests.

As always, the Polar Bear Alert Program remains a work in progress. More often than not, however, no one knows what the next challenge could be or where it might come from. Would X19173—the extremely aggressive polar bear caught and captured three times by Nick Lunn in 2004, 2005, and 2007—show up again in town some day? Would tourists become bored with polar bears? Would climate change result in the collapse of the polar bear's population?

No one, of course, has an answer. But ironically, Myrtle deMeulles, a celebrated Métis artist, who was born in 1941 and spent most of her life in Churchill, saw it all coming in 2000, when the media was reporting on how climate change might be the reason why conservation officers such as Wayde Roberts were handling more problem bears.

"The cities [down south] that cause the problem don't have the problem," she said. "The Arctic does."

© Edward Struzik

© Robert and Carolyn Buchanan

In late fall, polar bears will congregate at places such as Cape Churchill where the sea ice first forms in fall.

CHAPTER FOURTEEN

POLAR BEAR PATROL

On the evening of November 10th, 2011, a Saab 340 twin-engine airplane lands in Churchill. Before the turbo-prop plane comes to a complete stop, the flight attendant advises passengers to be on guard as they make the short walk to the terminal because a polar bear and her cub have been spotted on the tundra by the runway. The passengers—most of them tourists—spontaneously break out in applause.

It is a beautiful night. The sky is clear and the moon is full. There is a skiff of fresh snow on the ground, but no sign of polar bears lurking in the dark. Bob Windsor, district supervisor for Manitoba Conservation, greets me inside and takes me to his truck. He apologizes for Daryll Hedman, the regional wildlife manager who can't greet me as originally planned. "You came at the right time," Windsor says as we head down the road to the Bear House, where reinforcement officers for the Polar Bear Alert Program live at this time of year. "This is as busy as I've seen it during my three years here. If the warm weather holds, it's going to get a heck of a lot busier in the days ahead."

I am here by invitation to see just what it is that the conservation officers do during this season when hungry bears, sensing that the ice on Hudson Bay is about to freeze over, are on the move. Mid-October to late November is normally when things really start hopping. No one, however, has seen things this wild since 2003,

when there were so many bears coming into town that the Polar Bear Alert team nearly ran out of tranquilizing darts. The polar bear jail is full, and some of its furry inmates will have to be flown out to make room for other bears that will inevitably get into trouble before the ice-free season ends.

Windsor, I learn on the ten-minute drive into town, has worked with Manitoba Conservation since he was 16 years old. He spent 12 years working as a seasonal employee before being hired on full-time in 1990. He makes no secret of the fact that the Churchill posting has been the highlight of his career.

"People pay huge dollars to come from all over the world for a glimpse of a polar bear," he says as we pass D-20, the so-called polar bear jail. "But we actually get paid to work up close and personal with these bears. It's amazing really. It's a once in lifetime opportunity that you can't get anywhere but here."

Windsor initially thought that he and his colleagues were not going to have an especially busy time deterring bears from causing trouble this year. The previous year had been a slow one. Only 35 bears were caught and held at D-20.

The early summer weather, however, changed that expectation.

"The third week of June, there were people walking around in shorts in twenty-plus degree temperatures," Windsor said. "For Churchill, that's crazy, hot weather. In the end, the ice broke up quickly and the bears were forced to come on shore weeks earlier than what was considered normal thirty years ago."

The first sign of trouble occurred on the fourth of July when Churchill resident Helen Hart called the Polar Bear Alert hotline, saying she had spotted a bear on the beach at the edge of town. Although not unheard of, this report was pretty early for a bear to be walking around town.

Hart called in shortly after six in the morning. Both Windsor and Jack Batstone were on duty that day, and there was no reason to think that this incident would require anything more than a gentle hazing. But as the two officers drove toward the site, several more calls came in suggesting that this particular bear was homing in on a man walking along the beach.

Wayne MacRae, a railway contractor from Vancouver, was on vacation, taking video of beluga whales migrating up and down the Churchill River, when he spotted a polar bear walking along the edge of town. Seeing that the bear was moving in the opposite direction, MacRae thought he was in the clear. But when the bear stopped, sniffed and started circling back towards him he freaked out, knowing that there was really nowhere to run or hide since the bear was in between him and the safety of the townsite. MacRae's first instinct was to walk as fast as he could to get away from the bear. By the time Windsor and Batstone arrived on the scene, MacRae was running full speed to safety.

When a tour bus pulled up on the beach, Windsor knew they had a situation. Not only was this bear in a bad place to be hazed or handled, it was also unusually skinny and fearless—the kind of animal no officer likes to deal with because it can be unpredictable.

Moments after the officers' truck came to a stop, the bear began to walk towards them, circling a few times as it did so. Intent on driving the bear off, Batstone climbed out of his vehicle and fired off a couple of cracker shells. Undeterred, the bear continued to walk towards him.

Windsor had a bad feeling as he watched this encounter unfold. He drove the truck up to Batstone, who clambered in just as the bear charged.

Instinctively, Windsor put the truck in reverse and backed off as quickly as he could. That, however, did not end the incident. Although Windsor had hoped the bear would take flight towards the water, it headed west into town, towards another man who was apparently unaware of what was going on. However, Windsor set his wheels in motion, putting the truck in between the bear and the man. Once again the bear took another run at the truck, forcing Windsor to back off.

Playing this crazy game of hide and seek in pursuit of a bear appearing and then disappearing between buildings, Windsor assumed the worst when he lost track of the animal. Then he heard a blood-curdling scream. "When I finally found the bear, it was standing in the middle of the road, not far from a man who had been surprised, but unharmed by the close encounter," he tells me.

The bear still refused to back off when Windsor drove up. But this time, Windsor was not able to spin his tires fast enough to get out of harm's way.

"See that big dent in the hood of my truck," Windsor tells me as we pull up to a modest

non-descript bungalow, affectionately referred to as the Bear House. "When I drove up to him that time, he turned on me again, but I wasn't able to back up fast enough. When he caught up with me, he reared up and stomped on the hood of the truck. I have never seen a bear act so aggressively. For the safety of people in town, we had to put this bear down."

When I was last in Churchill at this time of year, in 2006, the temperature was in the minus twenties, the wind was howling and snow was blowing everywhere. The sea ice was already forming and the last bear was set to leave town before the month was over.

Although there is some ice on the banks of the Churchill River this time round, there is still no sign that Hudson Bay was going to freeze any time soon. With possibly two, three, or more weeks to go before polar bear season is over, some of the Polar Bear Alert team members are beginning to think that this might be another nightmare season like the one Conservation officers experienced in 2003.

Bob Windsor and Andrew Szklaruk are the two conservation officers stationed in Churchill year-round. Three resource management assistants back them up. April Lundie is a new addition. The two others, Jack Batstone and Donald Spence, have accumulated fifty seasons between them. At this busy time of year, reinforcements are brought in to help with daily patrols, hazing, capture work, and any relocation of problem bears.

Plans are already underway to fly several inmates of D-20 out to the North River, 40 kilometres outside of town. World Wildlife Fund and Polar Bears International are in Churchill with helpful donors, and are willing to pay the cost of airlifting three of the animals out in exchange for some of their guests being given the opportunity to watch.

Celebrities continue to come to Churchill, thanks largely to the efforts of Robert Buchanan and Polar Bears International, stationed in Churchill year-round. Television personalities like George Stroumboulopoulos (*George Stroumboulopoulos Tonight/The Hour*) and Rick Mercer (*The Rick Mercer Report*) also showed up. The celebrity "hot" factor was ramped up with the likes of Martha Stewart (in 2010), and actor Dan Aykroyd and director Rob Reiner were present at Halloween in 2006. The president of Coca-Cola, I learn, is in town this week to give a big cheque to the World Wildlife Fund's campaign to save the polar bear.

"When I bumped into Dan Aykroyd and Rob Reiner, they were trick-or-treating on Halloween night," Rob Kraychuk tells me as I join him on the first patrol the next morning. This daily drive in and about town is designed to clear the area of bears before children start walking to school and adults go to work. "I'm

not sure what they were up here for, but they were having fun knocking on doors."

A seasonal employee of Manitoba Conservation, Kraychuk is usually fighting fires or checking fishing licences during the busy spring and summer seasons. For rookies, the polar bear gig in Churchill is a relatively new and daunting challenge. But Kraychuk is in his second season with the Polar Bear Alert team. He is becoming increasingly comfortable with the daily operation and hopeful that he will get the call to come back in future years.

Kraychuk is a big, goofy, good-natured Ukrainian farm boy who likes to jog and play hard so that he can eat all he wants, which, I discover at mealtime, is a lot for a man his size. The Bear House may not be luxurious, but its fridge is full, with shelves stocked with pop and every type of junk food.

"These bears keep us hopping around the clock," Kraychuk tells me after a barbecued steak dinner that followed liberal helpings of potato chips, nachos, salted peanuts, and pretzels. "Most times we get to them before they cause too much trouble. But sometimes we don't."

On the drive through town, Kraychuk points to a large metal overhead door on the Health Authority building. "Two years ago there was this big mean bear we called 'Lard Ass' that busted through that door before smashing that other door over there on his way out. He weighed over 1,000 pounds. By the time we caught up with him, he was ripping apart some garbage bins. It was the second time he did it. The boys caught him again in August busting into a house on Button Street. He's been in D-20 ever since."

Moments later Kraychuk tells me that a few weeks earlier a bear broke a window on the door at Jack Batstone's place. "That kind of thing," he says, "is pretty typical. We get a lot of calls about bears trying to break into houses or cabins or bears eating puppies. They like eating puppies."

The Polar Bear Alert Program has come a long way since the "control" days when problem bears such as these usually ended up dead. Since the review of the program in 1984, there has not been a single death in Churchill proper and the number of euthanized bears is down sharply. But the nightmare of 2003 and a mauling outside of town in 2008 were wake-up calls which precipitated more changes.

The 2008 mauling at the Churchill Northern Studies Centre was ominous for multiple reasons. One, because it was rare, and two, because it occurred just as Churchill Mayor Mike Spence and the town's councillors were honouring current and former members of the Polar Bear Alert team at a town ceremony. Pierce Roberts, regional director for Manitoba Conservation attended the occasion, as did Steve Kearney, the former director. Bruce Bremner, assistant deputy minister in charge of Manitoba Conservation was there as well. Everyone was having a good time when Shaun Bobier, the district manager stationed in Churchill, got a call from Mike Goodyear, executive director of the Churchill Northern Studies Centre, informing him one of the Centre's employees had just been mauled.

Bobier consulted with Roberts before heading out to the hospital to see how the victim was doing. Goodyear was there, as he had hoped. So was Diane Howell, assistant executive director of the Centre. They told him everything they knew.

Rene Preteau, the victim, was apparently in good condition. He had received a few minor scratches to his face and deeper cuts to his knee. But he had been shaken so badly by the ordeal that doctors had to give him a sedative to keep his heart rate down.

Best as Goodyear and Howell could tell, Preteau had exited the north side of Centre's

©Lynn Holden

building and checked for bears (as he and everyone else at the Centre are supposed to do when exiting the premises). Preteau was bending down to work on a metal screen when he looked up to see a polar bear four feet away. The next thing he knew, the bear took three or four swipes at him. Preteau whacked the animal on the head with a ratchet without success in getting it to back off. The bear then pinned him up against the wall of the building. Just as Preteau stumbled, there was a cry from one of this female bear's cubs. The mother bear turned just long enough for Preteau to make a successful break for the Centre's door.

Shaun Bobier and Donald Spence made five sweeps around the building that day, and culvert traps were set, but the officers never tracked the animals down.

****

Rene Preteau was back at work after a few weeks with a lasting fear of being attacked again. The incident, however, was another wakeup call, as well as a reminder, that the maulings in 1983, 1984, and 2004 were not anomalies and that nightmare years such as 1976 and 2003 might be repeated.

"It was obvious to a lot of us after that what we went through in 2003 that something had to change," Daryll Hedman tells me when we meet up later that day. "It was clear that most of these bears weren't looking for trouble. They were just hungry and trying to find something to eat. It wasn't their fault. We're seeing the same kind of thing happen this year."

Hedman is on his way to D-20 to airlift a 600-pound animal that has completed its 30 days of detention. We are early in arriving at the site near the airport, but there are already twelve busloads of tourists and several vans lined up to watch the procedure. Several more are on their way. In relatively short order, there are about 500 tourists with cameras in their hands waiting for the airlift process to begin. News in Churchill, I gather, travels fast.

This kind of show has been going on since Conservation officer Laury Brouzes started experimenting with the idea of allowing tourists to see what he and officers do with the polar bears detained in D-20. Tourists, however, don't see a heck of a lot because wildlife officers won't let them beyond a point where they could be in danger.

In this case, the tranquilized bear is carted out on a small tractor-trailer and carefully lowered into a helicopter net. It looks surreal because the animal's eyes are wide open and apparently aware of what is happening.

As sad of a scene it appears to be, every effort is made to make sure that the animal's head is raised so that it won't choke under the force of its own weight when the helicopter lifts off. After making sure that all of the animal's limbs are tucked in, everything is set to roll. "Most bears don't come back," says Hedman just before he climbs into the helicopter to double-check that the release on the tundra goes well. "Since the closing of the dump, there is no good reason for them to return. But if they do, we put them back into D-20 for the rest of the summer. And if they have a record of causing trouble, we consider removing them from the population."

Thanks in large part to records that Ian Stirling, Nick Lunn and their colleagues at the Canadian Wildlife Service have been keeping diligently since the 1970s, Manitoba Conservation officials have, in addition to their own records, a remarkable database of information that they can use to make critical decisions about individual bears. That's why it came as no surprise to anyone when they learned that the bear which caused so much havoc on that particular fourth of July had a previous history. Lunn had caught it three times before, in 2004, 2005, and 2007. Each time, the animal behaved so aggressively, Lunn was left wondering what would happen if this bear encountered a human on land. Now he had his answer.

The big question now is what to do with Lard Ass, the big mean bear that keeps breaking into buildings. Every officer knew something needed to be done to prevent him from striking again and potentially threatening someone's life or someone's job. But no one at this point had either the time or the inclination to make a quick decision about the bear's future.

When the helicopter takes off with Hedman on board, Andrew Szklaruk offers to give me a lift back to town. Szklaruk has been stationed in Churchill for nearly four years, a little longer than most officers remain. Usually, three years is the maximum. Most personnel leave after that. Szklaruk confesses that he would stay longer if it weren't for the fact that doing so might hurt his chances of promotion.

There is not a road or laneway within five miles of town, Szklaruk tells me, where he hasn't chased a bear. One of his most memorable moments, however, did not involve the least bit of danger.

"Donald Spence and I were hazing a bear away from the Seaport Hotel one day with the

© Lynn Holden

strategy of keeping the bear between our two trucks as they travelled down the main street. We were trying to herd the animal into the river at the other end of town… It was really funny because there were people walking home from the bar, and we kept honking the horn to keep the bear between us as it ran along. We didn't allow it to run in front or behind us. It must have looked like we were directing a cow out of town."

"It's hard to believe, but sometimes, I find myself thinking that what I do here is routine," Szklaruk notes as he gets a call to

© Lynn Holden

check on a young bear hanging around L5—the building in which Churchill's garbage is stored until a way can be found to dispose of it. "And then something happens that makes me think that it is a miracle that no one has been killed by a polar bear in Churchill since 1983."

The prospect that problem animals like Lard Ass could become the next killer bear in Churchill came into sharp focus just weeks after that "Fourth of July" bear was finally caught and euthanized. Once again, both Windsor and Batstone were on duty on July 29th when Churchill resident Tommy Saunders called the Polar Bear Alert hotline to let them know that there was a bear between the Churchill Motel and the Northern Images Gift Shop. In separate trucks, Batstone and Windsor headed towards the scene, communicating by radio in an effort to try and find the animal.

Batstone had done this sort of thing more than anyone else on the team, except perhaps for Don Spence, his constant sidekick. A jack-of-all-trades, Batstone has plied his skills over the years, ferrying adventure paddlers from the mouth of the Seal River to Churchill, marshalling dog races, catching beluga whales for scientists, and responding to polar bear problems. Batstone thought he had seen pretty much everything he might see working with polar bears until he rounded a corner that day in late July and found Churchill resident Gloria McDonald backed up against a truck screaming at the top of her lungs as a bear headed towards her and her daughter. The animal was no more than a metre away from McDonald when Batstone leaned into his horn, causing the bear to take flight.

Following standard procedure, Batstone

did his best to lead the bear out of the area by herding it with his vehicle. Most times, this does the trick. But on this occasion, the bear suddenly veered into the path of Batstone's moving truck. Unable to stop in time to avoid it, Batstone ran over the animal.

The animal, however, was not killed. For a good fifteen seconds, the bear lay under the chassis struggling to find a way out from underneath. When it finally emerged, Batstone could see that it was hurt and limping, but not badly enough to prevent it from running away.

This is a very rare, but real nightmare for a member of the Polar Bear Alert team. There is no telling what a frightened animal will do in town when it suddenly runs into someone, or when it gets cornered in between buildings. An injured, frightened animal represents an even greater danger, especially with so many people on Churchill's streets during the middle of the day.

Pierce Roberts, who was now the regional director in charge of the Polar Bear Alert Program, happened to be in the Seaport Hotel at the time, having breakfast with Mayor Mike Spence, Roy Bukowsky and Bruce Bremner, the assistant deputy minister of Conservation for the Manitoba government. None of them, or any of the tourists having breakfast that morning, had any idea what had just happened when they saw the injured bear running past the hotel's window.

Bob Windsor was also unaware when he arrived on the scene, just as the bear turned and began to take a run at Batstone. What Windsor did see was Batstone firing off a cracker shell, which struck the animal in the chest. When the bear turned towards Windsor, blood was coming out of its nose. It was obvious that something was very seriously wrong, but Windsor could not figure it out, not knowing the earlier sequence of events. "I think it needs a bullet," Batstone shouted from the other side. "Something is wrong with it." Seeing how agitatedly the animal was pacing back and forth, Windsor responded, "I agree."

Watching this unfold, with tourists also standing by, Bremner had assumed that the gun aimed at the animal was loaded with a tranquilizer. Having been in this situation before, Roberts, who was a conservation officer between 1979 and 2001, could infer from his experiences in Churchill what the real situation was. He and Bukowsky both knew then and there that Batstone was about to put a bullet into the animal's head.

Roberts tells me this story later that night as he and I have a beer with Spence in the Seaport Hotel. "I knew that this was going to be a nightmare and potential public relations disaster," he says.

Bremner wanted a head delivered on a platter to account for what had happened. It

took a while, but after getting to the bottom of the story, Roberts managed to convince Bremner that Batstone really had no choice but to put the bear down, then and there, before it turned on someone and mauled them.

"The main reason the bear was put down was due to its injuries," Roberts explains to me. "It had reached a point where its strength was failing and Jack couldn't get it to move. At the time, Jack was the only one who knew that it was badly injured. Had the bear been healthy and capable of moving, the officers would have continued to haze it until they got it out of town, then they would have immobilized the animal if that were possible. We don't immobilize in town because it can take up to 15 minutes for the drug to take effect in an agitated bear, and a lot can go wrong in that time. We have learned this from past experiences which did not work out well. A necropsy of the bear later that day revealed severe internal injuries and bleeding from being run over."

****

In the early morning hours of the next day, the Polar Bear Alert team fields three calls to deal with a bear trying to break into two houses. All three times I fail to get up and dress in time to join Kraychuk as he runs out the door. Frustrated, I vow to go to bed with my clothes on the fourth time around. There is, however, not a fourth time that morning.

Following a breakfast that includes left-over nachos, peanut buttered toast, and several cups of very weak coffee, Roberts and I visit one of the homeowners, Jerry Cowley, who has had his house broken into earlier that morning. Jerry is still shaking. He tells us he was fast asleep when the animal tried to smash through the front door.

"I thought it was my son coming home from the bar and trying to get in because he lost his keys," Jerry says, as he leads us to the door where the bear made its entrance. "But the noise was so loud, I grabbed a golf club just in case it might not be my son. That's when I saw the big head of the bear looking right at me through the screen door."

I ask Cowley what he did then, and he does not miss a beat: "I told it to f--- off," he replies, wide-eyed and grinning. Jerry pauses for a moment with a look of deep concern on his face. Then his smile returns as he says "That's the first time anyone has actually f----- off when I told them to."

The damage done to Cowley's house is minimal. But the cost of dealing with polar bears coming to town has been rising steadily since the mid-1990s when a trend towards an earlier melt and later freeze-up resulted in a very noticeable rise in problem animals. Pierce Roberts tells me that not many years ago, it was normal to borrow funds from the forest fire fighting budgets to make ends meet in Churchill. "The fact was we had a dedicated budget for dealing with problem beavers but not for polar bears," he notes. "Something was not right with that picture."

Patrolling for bears in daylight was one thing, I learn the next night after I'd gone to bed with my clothes on. Chasing a problem bear in the dark, however, is another challenge altogether. It is 2 a.m. when the first call comes in. I am in a sleepy daze, but just quick enough to get into the truck before Kraychuk takes off. Neither one of us notices the fresh tracks of the animal that had passed through the back of the Bear House laneway just minutes, or possibly seconds, before we exited.

It is much colder outside than during the day, and snowing hard. I can only thank God there is no one on the street because Kraychuk is fish-tailing wildly, swerving on the icy road, trying to avoid slamming into telephone posts, parked cars and buildings. Even with the windshield wipers running full speed, it is hard to see where we are going, let alone try and figure out where the bear might be.

Attempting to find a white bear in such a snowstorm, I think, is going to be futile. But then we receive a radio call from Brian Barton, the newly appointed chief conservation officer responsible for the Churchill District officers and programs. He is in another truck with Andrew Szklaruk, and informs us that the animal is running past Gypsy's restaurant towards the road we are driving along.

Before I even register what this means, and what we do next, a big bear runs across the street directly in front of us. Then, like a ghost, it disappears in the snowy night. Kraychuk does a U-turn, and the chase is on for a good five minutes before we lose track of the animal in the frozen marsh on the edge of town.

We spend an hour searching, but cannot find the bear. Maybe, I think, this is X17286, the bear that eluded Shaun Bobier and Syd McGregor five times in one night by lying low behind a snowdrift. Perhaps this animal is somewhere out there waiting for us to depart so that it could return to town again?

© Lynn Holden

****

Unlikely as it seems, after more than forty years of handling polar bears in situations like this and others, occasionally an incident occurs which no one might have foreseen. In recent years, however, people have been streaming to the old dumpsite outside of town in fall to see dozens of bears acting very strangely.

I'm intrigued when Daryll Hedman and I drive out to look. We count twelve bears either fast asleep, looking very drowsy or acting like drunks coming out of a bar late at night. Hedman suspects the animals are getting drunk on fermented grain seeds disposed at the dump by the port authority.

"This has become a huge attraction," Hedman says as a tourist bus and several vans filled with people pull up at the site. "No sooner we solve one problem, by closing the dump, another one like this crops up. Whatever you want to say about this job, you can never say it's boring."

As we head back to town, Hedman suggests I take his place on a helicopter flight with biologist Steve Amstrup, who wants to find the carcass of a polar bear seen lying in shallow water along the tidal flats near Gordon Point, just outside of Churchill. "There is no indication how the animal died," says Hedman, "but given the rising number of reports of polar bear

cannibalism, Steve wants to determine if this, or perhaps disease or starvation might have been a factor."

Amstrup is, along with Ian Stirling, one of the giants in the world of polar bear science. He has been conducting research on polar bears in Alaska for 30 years. He made his mark in a big way in 2007, as lead scientist of a landmark study that suggested that two-thirds of the world's polar bears could disappear if sea ice continues to recede as quickly as climatologists have been predicting.

Amstrup is gracious when we meet and he expresses no objections to me coming along for the helicopter ride, as long as I am willing to be on the lookout for the dead bear.

Amstrup had just retired from the U.S. Geological Survey and is now chief polar bear scientist for Polar Bears International. This job, he says, gives him the freedom to do and say what is on his mind. Tall, lanky, and fit as you'd expect from someone who bikes to work year round in Alaska, Amstrup is pretty much everything I had anticipated after communicating with him electronically for years.

It is a beautiful late afternoon. Judging by the height of the sun over the horizon, we have about 90 minutes of daylight before darkness descends. Before we reach the coast, however,

Amstrup instructs our pilot to do a couple of turns over the grain dumping site a few kilometres out of town. Down below, we count a total of 18 bears, 12 vehicles, and a school bus. Most of the bears are lying on the snow, seemingly oblivious to all the cars and trucks around them.

Along the coast, *Ithaca*, a freighter once owned by Italian dictator Benito Mussolini, sits upright in the tidal flats. It ran aground in a windstorm in 1961, and has been slowly rusting away ever since.

With the tide coming in, Amstrup gives up hope that we will find our quarry. "I was told that one of the conservation officers who found it dragged it ashore," Amstrup says. "But I suspect he didn't drag it in far enough. The tide has probably washed it away. Too bad. It would have been nice to know how it died."

The next day, I am in the Conservation office with Pierce Roberts and Bob Windsor. Windsor looks a little uncomfortable talking to Roberts about Lard Ass—officially known as Bear 19173—with me in the room. But after a short pause, he decides to say what it is that is on his mind.

This 1,000 pound bear, he tells Roberts, is still in D-20 and he is there to stay until the ice forms on Hudson Bay so he won't be tempted to come back to town. First captured by Lunn in March 1999 as a cub of the year, this animal, he says, has become habituated to the town dump and then to L5, the waste management station set up in 2005. Between October 26, 1999, and August 3, 2011, he was caught and released no less than eight times. He had broken into garbage sheds three times, even tearing through the wall of a residential home before being hazed away.

"So what's the plan now that the animal is breaking into houses?" Windsor asks. Should the Patrol risk a 1,000 pound bear coming back the next year with the potential for doing more damage or even worse?

Given the bear's history, I felt I knew the answer. Windsor and Batstone had put down a similar-sized animal earlier in the year after it broke into and thoroughly trashed the Boy Scout Camp at Camp Nanuk. Was there any reason to think that this animal would fare any better?

© Lynn Holden

Manitoba biologist Vicki Trim explores a recently vacated polar bear den.

CHAPTER FIFTEEN

DENNING

In late March of 2011, we are standing on the edge of a frozen lake, eighty kilometres inland from the west coast of Hudson Bay. It is -33° C without taking the wind chill into account. The skies are clear, and the bright sun hovers over the horizon, lighting up the spindly forest around us with that alpenglow that makes everything look surreal—which it is. Twenty metres away is the polar bear den we have been looking for, nestled into the side of a south-facing hill.

Helicopter pilot Justin Seniuk keeps the engine running as Manitoba biologists Daryll Hedman, Vicki Trim and I crunch through the waist-deep snow, crossing days-old tracks of playful cubs zig-zagging in all directions around us.

Hedman, who has worked with polar bears since 1986, makes light of what we are about to do. He is fairly certain that the female and her cubs have left the denning area. Their tracks around the site suggest that they are now on the long march to Hudson Bay.

Hedman is not taking any chances, however. He has his gun loaded as we slowly approach. Then he lets out a shout, loud enough to startle both Trim and me as we peer over his shoulder into the den, searching, as he is, for movement within. There is none that we can see.

Still, I can't help recalling the story scientist Ian Stirling told me several years before, when

he was doing exactly what we are doing now. In Stirling's case, he did not notice the polar bear standing in a second chamber of its den until he was inside, adjusting his vision to the dim light. He backed out of the den as quickly as possible and managed somehow to tranquilize the animal with a dart gun when it emerged from the den seconds later.

"Unreal," says Hedman as he does his best to squeeze into the den a few minutes later. "Imagine spending a winter in a space like this where you can barely move and not have any food to eat or water to drink."

British explorer Samuel Hearne first described the denning behaviour of polar bears in this part of the world back in 1795, and today nothing much has changed. "The females that are pregnant seek shelter at the skirts of the woods," Hearne wrote, "and dig themselves dens in the deepest drifts of snow they can find, there they remain in a state of inactivity, and without food, from the latter end of December or January, till the latter end of March: at which time they leave their dens and bend their course toward the sea with their cubs."[1]

As climate change rapidly warms the Arctic, this centuries-old tradition may be in peril. Forest fires, once rare in this part of the world because it was often too wet and cold for wood to be ignited by lightning or humans, have migrated north as rising temperatures dry things up. A number of fires in northern Manitoba have already destroyed dozens of dens.

This is not good news for bears. Building new dens, according to research conducted by scientist Evan Richardson, while still a graduate student at the University of Alberta, could further tax the polar bear's already strained energy supplies.[2]

Most polar bears den on land, although some animals in Alaska den in huge sea ice snowdrifts. Not all dens are created in the same manner. Most are built into snow banks. Others, like the one we are visiting, are built into a peat bank.

Dens tend to have a single chamber big enough to allow a female to nurse one or two, and in very rare cases, three cubs. Some, however, have as many as three or four chambers to accommodate more adventurous cubs, or a two-year-old cub that has not yet been chased away from home by its mother.

A common denominator for construction of dens is snow. "Like Goldilocks' bed, snow has to be just right, not too soft and not too hard," University of Alberta scientist Andrew Derocher once told me.

Fresh snow, he explained, lacks structure and strength. Year-old snow may be too compact to allow for a sufficient amount of oxygen to get in."

Once I see that a bear is not there sitting inside the den waiting to pounce, I crawl in to have a look. I am struck by how warm, snug, and remarkably clean it is.

During his pioneering study on polar bear denning habits in the 1960s, Dick Harington, the first scientist to study polar bears in Canada, dropped a thermometer into two active dens and found that temperatures inside were 7.8° C and 21° C warmer than outside.[3]

Decades later, Ian Stirling studied another series of dens which had been excavated into peat banks south of Churchill. Stirling and his colleagues installed ten thermometers in dens that they expected would be re-occupied. In one case, the inside den temperature actually rose during a November snowstorm, probably because snow covered its entranceway. Although temperatures outside the den remained in the -20s and -30s in the following weeks, the temperature inside never fell below freezing point.

What really surprised Stirling, however, were the temperatures recorded in unoccupied dens. Even though there were no bears inside to heat things up, temperatures in these dens never descended below the -5° C mark. That suggested that Churchill's peat dens were much more efficient in conserving the polar bears' energy than the snow dens polar bears used in other Arctic regions.

Dens tend to be very clean because a polar bear female has the ability to go several months without defecating or urinating. Females will also move their dens in winter when the snow piles up too high to allow enough oxygen intake. The bears would suffocate otherwise.

When I met Hedman for the first time at the Bear House the previous November, he struck me as a little like Fred Flintstone—a likable,

The long walk to Hudson Bay can be hard on cubs. Not only they do they have to contend with deep snow, they are also vulnerable to wolves.

© Edward Struzik

blustery family guy with one foot in the Stone Age and the other in the future. Even then, it appeared to me that Trim, the regional caribou biologist, is the one that often keeps him grounded in the future.

"Daryll suffers from AAD," she tells me shortly after Hedman gives her a lecture, reminding her how lucky she is to be working for him.

"What's AAD stand for?" I ask.

"All About Daryll."

It was a joke, of course, but one that reflected the good-natured teasing that goes on constantly between most everyone involved in the Polar Bear Alert Team program. No one, not even Seniuk, the helicopter pilot, or a scribe like me, can escape the barbs that often come flying from unexpected directions.

Hedman, I suspect, likes to play the role of a Neanderthal, but the more I get to know him the more evident it is that his heart is in the science and the need to understand bears. He willingly admits that if he does not know the answer to a question, he calls Stirling, Steve Amstrup, or Andrew Derocher to get the answer.

Although there is still much to know about the denning habits of polar bears on the west coast of Hudson Bay, much has already been learned. We now know, for example, that 90 percent of the pregnant females in that location den in a relatively small area, 40 to 80 kilometres south of town, an overlap between Wapusk National Park and the Churchill Wildlife Management Area. A good year translates into 191 polar bear dens.[4]

We also know that, unlike most regions where den sites range over a large topography, Churchill's female polar bears den in clusters just as their counterparts do on Wrangel Island in Russia and in Kong Karls Land in Svalbard. There, dens are so concentrated they might be described as polar bear condominiums.

That's why Richardson's study, which was done under the supervision of Stirling, with collaboration from Bob Kochtubadja of Environment Canada, has caught the attention of wildlife managers like Hedman. Should a forest fire sweep down along the Owl River where Richardson conducted his study, some two dozen of the dens known to be in the area could easily be destroyed.

The problem in making a prediction like this is that historical forest fire data for northern Manitoba is scant. But, should climate models be correct, one could expect to see more forest fires in the polar bear denning region of western Hudson Bay, according to fire and vegetation specialist Mike Flannigan. All it would take, Flannigan says, is fuel, of which there is plenty, an ignition source, which in this case is most likely to come from lightning, and from warming temperatures, pretty much a given for most parts of northern Canada.

Why Churchill's polar bears choose sites so far inland when bears in Svalbard hunker down in clusters as close as ten metres from the edge of the seashore remains a mystery.

It is possible that Churchill's female bears are leery of hungry males tracking them down.

Sea ice patterns and snow conditions may be another factor. Human hunting may have also played into the bears' decision-making. Until 1957 (when the Hudson's Bay post at York Factory closed), First Nations peoples living on the coast harvested polar bears for food, fur and trade.

"I'm sure predator avoidance is another reason why these females go so far inland," Hedman tells me as the three of us walk back to the helicopter. "These bears are going as far away

Daryll Hedman cautiously approaches a den site to make sure there are no animals inside.

A female and her cub heading towards Hudson Bay in springtime.

from the coast as possible to avoid wolves, which we know prey on young bears. That's why Vicki and I are hoping to get a study underway to see if that might be the case. We really don't know much about the relationship between wolves and polar bears in this part of the world."

As large as polar bears can be, they still pay a price for denning so far inland. When the pregnant females come off the ice in late June or early July, most have so much fat stored up in their bodies that it sometimes looks as if they can hardly walk. By the time they settle into their dens, however, most of them haven't eaten for four months and it will be another four months before they get their first seal. Some of these bears are little more than a bag of bones by the time that happens.

Any further strain on the energy reserves of these female bears can result in the fact that many of them do not reproduce, as happened in the early 1990s when 28 percent of pregnant females failed to give birth because they simply did not have enough energy reserves to do so. Scientist Péter Molnár, working with Derocher's team, suggests that the percentage of polar bear females failing to reproduce in the future could rise 40 to 73 percent, should the spring ice break-up occur one month earlier than during the 1990s, and 55 to 100 percent should break-up occur two months earlier.[5]

The good news is that most dens in this part of the world are passed on from one polar bear generation to another, so all that most pregnant females need to do is clean up whatever debris that may have fallen from one year to the next.

How a young female bear instinctively knows where the home den is, after being out and about for four or five years is one of the enduring mysteries of polar bear science. These females are just roly-poly cubs when they emerge, and at least four years will pass before they are ready to reproduce. Yet, like salmon that return to the same spawning stream year after year, these female bears know instinctively where to go to find the place they were born.

Peter Scott and Ian Stirling conducted a study of tree rings, representing trees damaged by female polar bears digging their dens, and found evidence to suggest that this hand-me-down practice has been going on for more than a hundred years in some cases, and probably longer.[6]

Given the distances that these pregnant polar bears decide to travel, one would expect that their route would take the path of least resistance, along a relatively straight line. However, as we follow the tracks of another family group

Den site hidden in the trees along a frozen lake south of Churchill.

© Edward Struzik

along the Nelson River later that day, it is clear that this is not so. The bears made a full circle at one point before heading back in the direction they were supposed to be going.

It seems absurd that these animals would plough through shoulder-deep snow in an open meadow rather than follow the solid path of a frozen creek heading north, but that is what we observed here and in other cases. At the rate that this family group is progressing, Hedman figures it would take them three days or more to get to the coast.

The long walk is not the only challenge that these polar bear family groups face in late winter, as we see firsthand when we pick up a set of wolf tracks in pursuit of another family group. There is no shortage of wolves in northern Manitoba, and based on the experiences that Hedman and Trim have had had over the years, it is evident wolves are not shy about trying to take down a polar bear cub or even a young adult.

While one wolf would not have a hope of taking down a female bear protecting her cubs, a pack of five or more wolves stands a much better chance. Polar bear cubs, Hedman tells me, just don't have the energy to walk or run for an unlimited period of time. All wolves need to do is distract the mother bear long enough for one or more of them to detach one of the defenseless

The polar bears of western and southern Hudson Bay are the only population in the world that spends part of the year within the treeline.

© Edward Struzik

Fresh polar bear tracks around a den site 60 kilometres inland from the coast of Hudson Bay.

cubs from the group. "We don't know how often this happens, but I've seen tracks which suggest that this occurrence may not be all that uncommon," he noted. "It's something that we are going to be watching for in future surveys."

Conducting surveys such as these in such remote parts of the world, where wind, snow and ice fog is common, is a challenge. Too far away to fly back to a human settlement at the end of a day, we are compelled to take refuge in a one-room cabin at the mouth of the Hayes River along the coast of Hudson Bay. What little heat we get comes from a wood stove that takes its time warming things up. None of us dares to use the outhouse at night for fear of running into one of the many bears we know are heading in this direction. Seniuk, the pilot, however, has no choice when the generator that he uses to keep the engine and battery of the helicopter warm keeps cutting out.

Exasperated by the time the sun finally comes up, Seniuk tells Hedman that he is willing to absorb the cost of flying back that night to Gillam, Manitoba, where he can plug-in at the airport, and get a good night's sleep.

The costly decision, we learn the next day, may well have saved his life. Returning to that

A polar bear can fall asleep almost anywhere. In this October image photographed near Gordon Point, the bear is cooling off by a small pond with his back to the wind.

© Lorraine Brandson, O. M.

remote cabin to take on the fuel stored there in 45-gallon drums, we see fresh tracks of a polar bear that had evidently passed through the night before. Had we still been there, Seniuk may have well have bumped into the animal in the dark on his way to starting up that finicky generator.

****

Back at home in Edmonton, I sort through the photos that I have taken on my trip north. One picture that seems to be nothing more than a stand of trees close to the den I crawled into catches my eye for no apparent reason. There are no animals present in this picture, and nothing that I can see that makes it worth saving. I figure I must have taken the photo by accident. But just as I am about to delete it, I home in on some tracks I see in the snow. I follow them with my eyes, and discover that they lead to the rump of a polar bear, well-disguised in the trees. "Can't be," I think. There was, however, no doubt about it. There had been a polar bear hiding in the trees just as we were crawling into that den.

Polar bear stands outside a cage in which the author is sitting.

CONCLUSION

In the 30 years since I saw my first polar bear in the wild near Churchill, there was an incident that has puzzled me for a very long time. It happened in the fall of 1986. Northwest Territories biologist Peter Clarkson and I were at the polar bear tower at Cape Churchill, picking up where Gord Stenhouse and Marc Cattet had left off with the detection and deterrent experiments.

It was a crisp, clear, and bitterly cold night when we were both wakened by a blinding flash of light that seemed to have come from the southwest. Neither one of us was dreaming. As much as we tried though, we could not figure out what it was that could have caused it. It was too cold and clear to be lightning. The only thing we could think of was that there was an explosion in town, even though the town seemed to be too far away for us to see such a thing happen.

The following morning Clarkson called the Manitoba Conservation office by radio-phone to determine what might have happened in Churchill the night before to account for what we saw. Whoever it was on the other end didn't know what Clarkson was talking about. Nothing unusual, he said, had happened in Churchill.

Since then, I have tired of people looking at me as if I was a believer in aliens whenever I describe what occurred that night. At some point long ago, I filed the story away.

It all came back though, when I returned to western Hudson Bay in the summer of 2012, to join Daryll Hedman, Vicki Trim, and helicopter pilot Justin Seniuk once again; this time to do a survey of polar bears that had just come off the melting ice.

Before heading out, we dropped in at the Manitoba Conservation office where Dwayne James, a National Department of Defence official, was talking to town officials and tourist operators about the military's latest efforts to find unexploded bombs, rockets, grenades, projectiles and mortars that had been dispatched in the area during the 1950s and 1960s.

It was not a large group. Don and Marilyn Walkoski from Great White Bear Tours were there. So was Paul Ratson of Nature 1st Tours, and Wally Daudrich of Lazy Bear Lodge. Unexploded bombs, they and others at the meeting were told, were still washing up on the coast. Thirty-six of them had been found in 2010, eight kilometres east of Churchill towards the polar bear tower at the Cape. Another 29 were found in 2011. Ten of the 29 were still capable of creating a deadly explosion. In the latest sweep, nearly 800 kilograms of munitions scrap was screened and transferred for disposal in Dundurn, Saskatchewan.[1]

When asked, James could not say how many bombs had been dispatched in the 1950s and 1960s because Defence Department records were either scant or non-existent. But he estimated it to be in the thousands. He figured that as many as five percent didn't explode. These sweeps, he told us, had been going on since 2005 when the Department of National Defence's UXO Legacy Program got started. Residents and tour operators, he mentioned matter-of-factly, could expect them to continue washing up for some time.

After listening to this presentation, I felt a little sheepish asking James if perhaps that brilliant flash of light that Clarkson and I had seen at Cape Churchill in 1986 may have come from one of these unexploded ordinances. "It's very possible," he said without hesitating. "These ordinances have extremely sensitive fuses. If a polar bear or a wolf had come along, it could

have easily gone off if the animal had stepped on it, or batted it with its paw."

Sitting there, I couldn't help thinking about that "top secret" plan that was conjured up in 1949 when Canada's Defense Research Board and Great Britain's Atomic Weapons Establishment had proposed detonating twelve Hiroshima-sized atomic bombs along the west coast of Hudson Bay. Had the plan been approved, the bombs would have laid waste to a huge stretch of tundra in northern Canada and likely killed hundreds of polar bears in the region.

It never happened, of course. Yet, here we were in the 21st century, contemplating the possibility that polar bears might still be blown up by bombs, as a few had likely been in the 1960s when Fort Churchill was home to small arms infantry training.

That wasn't the only unusual thing we learned that morning. Following the meeting, Paul Ratson mentioned that a pod of orcas had killed several beluga whales near Seal River Heritage Lodge, which is owned by Mike Reimer, the man who shot the polar bear in 1983. Someone else noted that a polar bear had killed a grizzly bear on the coast between Churchill and the Nelson River just the previous day.

Back in the 1960s, both of these stories would have been dismissed as very strange talk.

There was no credible evidence of killer whales in western Hudson Bay before the 1940s, and sightings over the next half-century were sporadic and sketchy at best.[2] There was a reason for this. Unlike belugas and narwhals, which have developed an intimate relationship with sea ice, orcas avoid it. Ice, which chokes entry points into Hudson Bay for a good part of the year, is a barrier that they will not dare swim under for any appreciable distance.

As those icy barriers began melting away in the last twenty-five years, Inuit coastal hunters in the Arctic and tour operators in Churchill began reporting an increasing presence of killer whales. Churchill resident Morris Spence and several Port of Churchill workers swore they saw a pod of killer whales in the Churchill River in September of 2005. Still, some scientists were a little sceptical. The doubters, however, quickly turned into believers when tour operator Mike Macri and longtime Churchill resident Bill Ayotte spotted seven orcas on the night of August 22, 2007. "They were moving straight at the boat for a minute but stopped about 75 yards away as though having a meeting about what they should do with us," Macri recalled a short time later.[3]

Owner of Sea North Tours and a first rate photographer, Macri managed to get a photo of three of the killer whales that night. It was the second picture taken of orcas in western Hudson Bay that summer and only the third photograph on record in the Arctic at the time.[4]

In the years that followed, credible reports of killer whales in the Arctic continued to escalate. Inuit hunters, scientists, and tour operators were seeing them attempting to drown bowheads, tossing belugas up into the air, pulverizing narwhals into a flaccid mass of fat, or just happily swimming by. With 76 different orcas sightings recorded by 2009, Fisheries and Oceans scientist Steve Ferguson and the University of Manitoba's Jeff Higdon began thinking of the possibility that the killer whale could someday become the top predator in western Hudson Bay, if receding ice conditions decimate polar bear numbers in the future.

Like Ferguson, Daryll Hedman initially did not put much faith in similar reports of grizzly bears moving into the kingdom of the great white wanderer. Although the local Cree have a name for the grizzly, no one in any of the aboriginal communities had seen one in memory. The last reported sighting in Manitoba was an unconfirmed one far to the southwest in the Duck Mountains in 1923.[5]

But those doubts began to soften in 1990 when Jack Batstone and another local trapper reported seeing a grizzly on the tundra southeast of Churchill. Neither one was mistaken. Canadian Wildlife Service scientist Andy

Didiuk confirmed the sighting on July 27th, when he spotted what was likely the same animal in the area.[6]

In the ensuing years, more sightings, including one in which a grizzly bear woke up some Parks Canada campers, followed.[7] Between 1996 and 2008, there had been nine separate sightings in Wapusk National Park near Churchill.[8] Hedman was one of four people who saw a bear that last year.

Hearing of the grizzly report that morning in Churchill, Hedman was intrigued. Was this another grizzly? And if so, had a polar bear really killed it?

Heading out in the helicopter later that afternoon, we got an answer, or at least we thought we did when we found two polar bears eating what looked like a grizzly. There was no way of telling for sure from the Plexiglas window of a helicopter hovering a hundred metres up in the air. So Justin Seniuk used his flying skills to usher away the polar bears so that we could land and have a closer look.

Both polar bears eyed us from a stand of willows at a not-so-far distance, while Seniuk peeled the skin of the dead animal back over its head so that we could better see what was left of it. It had webbed feet, short claws and an elongated skull, all typical of a polar bear. But its fur was brown and the snout didn't quite have the Roman nose that you see on the head of the great white wanderer.

"Jesus Christ, I don't know what to make of this," said Hedman as he ran his fingers through the brown fur of the animal. "Right off the top, I'd say that this has to be a polar bear. But if this is a grizzly or a grolar, and it could well be, then we may be looking at a new chapter in the story of polar bears in this part of the world."[9]

The possibility that grizzly bears and killer whales will someday become the top predators in western Hudson Bay is not out of the question. Between 1987 and 2004, there was a 22 percent decline in the population of polar bears in the region. While the latest survey suggests the total numbers appear to be holding steady, or marginally rising, numbers found twenty and thirty years ago have not been restored. What's more, the latest survey suggests that there are now fewer family groups emerging from those den sites and fewer bears living beyond their first year of life.

One might have expected a population decline such as this one to result in a similar reduction in the number of polar bears coming into Churchill. But bear occurrences have been rising dramatically. Between 1992 and 2002, officers responded to a total of 1,495 calls. In the decade that followed, that number had nearly doubled, at 2,807.[10]

Although the Polar Bear Alert team has done a good job of reducing the number of bears its officers have to handle or kill—finally closing the dump in 2005 helped—doing so has been a strain on resources. In 2011, manpower costs were four times what they were in 2000, while operating costs had doubled in the same period.[11]

Ian Stirling and Martin Obbard, a bear biologist who works on the Ontario side of the Manitoba border, doesn't think it's going to get any better. The animals that they and other scientists are seeing now are younger and thinner than the typical bear seen 20 or 30 years ago. Typically, it's these hungry sub-adults that cause trouble.

Scientist Andrew Derocher had been giving some thought to future scenarios in western Hudson Bay and other regions of the Arctic since 2008, when Steve Amstrup, Ian Stirling, and several other scientists predicted that two-thirds of the world's bears could disappear by 2050 if sea ice continues to retreat.[12] Initially, colleagues in the polar bear community were sympathetic, but not enthusiastic about his suggestion that they start considering how polar bears might be better managed in the future when they are spending even more time fasting on land.[13]

This "wait-and-see" attitude began to change when Péter Molnár, Derocher's graduate student, and now a post-doctoral fellow at Princeton University, developed a mathematical model for the mating ecology of polar bears. That model, based, in part, on how many females in a population will be able to find a mate and get impregnated, suggests that the collapse of some populations, such as the ones in western and southern Hudson Bay, may occur much more suddenly and catastrophically than previously thought.[14]

Molnár's model was the wake-up call that forced other scientists into thinking about how to manage a crisis in the future. At the International Association for Bear Research and Management conference in Ottawa in 2011, nine scientists got together one night to discuss the possibilities.

They concluded that the day may soon come when the polar bears of western Hudson Bay, and bears from some of the other populations in Canada, Alaska, Greenland, Norway, and Russia, will have to be fed by humans in order to keep them alive during an extended ice-free season—or to prevent them from roaming into small northern communities like Churchill where they would pose a danger to people and property.[15]

In worst-case scenarios, the scientists envisioned the possibility of polar bears from southern areas being relocated to more northerly climes with sufficient sea ice cover. They even considered the possibility of euthanizing animals if relocation and rehabilitation were out of the question. One way or another, they figured, zoos (which are currently having a tough time acquiring polar bears because of stiff regulations), are going be offered as many animals as they can handle.[16]

****

I once thought that after 45 years of researching, deterring, and handling polar bears in western Hudson Bay, scientists, conservation officers and Inuit hunters would have pretty much figured out everything necessary to manage them. But each time I talk to Ian Stirling, Steve Amstrup, Andrew Derocher, Nick Lunn, Steve Ferguson, Daryll Hedman, or anyone else who has worked on polar bears in Churchill, something else comes along that makes me realize how wrong I am.

In Churchill, later that week, I heard talk of the possibility of a pipeline being built from the oil sands of northern Alberta to western Hudson Bay, in order to transport bitumen through Churchill's port. Even though the ice is receding in western Hudson Bay at a rapid rate, this plan seemed a little farfetched to me. There is still a lot of ice, and the shipping season would be a relatively short one.

Back at home, however, I discovered from various newspaper reports that quiet discussions between Calgary's oil sands community,

ARCTIC ICONS

the port authority in Churchill, railway companies, and refiners in Europe, the East coast and the Gulf coast had indeed been underway to see if such a scheme might work.[17] Not one of the numerous articles mentioned what this might mean to polar bears if there were an oil spill. I wondered what the late Nils Øritsland would tell the reporters who pilloried him 30 years ago for trying to figure what would happen to polar bears when they came into contact with oil.

****

I did not get to go to Churchill in the fall of 2012, as I had hoped. But I did learn what happened to Bear X19173—the big 1,100 pound animal that had been captured and locked up eight times in previous years. He had been released at the end of the 2011, and caught once again, breaking into the Health Authority building the following year.

Given his track record, something obviously needed to be done. Sending him to the Assiniboine Park Zoo was not a realistic option because of legislation passed in 2002, prohibiting the permanent transfer of adult bears to captive centres such as that one. His violent streak would have also made zoo administrators think twice about giving him a new home. Releasing the bear back onto the ice, however, and hoping for the best, was risky because of the possibility of him returning and doing something worse.

The three strikes policy no longer meant a certain death, but it seemed to me that this bear was like a cat that had played out its nine lives.

I was surprised to get a call from Pierce Roberts in early 2013, who informed me that they had decided to give the bear another chance before releasing it with a VHS radio transmitter affixed to its ear. The transmitter has a battery life of up to 1,200 days.

Vicki Trim, Pierce told me, was executing a plan in which receiving towers were to be set up on both sides of town. These receivers would home in on the bear if it got within four kilometres of town. Conservation officers would then go out and capture the animal and put it in D-20 until Hudson Bay froze over.

"I think it's worth a try," said Roberts. "The one thing that we've learned from the past is that there is always going to be a new challenge protecting both people and polar bears in Churchill. So we have to come up with new ways of dealing with these emerging situations. It's not going to be easy, especially if climate change does what everyone seems to think it's going to do. But if we can save one bear and protect people at the same time, I think it's worth it. Time, of course, will tell if it works."

It didn't. Bear X19173 came back in 2013, as anticipated. But the ear transmitters did not stand up to the pounding that took place as the animal travelled hundreds, if not thousands, of miles over the ice and in the water that previous year.

Fortunately, Bear X19173 was spotted by chance near the Seal River in August of 2013. Conservation officers were ready to catch and put him in D-20 when he wandered into town the following month.

Bear X19173's return in 2013, however, was the least of Roberts' concerns. As slow as the season had been, due to a long cold winter that kept most of the bears out of town longer than in previous years, it nevertheless produced some close calls and heart-stopping dramas that were reminiscent of 1983 when two people were mauled.

The first incident occurred on July 29th when Churchill resident Garth Hardy was on the beach with his dog and the children of some friends visiting from Winnipeg. Without much warning, a bear suddenly appeared from the rocks nearby and headed towards him and the children. Hardy was able to usher the children to safety before the bear charged at him. Thinking quickly, he fended off the bear, not once, but twice, by whipping it with the dog leash that he had in hand. To this day, Hardy is convinced that had the Polar Bear Alert team not responded as quickly as they had that day, he would have been seriously injured or possibly mauled to death.

Garett Kolsun had an even closer call when he was walking home shortly after midnight on September 7th. On temporary assignment in Churchill, the Canadian Border Services officer realized that something was amiss when he noticed something out of the corner of his eye moving in the dark. When he turned, he saw a polar bear coming towards him full tilt.

"The bear was just barreling towards me," he told me some time later. "There was really no place to go. So I ran towards some parked vehicles hoping to maybe get on top of one of them. But I had no chance. I ran maybe ten steps before it bit me on the hip."

Kolsun then spun around raising his arms up in the air, hoping to make himself look bigger. The bear, however, wouldn't back off.

Running in circles and then backwards to the front door of Gypsy's Bakery, Kolsun tried but failed to get into the building.

Pinned up against the door with the bear slapping him and scratching his chest, Kolsun reached into his jacket for his cell phone and flashed the LED light at the bear. Remarkably, the bear stepped back and knocked over a four-foot tall planter box. The crash distracted the animal long enough to allow Kolsun to run down the street, find a cab and get himself to the hospital.

The biggest drama of the season, however, began inauspiciously on Halloween, when all the stops were pulled to ensure that trick-or-treating children and partying adults were kept safe from any bears that wandered into town. Apart from an orphaned cub found at the L5 transfer station in mid-October, not much had happened since Kolsun had been attacked. All signs suggested that it would be a quiet night.

Keeping with tradition, however, schoolchildren from Grades One to Six were given a talk on safety and, once again, Hudson Bay Helicopters donated flight time so that Jack Batstone could make sure that there were no bears in the area. Everyone, including employees from Parks Canada, the RCMP, the Churchill Fire Department, Churchill Ambulance Service, Canadian Rangers, and Manitoba Hydro chipped in to make sure the night out on the town was a safe one for everyone.

The one bear spotted that evening didn't cause any trouble. But sometime around 2 a.m. the next morning, a female and cub showed up near Mayor Mike Spence's house. Bob Windsor and Jack Batstone were called in but lost sight of the family before they eventually found them eating garbage near the Town's Fire Hall. Following routine procedure, they pushed the animals out on the river ice before losing sight of them again.

A female and her cub resting on a rock.

ARCTIC ICONS

Twenty minutes after Windsor got back home, he answered another call, one from a woman who was screaming something about a bear attacking a person in the middle of town.

Moments earlier, Erin Greene had been walking home with a group of friends from a Halloween party, when they turned and saw a bear coming at them. The bear was on top of Greene before she had a chance to escape. With part of her scalp already ripped out, Greene would likely have been mauled to death had it not been for Bill Ayotte, who was watching TV when he heard the screams. The 69-year-old longtime resident of Churchill ran out the front door of his house, grabbed a shovel and began clubbing the 275-pound animal before it turned on him.

Ayotte may have also died if Didier Foubert-Allen and Mitch Paddock had not come out of their houses and fired several shots above the animal's head. Even when two of the shots struck the bear, the animal wouldn't back off until Foubert-Allen jumped into his truck, honked the horn, and chased the bear up the street after literally giving it a push.

Driving up the same street, Windsor saw that the bear coming towards him had blood on its muzzle and around its mouth. Realizing that someone had, indeed, been mauled, he immediately radioed Jack Batstone who was coming in another truck and told him to put some slugs into his shotgun.

With two people badly mauled, Windsor realized then and there that the animal had to be put down before it got away or ran into someone else in the dark. The bear, however, kept on running when Windsor shot and injured it.

Only a minute passed before Batstone found the bear in the willows near the parking lot by the railway station, not far from where it was last seen. Determined not to let it get away again, he shot and killed the animal. Batstone didn't see the cub that was hiding in the willows until it popped out and ran towards its dead mother. He realized then that they were the same bears they had pushed into the river a few hours before.

"I guess I am in trouble now," Batstone said when Windsor caught up with him a few seconds later. "I shot the wrong bear."

Unsure of what to do next, both men contacted Brian Barton, the regional field supervisor, who happened to be in town to assist with the Polar Bear Alert Program. After telling him what had happened, Windsor and Batstone captured the cub, loaded it and the dead female into the truck and took them both to D-20. In the meantime, Barton and Churchill Conservation officer Brett Wlock went out and found the bear that had mauled Ayotte and Greene. It had died from the injury that Windsor had inflicted when he'd put a slug into it earlier.

Both Ayotte and Greene eventually recovered from their injuries. But the attacks that fall led to a controversial change in the policy that prohibited Manitoba Conservation from sending bears more than two years old to zoos. As a result, the two orphaned cubs and the three-year-old bear that attacked Kolsun were sent off to the International Polar Bear Conservation Centre in Winnipeg.

Rob Laidlaw, the Zoocheck founder who was largely responsible for the legislation that prohibited the government from sending bears to zoos, complained that the Manitoba government had turned back the clock thirty years. "They're tinkering while Rome burns," he told the media. "These poor polar bears are suffering while they pat themselves on the back for doing wonderful things. This is bad news for polar bears."

Jim Duncan, director of the wildlife branch at Manitoba Conservation, insisted that the only alternative was to euthanize the animals. This, he said, would at least give them another chance at life.

No one knows why, after years without an attack in Churchill, there were two in one season, and a third that was as close a call as could be. All three bears were in good condition, and the previous two winters had been long and cold, with normal ice freeze-up and break-up times.

In an attempt to find new and possibly better management alternatives, Manitoba Conservation decided to do what had been done in 1976. It moved to set up an advisory committee, which would give locals a say in future management plans.

The difference between now and then is that killer whales continue to migrate into Hudson Bay, as was underscored in Winter 2013 when eleven of them made international headlines after they were trapped in the ice. Grizzly bears are also making their mark in the region. Not only have the number of sightings been increasing since 2008, but one of those grizzlies bears killed a polar bear in the summer of 2013. And, in spite of cold winters for 2012–2013 and 2013–2014, which allowed bears to spend more time on the ice hunting seals, there is good reason to believe that sea ice will continue to recede.

Will Manitoba wildlife managers then be dropping tonnes of seal meat along the coast in late fall to keep polar bears away from town? Will they be airlifting starving animals to more northerly regions where there is more ice? And will they have to start euthanizing animals that are too thin and troublesome to make it through the fall months?

No one, of course, knows yet. What we do know is that through trial and error, the 1,000 people of Churchill have found a way to live with the 1,000 polar bears of western Hudson Bay. Flawed and controversial as the management of these animals has sometimes been, it is arguably one of the most successful conservation success stories in North American history.

ARCTIC ICONS

289

ENDNOTES

Introduction

[1] McNamara, C. P., and William George Penney. *Canada's Defense Research Board and Ministry of Supply, England. Technical Feasibility of Establishing an Atomic-Weapons Proving Ground in the Churchill Area* (labelled Top Secret). 1949.

[2] Britain detonated its first nuclear test device, "Hurricane," on October 3, 1952, in the waters off the Monte Bello Islands off the coast of Australia.

[3] MacKenzie, Carol. "Letter to the Editor." *Northport News*, October 28, 1972.

[4] Jonkel C. J., "Some Comments on Polar Bear Management," *Biological Conservation*. Vol. 2, no. 2 (1970).

[5] The Coca-Cola Company. "Coke Raises More Than $2 Million to Save Polar Bears." Last modified October 16, 2012. <http://www.coca-colacompany.com/our-company/coke-raises-over-2-million-to-save-polar-bears>.

[6] United States. US Geological Survey. *USGS Science to Inform U.S. Fish & Wildlife Service Decision Making on Polar Bears. Executive Summary.* 2007. <http://www.usgs.gov/newsroom/special/polar_bears/docs/executive_summary.pdf>.

Chapter One

[1] Munk, Jens. *The Journals of Jens Munk, 1619–1620.* Edited by W. A. Kenyon (Royal Ontario Museum). Oshawa: Alger Press, 1980.

[2] West, John. *The substance of a journal during a residence at the Red River colony, British North America; and frequent excursions among the north-west American Indians, in the years 1820, 1821, 1822, 1823.* London, UK: L. B. Seelev and Son, 1824.

[3] Ibid.

[4] Ibid.

[5] While cleaning out scientist Ian Stirling's lab at the Canadian Wildlife Service in 2013, his colleagues found such a skeleton of a bear cub that was so human in appearance they did a double-take.

[6] Anawak, Jack (former MP and Inuit statesman). Personal Communication.

[7] Irniq, Peter (Inuit statesman, former MLA and former Commissioner of Nunavut). Personal Communication.

[8] Rasmussen, Knud. *The Netsilik Eskimos' Social Life and Spiritual Culture, Report of the Fifth Thule Expedition.* 8. Copenhagen: Glydendalske Boghandel, Nordisk Forlag, 1921.

[9] Hearne, Samuel. *A Journey from Prince of Wales's Fort In Hudson's Bay To the Northern Ocean.* New York: Da Capo Press, 1968. 366–67.

[10] Lemelin, Raynald Harvey, Martha Dowsley, et al. "Wabusk of the Omushkegouk: Cree–Polar Bear (*Ursus maritimus*) Interactions in Northern Ontario."

Human Ecology. 38.6 (2010): 803–815.

[11] Lytwyn, Victor P. *Muskekowuck Athinuwick: Original People of the Great Swampy Land*. Winnipeg, MB: University of Manitoba Press, 2002. 110.

[12] Ibid, 110.

[13] Ibid, 111.

[14] Moreau, William E. *Writings of David Thompson, Volume 1: The Travels*. Montreal & Kingston: McGill–Queen's University Press, 2009. 30.

[15] Manitou are the spirit beings of the Algonquian First Nations. Every plant, animal stone has its own Manitou.

[16] Moreau, William E. *Writings of David Thompson, Volume 1: The Travels*. Montreal & Kingston: McGill–Queen's University Press, 2009. 30.

[17] Ibid.

[18] Ibid.

[19] Ibid.

[20] Bernier, Captain J. E. *Report on the Dominion Government Expedition to Arctic Islands and Hudson Strait on the C.G.S. Arctic, 1906–1907*. Ottawa: C. H. Parmelee, 1909.

[21] Honderich, James Emerson. *Wildlife as a hazardous resource: an analysis of the historical interaction of humans and polar bears in the Canadian Arctic 2,000 B.C. to A.D. 1935*. Waterloo: University of Waterloo, 2002.

[22] Davies, Lawrence E. "Polar Bear Prey on Alaska Hunts." *The New York Times*, August 25, 1964.

[23] Murphy, Robert. "Are the Days of the Arctic's King running out?" *The New York Times Magazine*, May 28, 1965.

[24] In the light of what is known now, this was almost certainly an underestimate in total, though some subpopulations were being overharvested. Personal Communication with Polar Bear Biologist Ian Stirling, September 2014.

[25] Bartlett, E. L. "Opening Address, Proceedings U.S. Government Printing office." First International Scientific Meeting on the Polar Bear. U.S. Department of the Interior and the University of Alaska. Fairbanks, AK. September 6, 1965.

[26] deMeulles, Bob. Personal Communication. November 2012.

[27] Stirling, Ian. *Polar Bears: The Natural History of a Threatened Species*. Markham, ON: Fitzhenry & Whiteside, 2011.

[28] Stirling, Ian (Polar Bear Biologist, University of Alberta). Personal Communication, September 2014.

[29] Canadian Space Agency, Government of Canada, "Fort Churchill—a landmark in Canadian space research." Last modified September 8, 2004. <http://www.asc-csa.gc.ca/eng/sciences/fort_churchill.asp>.

[30] Daniel, Raymond. "Allied Experts in Churchill, Manitoba Try To Overcome Radio–Radar Interference." *The New York Times*, July 16, 1954.

[31] "70 Arctic pigeons Sent to Arctic for Training." *The New York Times*, November 22, 1950.

[32] Iarocci, Dr. Andrew. "Opening the North: Technology and Training at the Fort Churchill Joint Services Experimental Testing Station, 1946–64." *Canadian Army Journal*. Vol. 10, no. 4 (2008).

[33] Churchill Polar Bear Committee. *Recommendations to the Local Government District of Churchill and the Manitoba Department of Renewable Resources and Transportation Services.* June 1977.

[34] Ibid.

[35] Davidson, J. A. "How Fort Churchill Faced a Polar Bear Invasion." *The Globe and Mail,* October 29, 1971.

[36] Ibid.

[37] Iarocci, Dr. Andrew. "Opening the North: Technology and Training at the Fort Churchill Joint Services Experimental Testing Station, 1946–64." *Canadian Army Journal*. Vol. 10, no. 4 (2008).

Chapter Two

[1] Webber, Doug. Personal Communication. April 2013.

[2] Jacobs, Eileen. Personal Communication. April 2013.

[3] "Churchill Future Still Bleak." *Winnipeg Free Press*, May 11, 1968.

[4] Ibid.

[5] Culbert, Bob. "NRC Cuts Churchill Program." *Winnipeg Free Press*, October 21, 1969.

[6] Province of Manitoba. Manitoba Department of Mines and Natural Resources, Wildlife Branch. *Report on Churchill Polar Bear Depredation, Churchill, Manitoba*. Churchill, MB: Province of Manitoba, 1968.

[7] Ibid.

[8] Jonkel, C. J. "Some Comments on Polar Bear Management," *Biological Conservation*. Vol. 2, no. 2 (1970). 111–117.

[9] Hawkins, Tim. Personal Communication. May 2013.

[10] Senior, W. E. "Boys Battle Bear." *Winnipeg Free Press*, sec. front page, October 4, 1966.

[11] Jonkel, C. J. "Some Comments on Polar Bear Management," *Biological Conservation*. Vol. 2, no. 2 (1970). 111–117.

[12] Ibid.

[13] Harington, Richard. Personal Communication. April 2012.

[14] Godbout, Oscar. "Scientists to Study Polar Bears Via Transmitters in Orbiting Satellite." *The New York Times*, June 29, 1966.

[15] Bruemmer, Fred. Personal Communication. August 2013.

[16] Ibid.

[17] Bilgen-Reinart, Üstün. *Night Spirits: The Story of the Relocation of the Sayisi Dene*. Winnipeg, MB: University of Manitoba Press, 2000.

[18] "Two Injured, Polar Bear Attacks Dropping." *Winnipeg Free Press*, November 20, 1967. 59.

[19] Jonkel, C. J. "Some Comments on Polar Bear Management," *Biological Conservation*. Vol. 2, no. 2 (1970). 111–117.

[20] Ibid, 117.

[21] "Two Injured, Polar Bear Attacks Dropping." *Winnipeg Free Press*, November 20, 1967.

[22] Personal communication by author, with Carol Rogers and Tim Hawkins, April 2013.

[23] Hawkins, Tim. Personal Communication. April 2013.

[24] "Mauled By Polar Bear, Youth Dies." *Canadian Press report*, November 19, 1968.

[25] "Polar Bear Kills Eskimo Student At Churchill." *Ottawa Citizen* (*Canadian Press report*), November 18, 1968.

[26] "Polar Bears Kill Youth, Smash way into Home." *The Globe and Mail* (*Canadian Press report*), November 19, 1968.

[27] Taken from the transcripts of a series of interviews that biologist Brian Knudsen did with Jimmy Spence in 1972, courtesy of biologist Brian Knudsen.

[28] John Spence lived to tell the tale to everyone who asked, including *National Geographic* when the documentary crew came to town in 1980. A missing arm accentuated the fact that he wasn't exaggerating.

[29] Province of Manitoba. Manitoba Department of Mines and Natural Resources, Wildlife Branch. *Report on Churchill Polar Bear Depredation, Churchill, Manitoba*. Churchill, MB: Province of Manitoba, 1968.

[30] Emberley, Gordon (Former animal control officer, Province of Manitoba). Personal Communication. April 2011.

[31] "Mauled by Polar Bear, Youth Dies." *Winnipeg Free Press*, November 20, 1969.

Chapter Three

[1] Walz, Jay. "Polar Bears Airlifted Out, Return Because They Love the Dump." *The New York Times*, November 21, 1971.

[2] Lowery, Bob. "Norman Directors Scan Developments of the Future." *Winnipeg Free Press*, November 23, 1971.

[3] "Besieged by Polar Bears, Canadians Marooned on the Ice Fought Off Two Dozen Beasts." *The New York Times*, October 23, 1915.

[4] "Queen Faces a Blitz of Bugs." *Daily Mirror*, July 3, 1970.

[5] Ruley, Stephen. "Family Bears Up in Northern Manitoba." *Winnipeg Free Press*, July 11, 1970.

[6] Gordon, Alan. "The Great Bearlift." *Daily Mirror*, October 25, 1971.

[7] "Smallwood describes seal-hunt opponent as 'bigoted, a crank.'" *The Globe and Mail* (*Canadian Press report*), March 19, 1971.

[8] "Reprieve for Polar Bears." *Winnipeg Free Press*, sec.

front page, October 8, 1971.

[9] O'Malley, Martin. "Lured from Fleet Street to Polar Bear Country." *The Globe and Mail*, October 16, 1971.

[10] Cross, Dale. Personal Communication. August 2012.

[11] Province of Manitoba. "Memorandum, J. L. Howard to A. O. Jardine, Director of Operations, Ministry of Natural Resources." November 18, 1971.

[12] Ibid.

[13] "Value of Bear Lifts is questioned." *The Globe and Mail*, November 17, 1971.

[14] "Soviet Is Termed As Polar Bear's Ally." *The New York Times*, March 21, 1971.

[15] Gordon, Alan. "The Great Bearlift." *Daily Mirror*, October 25, 1971.

[16] Ibid.

[17] "Funds for Airlifting Polar Bears Assured, Director says After Trip." *The Globe and Mail*, November 4, 1971.

[18] "No Roundtrip Ticket, Bears Return to Churchill." *Winnipeg Free Press*, November 17, 1971.

[19] Gavin, Kent. Personal Communication. April 6, 2013.

[20] O'Malley, Martin. "Into the White Horizon, Operation Bearlift finally begins." *The Globe and Mail*, October 18, 1971; Cross, Dale, and Brian Wotton. Personal Communication, Spring 2011.

[21] Gordon, Alan. "The Great Bearlift." *Daily Mirror*, October 25, 1971.

[22] "Value of Churchill Bear Lift is Questioned After Two animals make 300 mile trek." *The Globe and Mail*, November 17, 1971.

[23] Province of Manitoba. "Memorandum, J. L. Howard to A. O. Jardine, Director of Operations, Ministry of Natural Resources." November 18, 1971.

[24] "Funds for airlifting polar bears assured, director says after trip." *The Globe and Mail*, November 1, 1971.

[25] Lowery, Bob. "Norman Directors Scan Developments of the Future." *Winnipeg Free Press*, November 23, 1971.

[26] "Yes, There was some good news in 1971, And Here's Our Personal Selection." *Winnipeg Free Press, Weekend Magazine*, January 1, 1972.

Chapter Four

[1] Lowery, Bob. "Polar bears Take Chill Out of Churchill Days." *Winnipeg Free Press*, October 14, 1976.

[2] "Fenced Zoos Promoted for Migrating Polar Bears." *Winnipeg Free Press*, November 6, 1975.

[3] Barry, Donald. *Icy Battleground: Canada, the International Fund for Animal Welfare, and the Seal Hunt*. St. John's, NL: Breakwater Books, 2005.

[4] Osland, Maureen Martin. "Sigrun Sigurdson

Martin, A Northern Business Woman." *Canadian Women's Studies*. Vol. 14, no. 4 (1994): 48.

5 Payne, Michael. "Fort Churchill, 1821–1900: An Outpost Community in the Fur Trade." *Manitoba History*. Vol. 20, Autumn 1990.

Chapter Five

1 Ian Stirling, and Claire Parkinson. "Possible Effects of Climate Warming on Selected Populations of Polar Bears (*Ursus maritimus*) in the Canadian Arctic." *Arctic*, Vol. 59, no. 3 (2006): 261–275.

2 Lunn, Nicholas John. *The Ecological Significance of Supplemental Food to Polar Bears On Land During the Ice-Free Period in western Hudson Bay*. University of Alberta (M. Sc.), 1985.

3 Ibid.

Chapter Six

1 International Union for Conservation of Nature and Natural Resources, ed. *Proceedings of the Seventh Working Meeting of the IUCN Polar Bear Specialist Group, Held at the Arktisk Institut*. Gland, Switzerland: 1980. 35.

2 Stirling, Ian, W. R. Archibald, and Douglas DeMaster, "Distribution and abundance of seals in the eastern Beaufort Sea." *Journal of the Fisheries Research Board of Canada*. Vol. 34, no. 7 (1977): 976–988.

3 Stenhouse, Gordon B., and Marc Cattet. Government of Northwest Territories. Wildlife Services. *Bear detection and deterrent study, Cape Churchill, Manitoba, File Report No. 44*. Yellowknife, NT: Government of Northwest Territories, 1983.

4 Bernstein, Adam. "Vagn Flyger, 83: Biologist was Expert on Squirrels." *Washington Post*, January 12, 2006.

5 Miller, Gary D. "Field Tests of Potential Polar Bear Repellents." *International Conference, Bear Research and Management*. (1987): 383–390.

6 Stenhouse, Gordon B., and Marc Cattet. Government of Northwest Territories. Wildlife Services. *Bear detection and deterrent study, Cape Churchill, Manitoba, File Report No. 44*. Yellowknife, NT: Government of Northwest Territories, 1983: 18.

7 Ibid, 13.

8 Ibid, 17.

9 Goulden, Richard. "Province of Manitoba, Interdepartmental memo, Richard Goulden to Dale Stewart." Province of Manitoba, November 8, 1983.

10 Bruemmer, Fred. "Two weeks in a Polar Bear Prison." *Audubon*. Vol. 83, no. 6 (1981): 28–37.

Chapter Seven

1 Constable Dennis Strongquill was killed in the line of duty on January 18th, 2001, when he approached a pick-up containing three robbers who were the subject of a Canada-wide warrant. The occupants shot at Strongquill's car, chased him into the town of Russell, Manitoba, and rammed his car in front of the detachment office. Trapped inside the vehicle, Strongquill never had a chance because of a pistol malfunction.

2 Province of Manitoba, "Community Profiles—Barrows." Last modified May 2003. <http://www.gov.

mb.ca/ana/community_profiles/pdf/barrows.>

[3] Durnin, Jim. Province of Manitoba. *Polar Bear Alert Program Report*. Winnipeg, MB: Province of Manitoba, 1983.

[4] Lowery, Bob. "Tundra Bus Opens North's Beauty to Tourists." *Winnipeg Free Press*, October 12, 1980.

[5] Struzik, Ed. "Interview with John Bilenduke." *Edmonton Journal*, December 12, 1983.

[6] Cleroux, Richard. "Polar Bear Kills Man in Churchill." *The Globe and Mail*, November 30, 1983.

Chapter Eight

[1] Montagnes, James. "Where the Wild Begins." *The New York Times*, June 22, 1958.

[2] Hudson's Bay Company. "Contest advertisement." *Winnipeg Free Press*, August 23, 1969.

[3] Churchill has 95 breeding bird species, with over 250 species recorded in total. Many of these species are tundra breeding shorebirds, or pond and marsh breeding waterfowl. Important Bird Areas Canada (IBA), "Churchill and Vicinity, Churchill, Manitoba." <http://www.iba-canada.ca/site.jsp?siteID=MB003&lang=EN>.

[4] Lowery, Bob. "Wildlife on Cue. Tour organizers bear baiting sparks fear of Churchill tragedy." *Winnipeg Free Press*, December 13, 1987.

[5] Huff, Sandy. "Does bear baiting make attacks more likely?" *Northern Times*, December 14, 1984.

[6] Ibid.

[7] Province of Manitoba. Manitoba Conservation, Polar Bear Alert Program. *Letter from Phyllis Moriarty to Don Jacobs, resident Conservation Officer, Polar Bear Alert Program Report*. Churchill, MB: Manitoba Conservation, 1984.

[8] Jacobs, Donald. Province of Manitoba. Manitoba Conservation. *Officers' Report*. Winnipeg, MB. 1984.

Chapter Nine

[1] Caswall Tower was originally referred to as Caswell's Tower by British explorers in the 19th century.

[2] Stirling, Ian. *Polar Bears: The Natural History of a Threatened Species*. Markham, ON: Fitzhenry & Whiteside, 2011, 92–93.

[3] International Union for Conservation of Nature and Natural Resources, ed. *Proceedings of the Seventh Working Meeting of the IUCN Polar Bear Specialist Group, Held at the Arktisk Institut*. Gland, Switzerland: 1980.

[4] Ian Stirling recalls attending an industry/government conference in the late 1970s when a senior marine mammal administrator in the federal government told the audience that "while oiled bears, like oiled birds, would make great photos in newspapers, the oil would have no significant negative effects on bears." Stirling, Ian. *Polar Bears: The Natural History of a Threatened Species*. Markham, ON: Fitzhenry & Whiteside, 2011. 272.

[5] Brief accounts by Steven Amstrup, Ian Stirling and Andrew Derocher reported that polar bears will not avoid petroleum products encountered in the wild and may actively investigate oil spills. Derocher, A. E., and I. Stirling, "Oil contamination

of polar bears," *Polar Record*, 27 (1991): 56–57.

[6] *Montreal Gazette, Canadian Press report.* April 3, 1979.

[7] Province of Manitoba. Legislative Assembly of Manitoba, *Hansard*. March 26, 1980.

[8] "Polar Bears Die in Oil Experiment." *Associated Press*, March 30, 1980.

[9] Degagne, Daly. "Outlook Poor For Polar Bear fighting to survive Oil Test." *Toronto Star*, March 28, 1980.

[10] *Toronto Star*, sec. letters to the editor, April 2, 1980.
[11] "There's no Goldilocks in this story of Three Bears," *Toronto Star* special, April 6, 1980.

[12] Stirling, Ian. Personal Communication. Dec-ember 18, 2012.

[13] *Manitoba Gazette*, October 5, 1985, Vol. 114, No. 40.

[14] Province of Manitoba. Manitoba Conservation. *Manitoba Policy Directive, May 1, 1985, Revision Number 01.* Churchill, MB: Manitoba Conservation. 1985.

[15] Province of Manitoba. Manitoba Conservation. *Polar Bear Alert Program Annual Report.* Churchill, MB: Manitoba Conservation, 1986.

[16] 68.3 percent of respondents to a survey agreed with the decision to remove bears from the dump. 25.7 percent did not. Province of Manitoba. Mani-toba Conservation. *Polar Bear Alert Program Annual Report.* Winnipeg, MB: Manitoba Conservation, 1983. 98.

[17] Province of Manitoba. Manitoba Conservation. *Polar Bear Alert Program Annual Report, 1985.* Chur-chill, MB: Manitoba Conservation. 1985. 1.

[18] Speirs, Doug. "Scavenging Polar Bears called Tourist Attraction." *Winnipeg Free Press*, September 17, 1985.

Chapter Ten

[1] Wildlife specialist Ian Thorleifson ended up showing Jacobs how to use the dart gun.

[2] Government of Canada. *RCMP Report. Statement of Cecil John Voisey, August 8, 1984.* 1984.

[3] Government of Canada. RCMP Reports. *Statements of Cecil John Voisey, Christopher Walter Campbell, Pat-rick Harold O'Connor, Dick Hunter, Brian Coma and John Reginald Bilenduke August 20, 1984.* 1984; Jacobs, Donald G. Province of Manitoba. Ministry of Natural Resources. *Ministry of Natural Resources Report from Donald G. Jacobs, to Mark Stringer.* Winnipeg, MB: Province of Manitoba. 1984.

[4] Stirling, Ian, C. Spencer, and D. Andriashek. "Immobilization of polar bears (*Ursus Maritimus*) with Telazol in the Canadian Arctic." *Journal of Wild-life Diseases.* Vol. 25, no. 2 (1989).

Chapter Eleven

[1] Ryan, Ted. The Coca-Cola Company. "The Enduring History of Coca-Cola's Polar Bears." Last modified January 1, 2012. <http://www.coca-colacompany.com/stories/coke-lore-polar-bears>.

[2] Harry, Linda Lee, and Jean Gibbs-Simpson. *Coca-Cola Collectible Polar Bears.* Dallas, TX: Beckett Publications, 2000.

[3] Karacs, Imre. "Ursula and the two bears, Kenny and Boris, were stars in East Germany, but with the State Circus gone, nobody wants them." *The Independent*, November 14, 1999.

[4] Buckles Blog, "Ursula Bottcher #3." Last modified December 26, 2008. <http://bucklesw.blogspot.ca/2008/12/ursula-bottcher-3.html>. The conversation was reported anonymously to this page.

[5] Owen, Bruce. "Polar bears in Mexico Circus; Province, activists appalled." *Winnipeg Free Press*, March 29, 1996.

[6] Ibid.

[7] Laidlaw, Rob. *Canada's Forgotten Polar Bears: An Examination of Manitoba's Polar Bear Export Program.* Toronto, ON: Zoocheck Canada Inc., 1997.

[8] Jonson, Tim. "Plight of Suarez 7 unbearable, Lawmakers state." *Philadelphia Inquirer*, November 10, 2001.

[9] Foss, Krista. "Move on To Free Polar Bears From Circus Act." *The Globe and Mail*, August 17, 2001.

[10] Jonson, Tim. "Plight of Suarez 7 unbearable, Lawmakers state." *Philadelphia Inquirer*, November 10, 2001.

[11] Alaska eventually did swim and she learned a form of sign language that the zoo's trainers devised to communicate with her.

[12] Hedman, Daryll. Personal Communication. November 2012.

[13] *Daily Mail* Online, "Ewan McGregor: The Bear Facts." Last modified July 7, 2001. <http://www.dailymail.co.uk/tvshowbiz/article-57756/Ewan-McGregor-The-Bear-Facts.html>.

[14] Hedman, Daryll. Personal Communication. November 2012.

[15] Murphy, Eliza. *ABC News Blogs*, "Polar Bears Get Chilly Birthday Surprise." Last modified November 23, 2012. <http://abcnews.go.com/blogs/headlines/2012/11/polar-bears-get-chilly-birthday-surprise>.

Chapter Twelve

[1] Burke, Kevin. Personal Communication. January 17, 2010.

[2] Stirling, Ian. Personal Communication. January 16, 2010.

[3] Windsor, Bob. Province of Manitoba. Ministry of Natural Resources. *Report, 2011*. Winnipeg, MB: Province of Manitoba, 2011.

[4] Climate change was just one of many factors that resulted in the explosion of snow goose populations. The expansion of agriculture in the Midwest and the southern United States in the 1980s provided the geese with a new and very large food source.

[5] Province of Manitoba. Manitoba Conservation. *Polar Bear Alert Report for 2003*. Table 12, P.B.A. Operation and Manpower Costs, 1969–2003. 2003.

[6] Province of Manitoba. Manitoba Conservation. *Polar Bear Alert Report for 2003*. 2003.

[7] Province of Manitoba. Manitoba Conservation. *Polar Bear Alert Report for 2003.* Table 13A Helicopter Costs Standing Offer and Contract. 2003.

[8] Province of Manitoba. Manitoba Conservation. *Polar Bear Alert Report for 2003.* 2003.

[9] Derocher, A. E., N. J. Lunn, and I. Stirling. "Polar Bears in a Warming Climate." *Integrative and Comparative Biology.* Vol. 44, no. 2 (2004): 163–176.

[10] Province of Manitoba. Manitoba Conservation. *Polar Bear Alert Program annual report for 2004.* 2004.

[11] Province of Manitoba. Manitoba Conservation. *Polar Bear Alert Program Costs, Background report.* Province of Manitoba, 2012.

[12] Brouzes, Laury. Personal communication. November 2012.

[13] Province of Manitoba. Manitoba Conservation. *Polar Bear Alert Program Annual Report.* Winnipeg, MB: Manitoba Conservation, 2003.

[14] In the November 2008 *Science Watch*, the journal that tracks trends and performance in basic research, credited the *TIME* paper as a timely overview and synthesis of the possible impacts of climate warming on polar bears. The paper has been used by a wide variety of scientists working on other Arctic marine mammals, sea ice dynamics, and climate warming, as a global biodiversity issue.

[15] Falkingham, John (Chief forecaster for the Canadian Ice Service). Personal communication. January 2011.

[16] Kempthorne, Dirk. United States Government. U.S. Fish and Wildlife Service. *Remarks by Secretary Kempthorne, Press Conference on Polar Bear Listing.* Washington D.C.: U.S Fish and Wildlife Service, 2008. <http://www.fws.gov/home/feature/2008/polarbear012308/pdf/press-conference-remarks.pdf>.

[17] International Union for Conservation of Nature (IUCN), "IUCN Red List of Threatened Species." <http://www.iucnredlist.org/details/22823/0>.

[18] Owen, Bruce. "Province protects polar bear habitat." *Winnipeg Free Press*, December 12, 2009.

[19] Province of Manitoba, "Rescue Centre and Exhibit to be Centrepieces of Polar Bears International World Headquarters." Last modified December 3, 2009. <http://news.gov.mb.ca/news/index.html?item=7272>.

Chapter Thirteen

[1] "Phony bear crusade." *The Globe and Mail*, sec. editorial. November 6, 1971.

[2] "Making the Fur Fly." *The Globe and Mail*, sec. editorial, October 12, 1971.

[3] O'Malley, Martin. Global News, "My Own Private Canada." Last modified June 28, 2012. <http://globalnews.ca/news/259896/my-own-private-canada>.

[4] Marshall Macklin Monaghan Limited. Government of Canada. Transport Canada. *Churchill Tourism and Transportation Study 4: Harbors.* Government of Canada, 1986.

[5] The review recommended cuts in the federal budget

across the board. Government of Canada. *Task Force on Program Review, Report: 1986.* Ottawa: ON, 1986.

[6] "The Care of Churchill." *The Globe and Mail*, sec. editorial, May 6, 1986.

[7] Ibid.

[8] Howard, Ross. "Spending More on Churchill Goes Against the Tory Grain." *The Globe and Mail*, May 5, 1986.

[9] "Call to Shoot Bears Provokes Fear." *The Globe and Mail.* August 17, 1984. 10.

[10] Ibid.

[11] Richards, Bill. "They Menace Manitobans, Tear Up the Town Dump, But Tourists Bear Cash." *The Wall Street Journal*, November 14, 1989.

[12] Ibid.

[13] Ibid.

[14] Murphy, Robert. "Are the Days of the Arctic's King Running Out?" *The New York Times Magazine*, March 28, 1965.

[15] Farnsworth, Clyde H. "Churchill Journal, Bears Yes, But Never in the Kitchen." *The New York Times*, November 23, 1992.

[16] "PCBs found in polar bears, scientists say." *Canadian Press report, The Globe and Mail*, May 7, 1985.

[17] Caroline, Pond. "Bearing up in the Arctic." *New Scientist*, February 4, 1989. 40.

[18] Amstrup, Steven C. Association of Zoos and Aquariums, "The Future of Polar Bears." <http://www.aza.org/Membership/detail.aspx?id=26836>.

[19] Abel, Allen. "Polar bear necessity raised in Washington." *Winnipeg Free Press.* March 3, 2012.

Chapter Fifteen

[1] Hearne, Samuel. *A Journey from Prince of Wales's Fort in Hudson's Bay to the Northern Ocean in the Years 1769, 1770, 1771 and 1772.* Toronto, ON: Champlain Society, 1911.

[2] Richardson, E., I. Stirling, and B. Kochtubajda, "The effects of forest fires on polar bear maternity denning habitat in western Hudson Bay," *Polar Biology.* Vol. 30 (2006): 369–378.

[3] Harington, Dick. Personal Communication, April 2014.

[4] Derocher, A. E. and I. Stirling. "Estimation of polar bear population size and survival in western Hudson Bay," *Journal of Wildlife Management.* Vol. 59 (1995): 215–221.

[5] Molnár, P. K., A. E. Derocher, T. Klanjscek, and M. A. Lewis. "Predicting climate change impacts on polar bear litter size," *Nature Communications.* Vol. 2 (2011): 186.

[6] Scott, Peter A., and Ian Stirling, "Chronology of Terrestrial Den Use by Polar Bears in Western Hudson Bay as Indicated by Tree Growth Anomalies," *Arctic.* Vol. 55, no. 2 (2002).

Conclusion

[1] Town of Churchill, ed. *Meeting minutes—Town of*

Churchill Special Council Meeting. Churchill, MB. April 19, 2012.

[2] Higdon, Jeff W., and Steven H. Ferguson. "Loss of Arctic sea ice causing punctuated change in sightings of killer whales (*Orcinus orca*) over the past century." *Ecological Society of America (ESA) Ecological Applications.* (2007): 1365–1375, <http://www.esajournals.org/doi/abs/10.1890/07-1941.1>.

[3] Macri, Mike. Sea North Tours, "Hudson Bay Nessie Revealed." <http://www.seanorthtours.com/orca.html>.

[4] Higdon, Jeff W., Brent G. Young, and Steven H. Ferguson. "Killer whale (*Orcinus orca*) photo-identification in the eastern Canadian Arctic." *Polar Research.* Vol. 30 (2011). <http://www.polar-research.net/index.php/polar/article/view/7203/html_155>.

[5] Clark, Douglas. "Recent Report of Grizzly Bears in Northern Manitoba," *The Canadian Field Naturalist.* Vol. 114 (2000): 692–694.

[6] Ibid.

[7] Gibbons, Melissa. Parks Canada—Wapusk National Park, "A Grizzly Encounter!" Last modified Summer 2010. <http://www.pc.gc.ca/eng/pn-np/mb/wapusk/ne/ne1/ne1_2010_ete-summer/ne1av.aspx>.

[8] Rockwell, Robert, Linda Gormezano, and Daryll Hedman. "Grizzly Bears in Wapusk National Park, Northeastern Manitoba." *Canadian Field Naturalist.* Vol. 122, no. 4 (2008).

[9] Analyses confirmed the animal was a very dirty polar bear.

[10] Data compiled by Author from Manitoba Conservation Annual reports, Churchill 1992–2012.

[11] Ibid.

[12] Amstrup, Steven C., Bruce G. Marcot, and David C. Douglas. United States. United States Geological Survey (USGS). *USGS Science Strategy to Support U.S. Fish and Wildlife Service Polar Bear Listing Decision—Forecasting the Range-wide Status of Polar Bears at Selected Times in the 21st Century.* Reston, VA: United States Geological Survey (USGS), 2007.

[13] Derocher, Andrew. Personal communication. December 2013.

[14] Molnár, P. K., A. E. Derocher, T. Klanjscek, and M. A. Lewis. "Predicting climate change impacts on polar bear litter size," *Nature Communications.* Vol. 2 (2011): 186; Molnár, P. K., A. E. Derocher, G. W. Thiemann, M. A. Lewis. "Predicting survival, reproduction and abundance of polar bears under climate change," *Biological Conservation.* Vol. 143 (2010): 1612–1622.

[15] Derocher, Andrew E., et al, "Rapid ecosystem change and polar bear conservation." *Conservation Letters.* Vol. 6, no. 5 (2013).

[16] Ibid.

[17] "Churchill seeks to become an oil export hub." *Alberta Oil*, February 26, 2013. <http://www.albertaoilmagazine.com/2013/02/arctic-oil-churchill/>.

INDEX

C

cages, 64–65

　　See also polar bear jail

Calvert, Wendy, 156

Canadian Association of Zoological Parks and Aquariums, 190

Canadian Council of Animal Care, 167

Canadian Department of Tourism, 147

Canadian Travel Bureau, 141–42

Canadian Wildlife Service, 160

cannibalism, 211

Cape Churchill, Manitoba, 111, 122, 124

Cattet, Marc, 111, 118–22, 124–25, 204, 275

celebrity interest in polar bears, 9, 246–47

　　Dan Aykroyd, 246–47

　　Ewan McGregor, 201, 204–6

　　Rob Reiner, 246–47

　　Sarah McLachlan, 201

Cessna 206 planes, 109–10

Chalmers, Barry, 138

Chambers, Joe, 83

Chartier, Al and Bonnie, 88, 96, 142–43, 144, 147, 148, 215

Chocomolin, Gregory, 95

Churchill, Manitoba, 35–36, 75, 83

　　committee recommendations, 91, 148

　　community committee, 7, 83–91

　　community opinion, 88–91

　　garbage dumps, 36, 48, 61, 73

　　honouring conservation officers, 221

　　men's and women's roles, 83–84

　　negative publicity, 235

　　polar bear problem, 5–7, 10–11, 36, 45–46, 62

　　Queen Elizabeth II visit, 57

　　tourism, 8–9, 142–45, 147–48

Churchill Northern Studies Centre, 8–9

Churchill Polar Bear Committee, 7, 83–91

circuses, 196–97

Clarke, Grace, 90–91

Clarkson, Peter, 275

Cleroux, Richard, 139

climate change, 211–17, 221–24

　　and Polar Bears International (PBI), 229, 230–32

　　and starving polar bear incidents, 244–49, 256

　　talks in Copenhagen, 226–27

Cloutier, Lillian, 88

Coca-Cola, 195–96, 201

Coca-Cola Canada, 9

Coca-Cola Collectible Polar Bears, 195–96

Comiso, Josefino, 222

commercial opportunities, 195–98

Committee on the Status of Endangered Wildlife in Canada (COSEWIC), 224, 226

community opinion, 88–91

Conservative government, 239–40

Cook, Greta, 52, 54

Cooke, Fred, 142

Cowan, Jay, 168

Cowley, Jerry, 256

COY (cub of the year), 181–82, 184–85, 189

Cronin, Pat, 178–79, 180

Cross, Dale, 49–52, 54–55, 60–61, 63–66, 71, 80, 111

CONSERVATION OFFICERS POSTED IN CHURCHILL

(Prior to 1976, Polar Bear Alert coverage was by rotation of staff)

Brian Wotton 1976–1978	Pat Cronin 2000–2003
Rob Dean 1978–1980	Geoff Smith 2001– 2002
Ken John 1980–1983	Richard Romaniuk 2002–2005
Don Jacobs 1984–1986	Syd McGregor 2003–2007
Rick Tease 1986–1989	Shaun Bobier 2005–2009
Gary Friesen 1989–1992	Andrew Szklaruk 2007–2012
Laury Brouzes 1992–1997	Bob Windsor 2009–Present
Wayde Roberts 1997–2000	Brett Wlock 2012–Present

WILDLIFE BIOLOGISTS AND TECHNICIANS RESPONSIBLE FOR THE POLAR BEAR ALERT PROGRAM

From 1969 to Present

Dale Cross

R.J Robertson

Roy Bukowsky

Steve Kearney

Dan Chranowski

Ian Thorleifson

Cam Elliott

Daryll Hedman

RESOURCE MANAGEMENT TECHNICIANS

(Residents of Churchill)

Jack Batstone 1984–Present

Louis Voisey 1985–1986

Donald Spence 1989–Present